Folk Beliefs and Practice in Medieval Lives

Edited by

Ann-Britt Falk
Donata M. Kyritz

BAR International Series 1757
2008

Published in 2016 by
BAR Publishing, Oxford

BAR International Series 1757

Folk Beliefs and Practice in Medieval Lives

ISBN 978 1 4073 0196 9

© The editors and contributors severally and the Publisher 2008

The authors' moral rights under the 1988 UK Copyright,
Designs and Patents Act are hereby expressly asserted.

All rights reserved. No part of this work may be copied, reproduced, stored,
sold, distributed, scanned, saved in any form of digital format or transmitted
in any form digitally, without the written permission of the Publisher.

BAR Publishing is the trading name of British Archaeological Reports (Oxford) Ltd.
British Archaeological Reports was first incorporated in 1974 to publish the BAR
Series, International and British. In 1992 Hadrian Books Ltd became part of the BAR
group. This volume was originally published by Archaeopress in conjunction with
British Archaeological Reports (Oxford) Ltd / Hadrian Books Ltd, the Series principal
publisher, in 2008. This present volume is published by BAR Publishing, 2016.

Printed in England

BAR titles are available from:

            BAR Publishing
            122 Banbury Rd, Oxford, OX2 7BP, UK
EMAIL   info@barpublishing.com
PHONE   +44 (0)1865 310431
  FAX   +44 (0)1865 316916
            www.barpublishing.com

Contents

1. Introduction ii
Ann-Britt Falk and Donata M. Kyritz

2. Place-names - a possibility of understanding the medieval and early-modern concept of ancient monuments? 1
Donata M. Kyritz

3. Myths and folklore as aids in interpreting the prehistoric landscape at the Carrowkeel passage tomb complex, Co. Sligo, Ireland 7
Sam Moore

4. Microhistory and Ethnoarchaeology of a cultural landscape: the parish of San Pedro de Cereixa (Galicia, Spain) 23
Xurxo M. Ayán Vila

5. Traditions of the Milesian invasion from the medieval Irish text An Lebor Gabála; *the context of their survival in connection with archaeological monuments and topographic features on the south-west coast of Ireland* 47
Simon Ó Faoláin

6. The power of tradition 59
Ann-Britt Falk

7. Pre-Christian and Christian: offering practices at two holy stones in Setomaa, south-east Estonia 67
Heiki Valk

8. The Medieval Udmurt Sacred Sites – an alternative interpretation 79
Alexei Korobeinikov

9. Symbolic meanings in the slip decoration of medieval redware pottery 85
Marianna Niukkanen

Introduction

This publication is a collection of articles proceeding from a session held at the 7th EAA conference in Cork, Ireland 2005. The session was aimed at exploring the impact of folk beliefs in daily life.

The medieval concept of the world included more than just the single voice of the Christian church and the cosmology of the time did not only contain heaven and hell but was also loaded with supernatural beings and practices related to them. One issue was the medieval reception of landscape where prehistoric monuments and places were of great importance for the people living among them. While the church tried to control the inner zone by Christianising monuments and places, the diabolised monuments of the outer zone still functioned as landmarks in the perception of space and time. Permanent pagan monuments like burial mounds and holy stones were not only visible in the landscape but also vital in the reshaping of the concept of the world.

Another issue to be discussed was folk believes regarded as a dynamic tradition where there is no clear boundary between paganism and Christianity. Folk beliefs were present in almost every aspect of daily life. A lot of rituals performed in housework probably had a pre-Christian origin. Some pagan rituals were adopted and modified to embrace Christian concepts, others simply continued through time in what had now become a Christian society. Some of these rituals can be traced in the archaeological records, but are difficult to interpret since they can be part of either a Christian or heathen context. The same ambiguity can be seen in medieval art, were many motifs might be explained in terms of both Christian and pre-Christian religion.

The session gathered speakers from countries all over Europe, and topics covering time periods from the Iron Ages to modern times. Nevertheless there were a number of important questions crossing both geographical borders and historical periods, during the session two main themes emanated.

The first theme is about folklore, landscape and monuments. Folklore can tell us about places and activities or incidents, but also about conceptions of monuments, buildings and places.
The second theme deals with folk beliefs in pre-Christian and medieval times. Archaeological records display a couple of examples on religious practices. To what extent is it possible to relate these material remains to 19th century folktales and mythology?

The first four articles deal with place-names, landscape and monuments. Donata Kyritz writes about place-names as a means of guidance in the landscape and their cultural significance as they mirror the cultural work of men, the sagas and fairy tales as well as the historical events of both local and supra-regional nature. Her work is based on a collection of place-names from the 1920s, covering the area of Germany in the early 20th century, with a connection to archaeological sites. The questions she deals with is whether this database might be used as a starting point from which to develop a better insight in how people in the middle ages and early modern times perceived ancient monuments. How far back can the creation of single names be traced? Is it possible to show in what way people combined and adapted the appearance of heathen monuments to make them a part of their Christian world view?

While Kyritz evaluates the impact of historical events on place-names and the perception of monuments, Sam Moore analyses a monument surrounded by silence. He tries to explain the fact that the Carrowkeel passage tomb complex, Co. Sligo, fails to attract attention in the legends and Irish literary sources. Neighboring areas like the Keshcorran Mountain, its caves in particular and the Moytura uplands abound in legendary and mythical tales from early sources. Many of these legends may date back to the Iron Age. But no folklore survives which relates to the Carrowkeel monuments. By looking at possible perceptions of the monuments in the past, along with the potential influence of Gaelic scribes and ecclesiastic settlements on the creation of these legends Moore investigates possible reasons that could explain the silence. He also looks at the importance of folklore in aiding our interpretation of such cultural landscapes. What are these tales really about, how much have they changed during the centuries? And even worse what does it mean when the sources are silent?

From the point of view of Landscape Archaeology, Xurxo Ayán Vila, tries to show the genealogy and development of a cultural landscape in a Galician little village. The research defines several spatial patterns built by the different societies which inhabited the area of San Pedro de Cereixa from recent ´prehistory to nowadays. He tries to demonstrate the existence of a mythical cartography over the agrarian space, reflected in microtoponymy and folklore. The peasant community develops a symbolic strategy of semantic appropriation of space. In this sense, the limits of the hamlet are ritualized through the use of permanent pagan monuments (megalithic graves) as landmarks, and the erection of stone crosses.

In contradiction to Moore and Ayán Vila, Simon Ó Faoláin starts from a rich source of oral material for folklorists from the late 19th to the mid 20th century. His article examines the connection found in local folklore between the mythological Milesian invasion as set out in the medieval text An Lebor Gabála and a number of archaeological monuments and topographical features on the Kerry peninsulas. The antiquity of these supposedly local traditions is critically assessed.

The concept of places could be analysed in terms of place-names, legends and monuments. Folklore and archaeology are dynamical counterparts that sometimes are closely linked. The articles show that folklore i.e. legends and place-names changes due to historical events, so does the perception of the monuments referred to in this legends. Simultaneously some monuments never show up in written records or oral traditions and there may be various factors for this silence. In some cases it might be the result of a church imposed silence but on the other hand the monuments could simply be situated in a forgotten cultural landscape that lost its importance for people since the erection of the monuments.

What do the folktales tell us about rituals and how do we apply that on a medieval material? The second part deals with just these questions. The connection between rituals performed in the 19th century as well as in pre-Christian and medieval times, and materiality as it is displayed in the archaeological records and in folklore, is examined.

Ann-Britt Falks article deals with building offerings as means of evil aversion in medieval times. Building offerings are to be understood as ritualized depositions connected to the building or rebuilding of a house. These types of depositions are identified as far back as to the Stone Age and up to modern times. From the 19th century there are ethnographic records dealing with the topic, but there are no written sources from the Middle Ages mentioning these kinds of depositions, neither connected to Christianity nor to pre-Christian traditions. This is remarkable considering the frequency of depositions from the Middle Ages. The question of the religious connotations of the depositions and the origin is discussed.

This is another example of the "silent sources". Just as in the case of the Carrowkeel passage tomb complex silence is an important aspect of the interpretation. Also in this case the silence can not be explained to be imposed by the Church.

Except from diabolization and silence the church also used assimilation as a strategy to control the use of heathen traditions. Assimilation could also evolve among isolated areas. This epitomized by Heiki Valk in his article about Setomaa an orthodox area in the south-easternmost corner of Estonia. Historical isolation from Russia and from Livonia/Estonia has caused extremely long persistence of beliefs and ritual practices of medieval, syncretic character among the native Finnic population.

These popular rites that have survived until present time are performed at holy stones related to the names of St. John and St. Anne at corresponding Church holidays. Practices, beliefs and legends bound with these stones have been recorded in folklore collections and ethnographic descriptions since the late 19th century. Some of these rituals seem to be of archaic origin but still the church tolerated and participated in the performance.

Alexei Korobeinikov has like Falk used ethnographic sources from the 19th century to explain archaeological evidence (comparative analysis). The site known as the Kuzebaevo settlement is located in the South of the Udmurt Republic (Russian Federation). The site has been interpreted as a fortification due to its banks and dikes. Korobeinikov states that the dikes and banks at this site are unsuitable as fortifications. He analyses offering practices known from ethnographic sources and the traces they would create on a ritual site. Comparing these results to the archaeological site of Kuzebaevo, he suggests that the site should be re-interpreted as a pagan cultic site.

Another approach to detect folk believes is through the materiality used in everyday life. Household objects together with many other common objects, had both a functional and symbolic significance in the lives of medieval people. Marianna Niukkanen examines the iconography on ordinary medieval and post-medieval redware vessels. In her opinion they could be used to influence the invisible, supernatural world. They could contribute to fertility, health and prosperity as well as keep the evil away. Many of the pictorial symbols may have a heathen origin and have survived in a rural milieu until the late 19th century.

Again we can detect a syncretic character in these pictorial motifs that makes it difficult to separate the origin from being pagan or Christian. Both Falk and Valk demonstrate that the question of pagan or Christian is difficult and depending on individual standpoints. Korobeinikov also demonstrates clearly that the modern interpretation is depending on the researcher's individual thoughts about paganism and Christianity.

Monuments as well as material objects and rituals are at times (in history) forgotten or losing importance; this is probably due to historical changes but also to socio-economical changes like altered agricultural use or climate. As an archaeologist, ethnographic sources must be handled with care - like the written sources that might be politically coloured; folklore is a most dynamical tradition.

Place-names - a way of understanding the medieval and early-modern concept of ancient monuments?

Donata Maria Kyritz

Introduction

Not only are place-names or field names a means of guidance in the landscape but they also are of cultural significance as they mirror the cultural work of men, the sagas and fairy tales as well as the historical events of both local and supra-regional nature. Or as it is put by Jakob Grimm in 1839: "When the old time still sticks to the new time, than it is in the naming of village lands, because the simple peasant throughout hundreds of years never felt to change them [...]"[1] (Kleiber 1996:405). On the other hand one should bear in mind, that the creation of new place-names still goes on and often follows certain historical trends.[2]

The database

The collection of place-names here presented is based on several articles about place-names written by Hermann Strunk, a German lawyer from Gdansk in the 1920s. Without any tangible structure he listed a huge number of place-names that had a connection to archaeological sites covering the area of Germany in the early twentieth century which today is Germany, parts of Russia and Poland (Strunk 1930, Strunk 1931, Strunk 1932).

Strunk´s aim was to create a scientifically sound collection of place names to be used by archaeologists when recording archaeological sites. Though the study of place-names was very popular among scholars in the 20th and 30th of the 20th Century, there was no connection established to prehistory. Strunk was convinced that certain place-names point to the existence of archaeological sites in the area, but he never finished his work that was published outside mainstream.

The aim of this work is to see if working on this compilation, structuring it eventually would become a possibility of understanding the medieval and early-modern concept of ancient monuments. One of the questions asked is how far back the creation of single names could be traced, and whether this database might be used as a starting point from which to develop a better insight in how people in the Middle Ages and Early Modern times perceived ancient monuments, and also in what way they combined and adapted the appearance of heathen monuments to make them a part of their Christian world view.

In the end – after having it categorized and its reliability tested against current archaeological literature the database so created consists of 642 place-names that are closely linked to archaeological sites or finds of different kind. In addition to a statistical interpretation of these place-names an etymological analysis was undertaken and folktales serve as supplementary information.

Though this study is still very preliminary, certain patterns shine through and it becomes clear how deep an impact some historical events had on people and how these incidents shaped their perception of ancient monuments as well as of the past itself.

The aim of this effort is not, as with Stunk, to work out a probable relationship between place-names and archaeological inventory but to check if this material makes it possible to find out about the relative importance of ancient monuments as characteristics of landscape. Of course this database is expansible – both in terms of number and combination of terms but this is to be done after the collection at hand has been put to the proof.

Statistics

A statistical analysis of the place-name-collection was undertaken in following categories: **Region** (*8 regions that correspond to the newly formed as well as old German States and the former geographical boundaries of Prussia and Silesia*); ***type of site*** *(settlement, grave, fortification, without specification, path)* and ***type of place-name*** *(17 expressions, based on the determinative element).*

Limitations

What has to be borne in mind when working on the database? First of all, the place-names spread very unevenly over the eight regions. The major share of place-names was collected in Lower Saxony (22,3%), followed by Prussia (17,6%), Baden-Württemberg (14,6%) and Hessen and Brandenburg (12,1%). Far

---

[1] "*Wenn aber die uralte Zeit noch irgendwo haftet in der neuen, so ist es in der Benennung der Dorffluren, weil der einfache Landmann lange Jahrhunderte hindurch kein Bedürfnis fühlt, sie zu verändern.* (Wie sich Waldstege und Pfade durch die Getreidefelder unverrückt bei den wechselnden Geschlechtern der Menschen erhalten, und da kaum ein Fuß hintreten kann wo nicht schon vor vielen Jahrhunderten gewandelt worden wäre, weil der Lauf des Wassers und die Bequemlichkeit des Ackerbaus oder die Viehtrift dafür notwendige Bestimmungen gab; ebenso getreu pflegt auch das Landvolk die alten Namen seiner stillen Feldmark zu bewahren) [...]." (Jacob Grimm (1840); zit. nach: Kleiber (1996))

[2] Since there is no room for a theoretical discussion, for those interested I recommend a reader that discusses the phenomenon place-names from very different viewpoints: Debus, F. and Seibicke, W. (eds.). 1996. Reader zur Namenkunde III,2. - Toponymie. Georg Olms Verlag, Hildesheim.

behind but still part of the interpretation there is Saxony (8,7%), North-Rhine-Westphalia (6,5%) and Silesia (5,9%).

From an archaeological point of view, it will become clear that in fact it is a northern and southern zone that is relevant for my work so that the strict division in regions will be obsolete. It is two (archaeological) aspects that suggest a splitting up in two larger zones: First: the appearance of the megalithic tomb as we meet it in Lower Saxony (northern zone) and the border of the Roman Empire (southern zone). For the regions of Hessen and North-Rhine-Westphalia this is slightly complicated, since they constitute of a transitional area, but thinking of the impact the Roman era had on these regions, they rather belong to a southern zone. The zones therefore consist of following regions: Northern zone: Lower Saxony, Prussia, Brandenburg, and Saxony. Southern zone: Baden-Württemberg, Hessen, North-Rhine-Westphalia and Silesia. These zones also correspond with those created by the language boundary that divides the German-speaking area in two, with Middle Lower German in the north and Middle High German in the South. Another linguistic aspect has to be taken into account: the regions east of the river Elbe became German-speaking not until approximately 1400 as a result of the German colonization of the east (König 1994:73f).

The fact, that with 66,6 % of all place names the northern zone is overrepresented, probably results from Strunk himself being from Prussia and thus having easier access to this and his neighbouring regions. But – keeping the afore said in mind - it is still possible to compare the zones.

Another aspect to be mentioned is that the category *type of place-name* only contains terms that seemed relevant to Strunk and leaves out further expressions that might point to archaeological sites. Since Strunk was looking for place-names that might consist of a time- value he didn't bother to collect place-names of general nature, like for example combinations on house-, old- or castle-. The same could be said of place-names with the determinative element "roman" which Strunk included only occasionally in his collection. Strunk points out to his readers that "roman" was an "in-word" in the 18th and 19th century, applied on everything that looked old and often was used by cartographers of the time, so that we here have a type of place-name of a very young age (Strunk 1931:30f). Besides mistakes made during the cataloguing – different sources and focuses – should be taken into account

Included in my database were expressions with following determinatives: Galgen/gallows, Gold/gold, Heiden/heathen, Heilig/sacred, Hexe/witch, Hüne/giant, Jude/jew, König/king, Topf/pot, Riese/giant, Römer/roman, Schelm/rogue, Schloss/palace or mansion, Schweden/swedish, Stein/stone, Teufel/devil, Toten/dead.

There is one term that needs explanation, since it is of importance for the interpretation of the figures below. Hüne – Giant in English – derives from Huns (the Asiatic peoples who ravaged Europe in the 4th and 5th century) and was applied on features the same way as Riese (which is another word for giant). Since the middle-ages the expression Hünengrab has been the name for what now is called megalithic tomb or dolmen.

Since space is limited, only some of the above mentioned expression that find their equivalents in English will be discussed here, following a general outline of the statistics.

Finally some remarks concerning the category *type of site*. The sub-unit *grave* includes any kind of grave, like megalithic tombs, burial mounds, flat graves as well as places of worship. The term *fortification* takes account of different types of hill-forts as well as roman and medieval fortresses. Altogether 54,5% of all sites fall to the subunit *grave*, 20,9% are *fortifications*, 14,8% are *without specification*, that is, no information was provided by the author[3], 7,9% of all sites comprise of settlements and only 1,9% are said to be pathways.

Although a category *date of the site* (provided by Stunk) was included in the database it is not part of the analysis since it is very unreliable.

The interpretation of **Figure 1** shows that there are three terms that appear more often than the others. Those are: Hüne-/Giant (15,1%), Heide-/Heathen (12,8%) and Galgen-/Gallows (12,%) followed by Gold-/Gold and Schweden-/Swedish. One question to ask would be: which term dominates what region? Whereas in Baden-Württemberg and Hessen place-names with the determinative Heiden-/Heathen predominates, in Brandenburg, Lower-Saxony, North-Rhine-Westphalia and Prussia place-names on Hüne-/Giant are in the majority. In Saxony most place-names were combinations with the word Galgen-/Gallows, in Silesia the most frequent place-name is on Schweden-/Swedish.

Another question that leaps to mind is to ask what kind of site is hiding behind what kind of place-name and in which region which kind of site can be found (in connection to the here presented place-names). While in Lower Saxony the sub-unit grave is the one most frequently met (27,7%), in Baden-Württemberg most sites that are listed in connection with a place-name are settlements (58,8%). The fortification is the kind of site that is mentioned repeatedly in the area of Prussia. This is also true for the sites that are listed without specification. Since the sub-unit pathway only turns up four times it isn't really comparable and will therefore not be mentioned again.

---

[3] Since most of these unspecified sites are linked to place-names on *Swedish* or *mansion* and are situated in Prussia it is most probably fortifications we are dealing with. This is only one example of how unreliably Strunk was working.

642	Lower Saxony (143)	Prussia (113)	Baden Württemberg (94)	Brandenburg (78)	Hessen (78)	Saxony (56)	North R. Westphalia (42)	Silesia (38)
Giant	27	18	11	12	18	2	9	-
Heathen	14	9	18	6	20	5	4	6
Gallows	14	13	7	8	4	24	3	4
Gold	2	13	12	3	10	7	-	1
swedish	5	15	4	5	2	4	2	8

Figure 1: Place-names and regions

What word-combinations are used for what kind of site? Even here, tendencies become obvious. With almost 15%, graves triggered the creation of place-names that allude to Galgen-/Gallows, closely followed by those alluding to Hüne-/giant. Settlement remains most often figure as place-names that are based on the term Heide-/Heathen (17,6%) and next in line Gold-/Gold. Finally a look at the subunit fortification: In 30,6% of all cases a connection to the term Hüne-/giant was established in place-names referring to fortifications.

Place-names

Giant (Hüne-)-
The North German term Hüne, in its current form, means giant, huge, strong man and was spread out in the 17th century via written language. In Middle Low German (1200 - 1600) singular Hüne means Giant, in the plural an eastern non-Christian people, Huns, Hungarians, sine the 13th century even Giant. The early New-High German 14th century "Heune" means the same. All terms are founded on the native name of a wandering Turkic/Asiatic people that ravaged Europe in the 4th and 5th century.[4]

The traditional name for megalithic tomb – Hünengrab, is known since the 16th century but already in the 14th and 15th century in the Upper (southern) German language-area we find place-names like "ze hiunengrebern" or "an hiunengreber weg" (Etymologisches Wörterbuch des Deutschen 1995:565f).

In the database 97 place-names are built on Hüne/Giant (for example Giant's stone, Giant's grave, Giant's hill, Giant's bed, Giant's oven etc.) and most of them are located in Lower Saxony but they spread over all regions with a slight predominance in the northern zone were they most often point to stone graves and hill-forts. In many cases we find folktales related to the single name and site that mention names of historical or mythical persons/kings that are said to be giants buried there. In folk beliefs Attila the Hun for example was said to be a giant-king (Handwörterbuch des deutschen Aberglaubens Band 9 2000:1126). Generally giants were believed to have preceded the human race – heathen natives in the lands that then were inhabited by Christians, so to speak. The traces they left are today visible as graves, hill-forts, standing stones, that couldn't – because of their size – be

---

[4] After having the stories about the Huns and Hunnish invasion orally transmitted to the Middle Ages they later become an element in the Old Norse Sagas and the Old German Nibelungenlied were their memory was kept alive.

man-made. Saxo Grammaticus for example is a medieval writer who informs us on this. Another source is the old English poem: the Wanderer (The Exeter Book 1961).

Heathen-
The term Heathen is problematic since on the one hand it stands for follower of a non-Christian religion and on the other hand means heath (land). Working on the assumption that the place-names here listed are linked to archaeological sites the term has to be understood in its former meaning, which doesn't rule out exceptions.

In the eyes of the Christians the Heathen were the Germanic tribes in the North as well as the Romans in the south and the Slaves in the east. In its early meaning the term describes foreign people in the whole (can also be seen in connection with the missionary work among the Germanic tribes). Not until the 14th and finally the 16th century the term obtains its final form when it describes non-Christians, non-Jews and Moslems (Etymologisches Wörterbuch des Deutschen 1995:522).

Place-names that build on Heide/heathen predominate in the southern zone were they are found in connection to settlement remnants. Most probably we are dealing with roman remains containing of bricks and stone that were easy to detect. Roman remains distinguish themselves from other ruins because they were abandoned and differ from the medieval style of architecture. People came into contact with these sites when they were looking for building material. Heathen means here a foreign and strange people that were unknown to those finding the remnants. In some regions dwarfs were thought to be the inhabitants of these places (Handwörterbuch des deutschen Aberglaubens Band 9 2000:1111) The Romans as a people were not known by then. On the other hand - when in early modern times the Romans suddenly become of interest, an increase in place-names building on römisch/roman naming everything that is old (this is true especially for the 18th and 19th century) can be noticed. Anyway this allows us to assume that the creation of place-names that build on Heide/heathen can be dated back to the middle-ages. A similar situation prevails in the northern zone were place-names on Heide/heathen often turn up in connection with graves. As mentioned before this has to be seen as a result of the missionary work undertaken since Charlemagne in what is called the northern zone.

When it comes to cult and rites there were different ways for the missionaries to deal with these phenomena. Either they had to incorporate them and make them part of the new religion or make them illegal and inferior to Christianity. To lean on already existing heathen ideas was of course a less painful way of introducing a new religion. So ritual sites, gods and religious holidays were filled with new meaning. Those sites and rituals – this includes for example burial rites and places - which the church couldn't accept or modify were to bear the imprint of the negative, the evil and dangerous. In folk beliefs the heathen, like the giants, became human predecessors who could perform unimaginable deeds, like building huge stone graves and fortresses. At the same time it was these features that kept alive the memories and knowledge of what took place in times past.

Gallows-
A very common place-name in combination with gallows is Galgenhügel/Galgenberg or Galgenbaum - Gallows-hill or Gallows-tree in English. The Gallows, a wooden framework on which criminals were put to death by hanging, were mainly situated visibly on a hill of natural origin or one made by man, in close proximity to settlements, outside the city-walls, along with arterial roads or at cross-roads. Even other aspects, like the proximity to lepers´ colonies or Jewish cemeteries could be the deciding factor for the founding of gallows. In addition to the use of a wooden framework the simpler or initial form of hanging - using a tree or branch – was never given up on. Hanging was part of the High justice, so that gallows on the one hand were symbolizing claims to power and throne but on the other hand meant to scare off potential criminals by being far visible (Auler 2003).

Apart from written sources, historical maps, paintings or still existing ruins, place-names testify to the existence of gallows that were used until the 19th century. In several narrow/minor investigations carried out by Auler, a German archaeologist, he was able to give evidence for a large number of gallows and he estimates that in central-Europe there must have been tenthousands of such constructions (ibid 2003). Fact is that place-names built on the term Galgen-/gallows rank third in the database. They are most often found in the northern zone, especially in Saxony.

The appearance of the prehistoric burial mound very much resembles the hill constituting the base of gallows, so it wouldn't be surprising if the picture of gallows would form before the eyes of the ignorant viewer of a burial mound. The sight of real gallows probably was an everyday matter for most people.

Place-names with Galgen-/gallow we find in equal parts in the naming of open fields and village lands that are containing graves, settlements or sites without specification[5]. Even settlement-remains might appear as rises in the landscape. Moreover finds of skeletons in burial mounds could have led to the assumption that there once has been gallows. The dead criminals usually were buried in the ground nearby or beneath the gallows. Gallows were believed to be the place of residence of witches and demons of the dead and the lure of the forbidden place was holding an attraction for people until modern times. Not only in body parts and belongings of the dead secret and sacred powers were hidden. The rope used for the hanging or nails of the gallows were said to

---
[5] Since I assume these to be graves, it is two thirds of the place-names that point to this kind of site.

be lucky charms (Handwörterbuch des deutschen Aberglaubens Band 3 - 2000:261ff).

For economical reasons grave-mounds were indeed used as gallows hills, as Auler could demonstrate at several sites, like Münster or Hundisburg in North-Rhine-Westphalia. Also notes from excavations in the early 20th century, when burial mounds were searched for urns and other finds, speak of remains of medieval and early-modern gallows in the mound (Auler 2003).

In Hundisburg on a hill called Galgenberg/Gallows hill a burial ground is situated. Since the 13th or 14th century the site was reused as place of execution. Archaeologists brought to light 14 skeletons without grave goods and building material that could be linked to gallows. Traces of the wooden construction were found as postholes in prehistoric features (ibid 2003).

I think it became clear that graves or burial mounds of course were perceived as part of the cultural and inhabited landscape. Rarely as what they were, but rather with a new connotation since the use of mounds was known only in combination with gallows not burial-places. Besides - even a closer look at a burial mound could have lead to the wrong conclusion. A dead body in a hill, a non Christian burial that is, could only be a criminal so the feature has to be a gallows hill. Since Gallows were in use for many hundred years it is of course difficult to tell when a single place-name was created, but I think it is safe to say, that place-names referring to Gallows could mainly have been coined in the Middle Ages.

Gold-
Place-names with gold- (including the terms silver, iron, and treasure) is another grouping we meet quite often in the database (ranking fourth). They spread evenly over the regions so that there is no observable difference between the northern and southern zone. It is mostly settlements that were found in combination with place-names speaking of gold. It has probably been single finds made during working in the fields that were the deciding factor for the naming of a place. It could have been coins or jewellery that were buried or left behind at deserted settlements. Strangely enough these place-names seldom occur with the sub-unit grave, although one would think that precious metals or treasures in a wider sense are rather linked to graves.

The results of the statistical analysis suggest that grave-robbery didn't occur too often or that it wasn't gold that was found. Believing in subterranean treasures and magic to get them always played an important role in folk beliefs. Lucky finds of course put life in the believe in treasures as well as treasure hunters. Urns for example were believed to have grown of the earth or being vessels belonging to dwarfs, carrying the ashes of witches or pagans. Some thought they were containing treasures (Handwörterbuch des deutschen Aberglaubens Band 3 - 2000:1110, Band 7 - 2000:1002ff). But even though people were ascribing magical powers to these vessels, the fear of evil spirits stuck to them probably was predominant.

The 17th century – especially the Thirty Years War – was a century that saw many treasures buried and dug up again. The correspondence to the category type of site is of course missing in this explanation, but the possibility shouldn't be neglected.

In this connection it is almost impossible to make a statement about the date of appearance of this kind of place-names, since we are dealing with lucky finds that can occur at any time.

Swedish-
Another kind of place-name that is definitely tied to the Thirty Years War both in the northern and southern zone and the 90 years that followed[6] is Schweden- or Swedish or put in concrete terms the place-name "The Swedish fort". Though there are other place-names, like "the Swedish cemetery" they are an exception. "Swedish forts" are mostly found in regions were battles took place and which were under Swedish occupation during the time when Sweden was a great power until the Nordic wars (the Swedish – Polish War (1655-1660) and the great Nordic War (1700-1721) that is) (Großer Historischer Weltatlas 1991:24ff). In Silesia for example the most frequent place-names are those alluding to the Swedes, in Prussia we find them positioned second after Hüne/giant. Of course there existed forts that were really built by Swedes but these are not part of this database. We actually find place names referring to Swedish forts in every region, yet far off the actual theatres of war. This points to the impression the Swedes and these times of war must have made on people.

The origin of the new names for hill-forts and in a few cases graves was in the decades to come – in a time of digesting and creation of legends – attributed to the belligerent Swedes.

In several cases we have two different place-names for the same spot, which leads to the assumption that a (probably) younger one (the Swedish fort) replaced the older ones that are composed of combinations with the terms: Hüne/Giant (frequently used in combination with fortifications), Gallows- or King, but which continued to exist in the memory of people.

Conclusions

In folk beliefs history was the age of small people (dwarfs) and, more important to us, big people like giants. Soon the heathen and the Huns developed gigantic features and even later the Swedes were about to go through the same process of becoming giants as is told in

---
[6] Here it is mainly the area around the Baltic sea that was effected.

a handful of folk tales but the transformation was never fulfilled (Handwörterbuch des deutschen Aberglaubens Band 3 - 2000:1649f). So one could say that the mystical picture of popular history was shaped by historical incidents that took place in the Early Middle Ages (the Huns ravaging), the developing Middle Ages (Christianization of the northern zone) and Early Modern Times (the 30 Years War and Swedish claims to power). So, if nothing else, this work once again shows how deep an impact historical events had on people and how they shaped their perception of landscape which in this case mirrors the fears of people (of mythical creatures, warlike people, hanging and in consequence a non-Christian burial) and at the same time inspired imagination. Only place-names built on gold lack these negative connotations although they are a product of the same way of thinking between fear and curiosity.

The analysis of place-names – it doesn't need to be on the basis of a large scale documentation – certainly helps us in understanding the way people were observing their landscape and the pre-historical monuments being part of it since the middle ages. Unfortunately the place-names themselves and the tales connected to them are about to become extinct (as did and do most of the archaeological sites mentioned in the database) so the material that is left to work on is very limited – but more than nothing.

References

Auler, J. 2005. Richtstätten des ausklingenden Mittelalters und der frühen Neuzeit im Fokus moderner Archäologie. http://www.archaeologisch.de/forschung/richtstaetten/richtstaetten.html. 26.04.2005

Bächtold-Stäubli, H. & Hoffmann-Krayer, E. (eds.). 2000. *Handwörterbuch des deutschen Aberglaubens – Band 3*. Walter de Gruyter, Berlin

Bächtold-Stäubli, H. & Hoffmann-Krayer, E. (eds.). 2000. *Handwörterbuch des deutschen Aberglaubens – Band 7*. Walter de Gruyter, Berlin

Bächtold-Stäubli, H. & Hoffmann-Krayer, E. (eds.). 2000. *Handwörterbuch des deutschen Aberglaubens – Band 9*. Walter de Gruyter, Berlin

Engel, J. & Zeeden, E.W. (eds.). (1991). *Großer Historischer Weltatlas – Neuzeit*. Bayrischer Schulbuch-Verlag, München.

Kleiber, W..1996. Vom Sinn der Flurnamenforschung. Debus, F. & Seibicke, W. (eds). *Reader zur Namenkunde III, 2 – Toponymie*. Georg Olms Verlag, Hildesheim. 405-417.

Krapp, G.P. & van Kirk Dobbie, E. (eds.). The Wanderer. *The Exeter Book*. Columbia University Press, New York.134 -137

König, W. 1994. *dtv-Atlas zur deutschen Sprache*. Deutscher Taschenbuch Verlag, München.

Pfeifer. W. et. a. (eds.). 1995. *Etymologisches Wörterbuch des Deutschen*. Akademie Verlag, Berlin

Strunk, H.1930. Flurnamen und Vorgeschichte. *Altpreußische Forschungen 7. und 8. Jahrgang 1930 und 1931. Sonderschriften des Vereins für Familienforschung in Ost- und Westpreußen e. V. Nr. 65/4*. Hamburg. 17 – 32.

Strunk, H. 1931. Flurnamen und Vorgeschichte. 2. Teil. *Altpreußische Forschungen 8. Jahrgang 1931. Sonderschriften des Vereins für Familienforschung in Ost- und Westpreußen e. V. Nr. 65/4*. Hamburg. 1 – 45.

Strunk, H. 1932. Flurnamen und Vorgeschichte. 3. Teil. *Altpreußische Forschungen 9. Jahrgang 1932. Sonderschriften des Vereins für Familienforschung in Ost- und Westpreußen e. V. Nr. 65/5*. Hamburg. 1 - 8.

Myths and folklore as aids in interpreting the prehistoric landscape at the Carrowkeel passage tomb complex, Co. Sligo, Ireland

Sam Moore

> "Then Finn sat upon his hunting *tulach* [mound] on top of high Keshcorran; at which instant there tarried by him none but his two wolf-dogs; Bran and Sceolaig; . . . and at this point each wrathful and eagerly fierce wolf-dog slipped from his leash to course the tulach. Howbeit the ruler that at such time had sway in Keshcorran was Conaran son of Imidel, a chief of the Túatha Dé Dannan; . . .bade his three daughters (that were full of sorcery) to go and take vengeance of Finn for his hunting. The women sought the entrance of the cave that was in the *tulach*, and there sat beside each other."
>
> *Bruidhen Chéise Chorainn*, (O Grady (ed.) 1892:343).

Introduction – monuments and myths

Some scholars such as Chapman (1997), Bradley (1993; 2002) and Holtorf (1998) have suggested that some ancient monuments may have acted as 'timemarks' that possessed an 'afterlife' or a 'life-history'. Many of these were re-appropriated and given political meanings by later generations. These 'timemarks' have been preserved in, and made part of many different history cultures over the ages, in which they played various social and political roles. Secondary burials in cairns, for instance, may have been a convenient method for inventing genealogies on which claims for political power or ideological supremacy could be based. Similar political or ideological intentions may also have led to activities which can account for later prehistoric finds at or near ancient monuments, for the re-use of building material or objects from earlier periods, for the imitation of ancient monuments, and for the revival of past traditions. All these activities can be seen as appropriations of the past in order to legitimatise ideological interests of different kinds. In many ways the association of a monument with a particular god, pseudo mythical king, important mythical or legendary event etc. could be seen as an act of re-enforcing a particular ancient monument's ideological signifiers. Potential examples of this phenomenon can be seen through the reuse of the passage tomb of the Mound of the Hostages at Tara, Co. Meath (Newman 1997; Bhreathnach 2006), later activity in the vicinity of Newgrange, Co. Meath (O'Kelly 1982; Eogan 1986), the La Tene decorated bone pieces from cairn H at Sliabh na Cailleach passage tomb complex, Co. Meath (Conwell 1873; McMann 1991) or the Iron Age burials at tomb 26 Carrowmore, Co. Sligo (Burenhult 1984; Bergh 1995).

Taçon remarks that to many cultures throughout the world landscapes were filled with spirits, that in many ways the landscape could be viewed as being alive with the supernatural (Taçon 1999). Every landscape is made up of an unlimited number of individual locations that may have acquired a meaning from the contextual experience of them. Tilley explains that daily passages through the landscape - encountering cliffs, rivers, outcrops etc. - become 'biographic encounters' and recall traces of past activities and previous events, hence the landscape becomes an embodiment of social and individual times of memory (1994). This theme is shared by Ingold who sees that placenames, movement along paths and specific locales in a landscape form the basis of memories and remembrance. Thus it can be demonstrated that the lives of people and the history of their relationships can be traced to the textures of the land (2000). Within this framework of movement in a landscape these locations may have acted as reference points where a tree, a rock, an outcrop, a stream or a vista may have acted as a source of identification or where similar features could have indicated a special place of the ancestors or a place for worship, ritual or communal activities (Bergh 2002). Bradley examines ethnographic evidence in order to understand why many features in the landscape may possess special powers; play a part in a mythical narrative; where paths crossing the landscape might recreate the movement of an ancestor or that an entire area might take on a sacred character (2000). These special places often occupy a liminal space in the landscape such as mountain tops, valley passes, islands, bogs, lakes, fording points of rivers, intertidal areas, megalithic tombs or visible monuments etc. A significant sacred place could have been perceived as a site where different cosmic levels come into contact – earth, sky and otherworld – the *axis mundi*. Ceremonial events at these sites play important roles in maintaining order and averting chaos – the two elements of religion – the sacred and the profane. The importance of mountain tops and the construction of monuments has been well described by Bergh's analysis of Knocknarea (2000; 2002) and even some mountains without monuments on their summits possess a ritual significance in prehistory such as the Sugarloaf Mountain in Co. Wicklow (Corlett 1998), or Croagh Patrick in Co. Mayo (Corlett 1997; 2001). These considerations of place, memory, remembrance etc., can often be linked to associated folklore which may contain "material residues of the past" (Layton 1999:32) and reflect a "mythical geography of the later inhabitants of the landscape" (Roymans 1995:4).

Many important archaeological complexes and archaeological remains in the Irish landscape have a wealth of stories associated with them, some offering creation myths about a site, telling of great deeds or battles that occurred there and all add to the their cultural significance. Also, many liminal sites retain certain elements of 'Otherworldness' that are reinforced by myths and legends associated with that place. This is hinted at by Gazin-Schwartz and Holtorf who suggest that in certain instances references to Otherworldly entrances in folklore might represent a continuation of local knowledge regarding the original function of prehistoric mounds (1999:16). The meaning behind a monument changes through time as successive communities alter their perception of the past but it is important to bear in mind the memories and histories associated with monuments. Myth and legends; folktales and superstitions do not contain accurate or reliable aspects of the past but they do reflect parts of the life history of particular monuments that extends from their construction to up to the present (Holtorf 1998; Gavin-Swartz & Holtorf 1999). Until recently many archaeologists focused on the construction of a particular prehistoric site and its intensive or initial stages of use without analysis of the apparent array of meanings that they gather through time and how they are perceived today. Folklore is one of the various layers of meaning that monuments accrue through time. It often reflects some of the later interpretations of prehistoric sites with recent and contemporary folklore being an important part of how people of recent times and today might perceive monuments.

Ireland has a vast collection of fairy stories dealing with both malevolent and benevolent beings such as sheeogues, dullahans, leprechauns, banshees, and púcas. Most of these beings belong to the *Sidh* (pronounced Shee) who are the otherworld dwellers that inhabit the Irish countryside but remain, for the most part, invisible to humans. The fairy palace, a place of great beauty with wonderful food, drink and music, was where they dwelt. These are often the numerous cairns and burial mounds that dot many Irish hilltops – Knocknashee in Co. Sligo, Sheebeg and Sheemore in Co. Leitrim being examples. Also ringforts, mottes and other archaeological sites were associated with the fairies, along with lone bushes, springs and rivers, caves and enchanted lakes within hills and mountains. Irish folklore accounts have many stories relating to misfortune or even death befalling people who interfere with the *Sidh* or their dwellings and this has in some cases helped preserve numerous monuments in the Irish landscape (Champion and Cooney 1999). The *Sidh* are associated with the Túatha Dé Dannan and are generally referred to as the 'good people' so as not to offend them by using diminutives or disrespectful terms. The so-called 'little people' are derived from the introduction of English traditions of imps and elves while in authentic Irish folklore fairies were rarely small. Following the mythical invasion of the first humans to Ireland the Túatha Dé Dannan were relegated to these otherworldly realms (Ó hÓgáin 1991; 1999; Champion and Cooney 1999).

In many ways the Nationalist aspects of how archaeology was used is similar to that of folklore. Following the rise of 18th century romanticism popular culture was no longer seen as something to be looked down upon, but as a source of artistic inspiration and as a resource of national culture. Folklore became closely associated with the rise of cultural nationalism and can be seen in its use by Thomas Davis and his Young Ireland movement where the peasantry, their language, music, dance, stories and traditions were seen as the most authentic part of the Irish nation. This impacted on the formation of the Gaelic League and the Gaelic Literary Revival of the late 19th and early 20th centuries, including the works of W. B. Yeats. Greatly influenced by the German brothers Grimm, oral tales and traditions began to be collected in Ireland by the middle of the 19th century, and they continue to be so by the Department of Irish Folklore in University College Dublin and by the Ulster Folk Museum. Irish folktales are famous for their variety and the sheer number. Two main groups can be identified – firstly there are those dealing hero-tales, and wonder-tales many of which are derived from late medieval romances based on the earlier traditions from the Fionn Cycle of tales and secondly there are a number of international folktales, some of which arrived in Ireland as popular stories during the Middle Ages, but many appear to be relatively recent in date. Many of these tales are altered or popular renditions from earlier traditions while many are sources of entertainment. Today, the use of myths, legends and folk tales has become key marketing tools for the tourist industry and other commercial ventures. Certain aspects of the 'life history' of a number of monuments have become associated with cultural Nationalism, commerce and tourism and are often expressed through, or strongly associated with, folklore. Tara and Brú na Bóinne being good examples (Woodman 1995; Cooney 1996; Ronayne 2001).

The Carrowkeel/Keshcorran Megalithic Complex: an overview

It is remarkably clear that, despite the fact that Carrowkeel is one of the four major passage tomb complexes in Ireland, and despite its significance in terms of western European Neolithic studies, remarkably little archaeological research has been carried out on this site by way of modern excavation or detailed survey. The excavations carried out by Macalister, Armstrong and Praegar in 1911 (1912) provides the foundation of our knowledge on Carrowkeel. Thus, the architectural aspects and cultural assemblage that the excavators uncovered provide the basis of how Carrowkeel is seen in terms of the other complexes, and how it fits into our understanding of the Neolithic. Prior to Macalister's investigations the area had received no archaeological investigation, and since 1911 no major archaeological field work has been carried out until Stefan Bergh studied the area as part of his PhD thesis on the passage tombs of the Cúil Irra region of Co. Sligo. The work carried out by Bergh has addressed this lack of archaeological analysis of this region somewhat, however, his work was focused on the Cúil Irra region of Sligo and his study of Carrowkeel was directed towards an understanding of Cúil Irra, to which Carrowkeel is intrinsically connected. (1995).

The Carrowkeel/Keshcorran complex is found in the range of hills called the Bricklieve Mountains in south-east County Sligo, which cover an area of $c.25$ km². The range is to the west of Lough Arrow, a 3,140 acre spring fed lake, which is drained by the north flowing River Uinshin. A number of small lakes occur within and along the flanks of the Bricklieves and due to the karstic formation of the mountains a complex diffuse hydrological recharge occurs with sinkholes, springs, relict caves and small streams being present. The form of the mountains, created by physical and chemical processes over immense time periods, gives them a highly distinctive and dramatic shape.

The Bricklieve Mountains are covered in poor quality pasture and blanket bog. Parts of this blanket bog reach a depth of 5 m. The geology of the range and subsequent glacio-karstic processes have given a north northwest to south southeast prevailing direction of the valleys, rifts and long axis of the hills. The range can be separated into two topographical zones. The first zone is to the east and is dominated by the Carrowkeel group of fifteen cairns, and is where the majority of passage tombs are located. It comprises a limestone upland with three dramatic rift valleys that make up four distinctive ridges, with a fifth slightly less distinctive ridge to the west (cairns A to P and cairn X (see figure 1), ranging between $c.240$ to 320 m OD. The western zone is made up of five hills with the western most being Keshcorran with cairn Q on its summit standing at 359 m OD, while the remaining hills range between $c.240$ to 210 m OD. However, the western side lacks the cliff walled rifts of the east side of the range and its limestone hills are more rounded but are still considerably prominent when viewed from the north. A solitary cairn – cairn Y, isolated in many respects from the other groups, is found on a prominence ($c.240$ m OD) in the south of the Bricklieves in Carricknahorna West townland. In total there are twenty three cairns within the complex and eleven of these have identifiable chambers – four undifferentiated; seven cruciform. All but one (cairn Y) of the twenty three cairns has a preference for being located on the north end of the ridge or hill they occupy, and these are on the northern side of the Bricklieves. The eleven identifiable chambers are orientated between north east to north west. Many of them appear to reflect an 'ideological communication' between Carrowkeel and the Cúil Irra group of passage tombs – Knocknarea, Carrowmore and Cairns Hill, which are located $c.20$ kms. north of Carrowkeel (Bergh 1995:162). A further eight prehistoric monuments occur within the upland area including court tombs, unclassified megalithic tombs and barrows (figure 1).

The surrounding prehistoric landscapes

Many comparisons and differences can be drawn between the four major passage tomb groups in Ireland – Carrowkeel/Keshcorran, Brú na Bóinne, Sliabh na Caillighe and Cúil Irra, (Cooney 1990; 2000:152-164). One difference is the height above sea level of the cairns and their high visibility towards the north. The other difference is the large concentration of other Neolithic and prehistoric burial and ritual type monuments within 10 km northwest, south and east of this complex. This concentration indicates both intensive settlement and extensive ritual activity in the landscape around Lough Arrow during the Neolithic. To the north of the Bricklieve Mountains are a belt of drumlins that follow the same axis as the Bricklieves, having a north northwest to south southeast prevailing direction and these are also present to the north east along the River Uinshin's. On the summits of two of these drumlins are two sites considered by Herity as outliers of the Carrowkeel/Keshcorran complex – Ardloy and Sheereevagh (1974:58), however, Sheerevagh is actually a bowl barrow. There are also a portal tomb and a court tomb in less prominent locations. Approximately 2.5 km to the north of Keshcorran Mountain is a small area of limestone upland (above 100 m) at Doomore, with a cairn north east of its highest point. On the summits of drumlins nearby Doomore are a considerable number of bowl barrows and mounds. Further to the north west and c.4.5 kms north of Keshcorran is the upland limestone area of Carrigans Upper (above 100 m), which extends north to the Carrickbanagher area which has a dense concentration of barrows and an apparent bronze age landscape is preserved here (Condit & Gibbons 1991:9; Mount 1995; 1998; 1999; Farrelly & Keane 2002; forthcoming). To the west is the river plain of the Owenmore river - the Plains of Corran, predominantly made up of drumlin swarms. To the south of the Bricklieves are the Curlew Mountains, a range made up of Red Sandstone with an east-west axis, that are seen by some as a natural frontier between north and south Connacht and a gateway to west Ulster (Kieran O'Conor, *pers comm.*). There is practically no archaeology evident in these mountains, however, a medieval road – Bóthar an Chorainn is present on the west side and another on the east side – Bóthar an Iarla Rua. A possible cairn is to be found on the most eastern hill at Sheegorey. Just south of the Curlews is the Plains of Boyle, a limestone upland surrounded by drumlins on a west south west to east north east axis. A massive concentration of barrows, along with four hengiform monuments occur here in two main areas at Knockadoo-brusna and Killaraght, just south east of Lough Gara (Knox 1914; Condit & Simpson 1998:47; Fedengren 2002:146-7). To the east of the Bricklieves and on the opposite side of Lough Arrow is the Moytura limestone upland (McGloin & Moore 1996a; Mount 1996; Moore 2000) that runs parallel to the

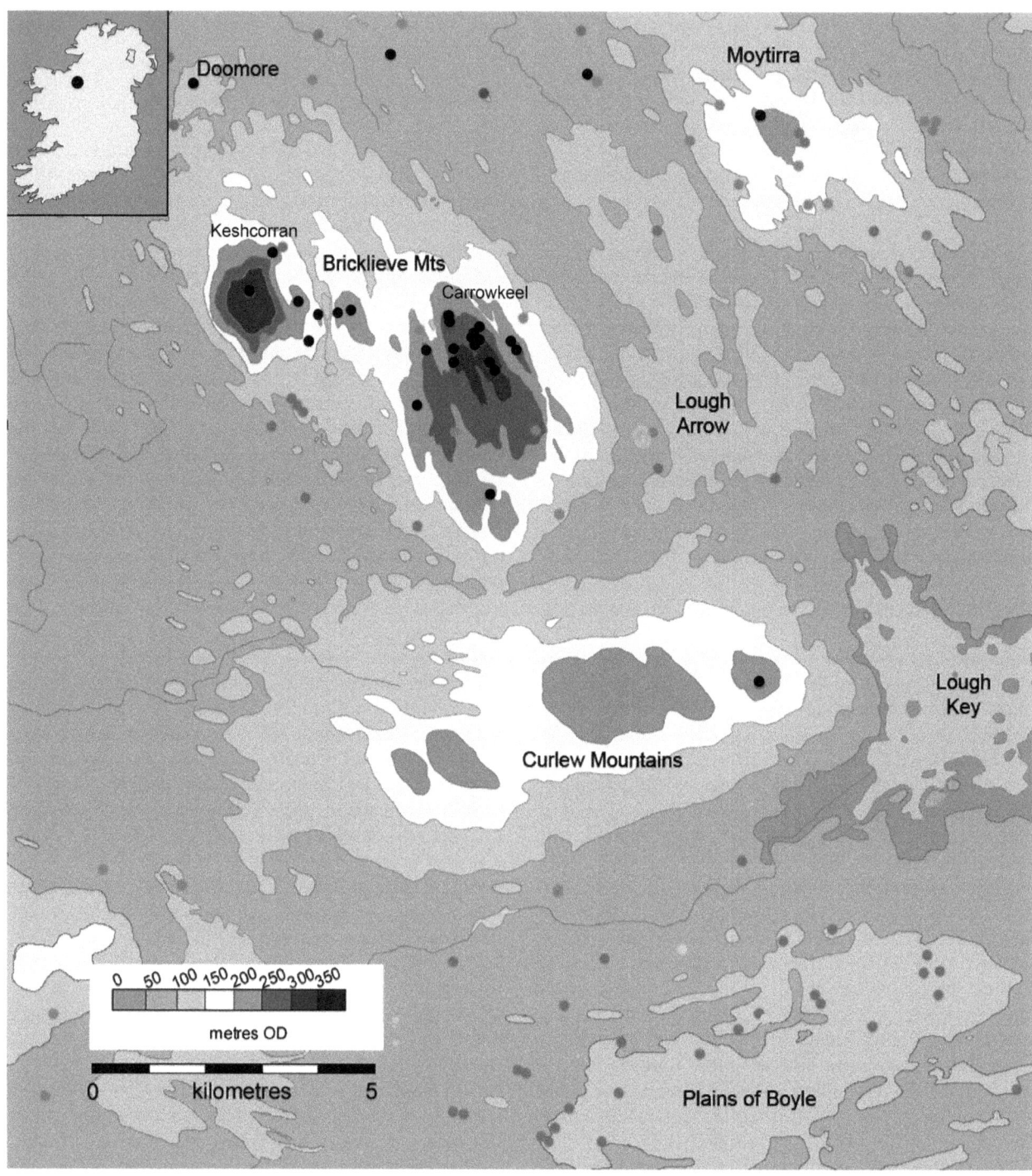

*Figure 1. Map of the Bricklieve Mountains and surrounding prehistoric landscapes.
(The black dots represent cairns, while grey dots represent megalithic monuments and barrows).*

Bricklieves with the outlier cairn of Seelewey being at the highest point (226 m OD). This area has a collection of megaliths of all types along with mounds and barrows amounting to twenty two sites. North west of Moytura lying at *c.*68 m OD is the 58 m diameter Heapstown kerbed cairn, one of the largest yet unopened cairns outside of the Boyne Valley, and this was also considered to be an outlier by Herity, but not discussed by him (1974:58).

Carrowkeel: A cacophony of silence

The Bricklieve Mountains are not high mountains - and in today's landscape they are relatively easy to access by car and foot. However, they are seen as a place apart; a wild place and one not regularly visited by many people living on the flanks of the mountain range, although they, and the cairns on them, cannot be missed when looking along the horizon. A farmer living at Murhy Townland,

and who owns the land occupied by Keshcorran and the small cairn on Kelly's Hill - Cairn W - commented that he believed "there were human bones and the like found up over there" and nodded towards the Carrowkeel cairns, admitting he had never been there. In the near past it was the remoteness and poor quality of the land of this place that aided the preservation of the monuments and, perhaps, the absence of antiquarian interest in the site. This is particularly evident in the OS survey of 1836; the fact that the monuments were first 'discovered' by antiquaries as late as 1896 when Robert Lloyd Praeger was conducting botanical field work in the vicinity (Praeger 1934); the lack of early historical references to the cairns and the small amount of archaeological investigations until Bergh in the late 1980s (Bergh 1995).

Apart from Carrowkeel the other three main passage tomb complexes in Ireland, and many of isolated or smaller groups have a wealth of myths, legends and folklore associated with them. It is not my intention here to discus the various origins of these tales or their potential meanings only to say that they are another aspect of what Horltorf calls a monument's 'life history' (1998). Jean McMann discusses the hag or Caileach and her association with the Loughcrew cairns, but appears to believe somewhat that the legends of the hag of Beare has some link to the possible meaning behind the passage tombs there (1991). Gabriel Cooney and Sara Champion's article on Loughcrew is clear in that the oral traditions on the cairns form another part of the story of the site and the monuments become more mythic and ambiguous, places where the real world and the otherworld collide (1999). Cathy Swift's work on Brú na Bóinne suggests that the O'Kelly's understanding of the myths surrounding Newgrange are not 'windows on the Late Neolithic', as they suggest, but appear to reflect a later Iron Age origin for the mythical characters associated with the site. These characters are associated with the Túatha Dé Dannan (2001). Miranda Green sees the monuments at Loughcrew and Brú na Bóinne as a reaction of the composers of medieval Irish myth to their ancestral past and that these monuments were held in high esteem by local communities throughout the early medieval period. She too identifies many Irish myths and legends, particularly those containing cult imagery or evidence of ritual practice as being late prehistoric in origin but were later woven into medieval literature (1999).

With Carrowmore and Knocknarea there are few literary sources relating to the monuments but there is a considerable amount of oral tradition recorded by the Ordnance Survey Letters for example and through presumptions by Petrie (Ordnance Survey of Ireland 1837a 1837b; Wood-Martin 1882; Bergh 1995). The Carrowmore tombs were seen as the burial places of the Firbolg following their defeat by the Túatha Dé Dannan in the late medieval version of the first Battle of Moytura, which was a literary fabrication to explain the older second Battle of Moytura. On the summit of Knocknarea Mountain is the cairn Miosgán Meadhbha and local folklore suggests Queen Maeve, Queen of Connacht who ruled from her royal capital at Rathcroaghan, Co. Roscommon was buried here sometime around 500 AD (Bergh 2002). Queen Maeve, Meadhbha or Medb's name means 'one who intoxicates' and in early Irish texts she symbolises the traits of the ancient goddess of sovereignty and war-goddess. However, her depiction as being a power-hungry sex-object was a creation of later medieval writers. She is also said to be buried at Knockma near Tuam. Co. Galway and at Rathcroghan, near Tulsk in Co. Roscommon (Ó hÓgáin, 1991). In local tradition Maeve is said to be buried standing upright in the cairn of Miosgán Meadhbha armed with sword and spear and dressed in armour and facing her enemies in Ulster, but this has possibly derived from the story of Eoghan Bel's request to be buried the same way. He died during a battle in 543 AD with the Ulster men and was buried on a hill somewhere south of Sligo Bay (Wood-Martin, 1882:134; O'Rorke 1886, Vol. I 53-61). The cairn impressive size and prominence has most likely caused such a famous legendary character from Connacht to become associated with it.

The cairns on the Carrowkeel side of the Bricklieves fail to attract attention in the legends and myths of early historic sources, unlike the repertoire of tales associated with many of the other passage tomb complexes. However, the area around Keshcorran, the western zone of the Carrowkeel/Keshcorran complex, abounds in legendary and mythical tales from early sources. Likewise, the upland area of Moytura to the east of Carrowkeel is the site of the epic of the Irish Mythological Cycle of tales - *Cath Magh Tuired* (Gray 1982). There are some references to the Curlew Mountains also, but no such lore survives which relates to the Carrowkeel monuments or the associated landscape.

The Curlew Mountains

The range of Red Sandstone hills to the south of the Bricklieve Mountains, the Curlew Mountains - *Corr Sleibh na Seaghsa* - are practically devoid of any archaeological remains, particularly in comparison to its neighbouring upland areas of Moytura, the Plains of Boyle and the Bricklieves. However, the possible cairn of the Corr-Shliabh, possibly that on Sheegorey Hill, is mentioned in a number of early sources, including one of the later versions of the Story of the Sons of Tuireann where Lugh crosses the Curlews to Sean-Slieve (Keshcorran) onto the place of the bright-faced Corran (the plain of Corran) (Joyce 1907:32; Gregory 1970:45). The cairn is also mentioned in the Book of Ballymote in the tale *Imthreacht an Dá Nónbhar;* a modification on how Finn MacCumhall acquired his wisdom through his thumb (O'Rahilly 1984:328). In *Acallamh na Senorach*, the Curlews is called the 'Pointed Mountain of the Fian and the 'Cataract of the Sons of Erc', then, according to the text Cáilte went north "to the Mountain of Seagais, the descendant of Ébricc, to the Gap of the Hundred, now

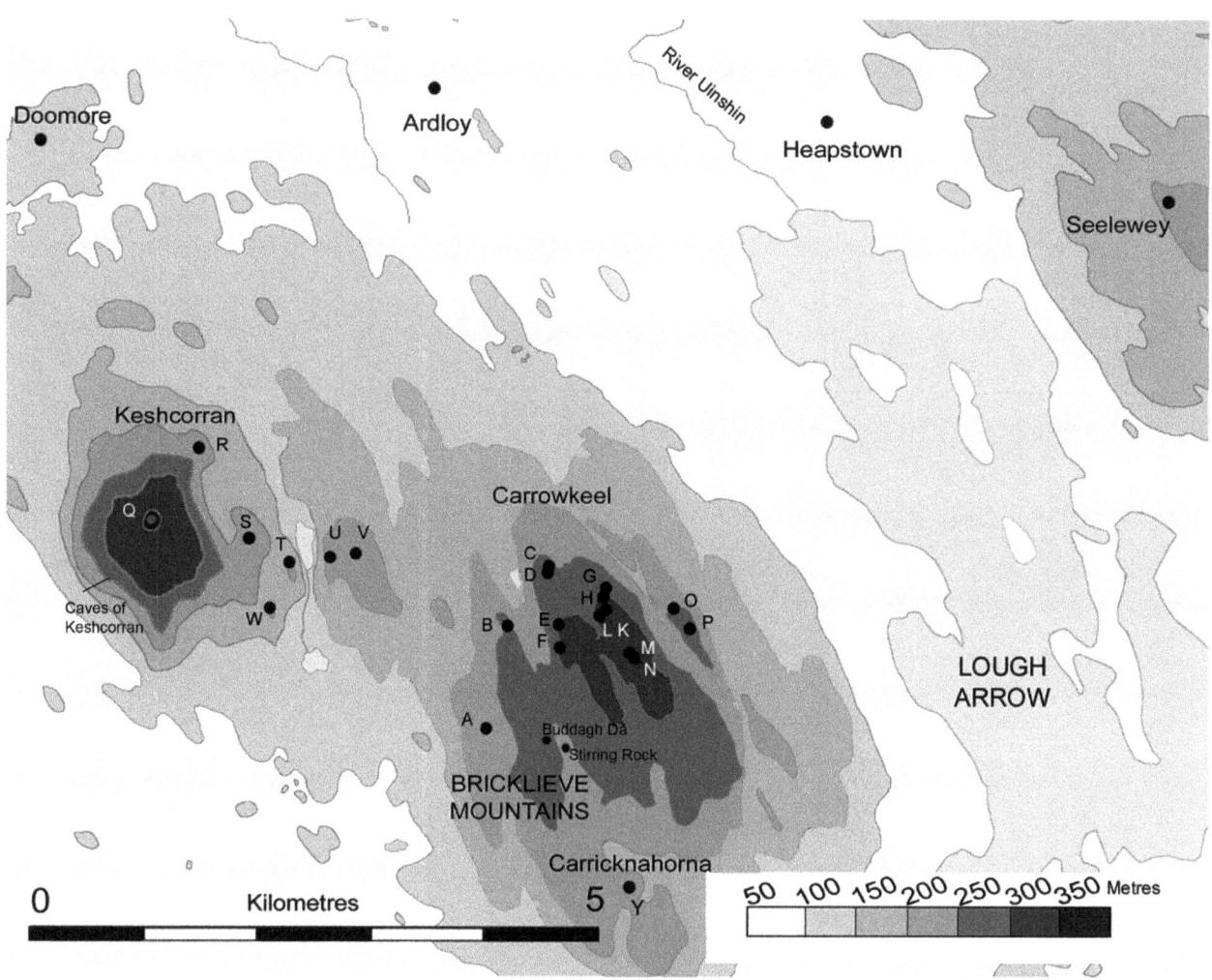

Figure 2. Map of the Carrowkeel Keshcorran Megalithic Complex.

called Keshcorran and out onto the Level plain of Corran (Dooley & Roe 1999:47). In the *Dinsheanchas* the cairn was said to be the burial place of Cé, the druid of Nuadha Lámhairgead, king of the Túatha Dé Dannan (Ordnance Survey of Ireland 1837b).

Keshcorran

Keshcorran Mountain is the highest point in the Bricklieves at 359 m and has the second largest cairn in the complex, Cairn Q, locally called the 'Pinnacle'. This cairn is on the most dominant of the hills and can be seen from considerable distances in all directions. The hill, the cairn and the series of caves on the western flank of the mountain all feature in a wide range of myths and legends and all are part of Garland Sunday Festive Assemblies (figure 2).

According to the *Dinsheanchas* the name Corran stems from the name of the harpist of the Túatha Dé Dannan, who was given the mountain and the plain that extends to the west, *Magh Chorainn* for his excellent harp playing; and Ceis stems from *Caelchéis*, an enchanted sow, which was killed there with the help of Corann's harp playing (Gwynn 1913, III: 438; 1924, IV: 292). However, Ó hÓgáin believes that *ceis* is a 5th -8th century Gaelic word meaning circuit (2001:219). and Wood-Martin claim's *ceis* means 'small harp' (1882:101).

The Ordnance Survey Letters of 1837 record the story of *Cailleach an Smugairle Buidhe* (the Hag of the Yellow Spits) which relates the story of the three daughters of Mannanán MacLir who dwelt in an enchanted lake in Keshcorran Mountain - Cé, Arabach and Léibe, who gave their names to the three principle lakes in the vicinity - Lough Key, Lough Arrow and Lough na Leibe (Wood-Martin 1882; Sharkey 1930:151-58).

Keshcorran features strongly in the Fenian Cycle of tales. It was sometimes called *Céis Chorainn na bhFiann* (Keshcorran of the Fianna) (Hogan 1910:172) and is the location for various stories associated with the adventures of the Fianna. The district around Keshcorran belonged to the clan of Gráinne, and her father, king Cormac Mac Airt. Gráinne settled there with Diarmait after making peace with Fionn MacCumhall, and it was from here that Diarmait set off from to the fatal hunt of the enchanted boar of Benbulben (O'Grady 1857:170; Breathnach

Figure 3. Aerial photograph of cairns G and H, Carrowkeel (Sam Moore).

Bruighion Chéisi Coruinn and this possibly relates to the cairn on Keshcorran, Cairn Q, the Brú of Conaran mac Imidel and this four hag daughters. As per the opening quotation in this paper, Fionn is watching the Fianna hunt on the plains below from the Brú, also referred to as the 'Hunting Mound', when a doorway opens in the side of the mound and Fionn and the Fianna are taken into the mound to be killed but are finally rescued by Goll mac Morna (O Grady (ed.) 1892:343-47; Ó Cathasaigh, 1977:35; MacNeill 1982:186).

Ireland's famous legendary hero and high king, Cormac Mac Airt was born at Keshcorran and a variety of versions of the story appear in a number of early texts. However, many of these versions contain the motif used in his birth story where the hero is suckled by a she-wolf in Úaim Cormaic (Cormac's Cave). The theme of wolves/hounds being connected with the area of Keshcorran is interesting as the association appears a number of times. The root word in Conaran's mac Imidel's name (mentioned above) is *cú*, meaning wolf (but also hound), Cormac is rescued from *úaim Céise Coraind* (the Cave of Keshcorran) where Cormac was being reared by a wolf by Conamail Conriucht (literally Wolf-like Wolf-shape), the leader of the wolves of Connaught (see Ó Cathasaigh, 1977 for discussion). It is worth noting that wolf or dog bones were found in the Caves of Keshcorran (Scharff et al. 1903:202; Woodman et al. 1997:140).

1968:141). Interestingly, the earliest surviving account of the Pursuit of Diarmait and Gráinne was penned by a local scribe, Dáithí Ó Duibhgeannáin, of Shancough and Ballindoon in 1651and is contained in R.I.A. MS 24 P 9 (Breathnach 1968:140). In the possible 12th century tale *Duanaire Finn,* Fionn and the Fianna are lured into one of the caves of Keshcorran Lon mac Líomhtha where he made weapons for them Lon was a "hugely tall warrior with a single foot" (Murphy 1933:5). His single foot was enormous and blue in colour; he bounded from hill to hill in a single leap. He had three arms, his face was as black as coal and he had one eye in the centre of his forehead. Lon was the master of all crafts and teacher of the smiths of the king of Lochlann. The best known of the stories is

MacNeill (1982:186) makes a note of a tradition concerning Áine an Chnoic living at Céis an Chuirin; a woman of great age with similar traits to the Cailleach Bhéara. The occurrence of the Cailleach and her association with passage tomb areas such as Loughcrew, Co. Meath, Slieve Gullion, Co. Armagh and Cailleach-a-vera's House in the Ox Mountains, Co. Sligo is discussed by McMann (1991).

Figure 4. The Caves of Keshcorran.

One of the best known stories about the caves concerns an old woman who lived at the ancient capital of Connacht at Rathcroghan in County Roscommon many, many years ago. At Rathcroghan, another place steeped in myth, is the cave/souterrain known as Oweynagat (*the Cave of the Cats*), but was formerly called 'The Hellmouth Door' as it was considered to be an entrance to the other-world. The story tells of the old woman holding the tail of an unruly calf; the only method she had to bring it home. However, the calf bolted and ran into the cave but the woman refused to let go. The calf kept running through twisting passages and caverns until the following morning, when the calf and woman, to her amazement and that of the locals, finally exited the darkness to arrive, twenty four miles from her home, at the caves of Keshcorran (Beranger 1779:10; Wood-Martin 1882 Vol. I:351-2)

The dates of these various tales come from numerous literary sources. The saga of the conception, birth and early years of Cormac Mac Airt, legendary high king of Ireland, is contained in the *Cath Maige Mucrama*. The earliest version of this story was written down *circa* 800 AD. Some of the other stories appear to date mainly from the 17th century and many are still reflected in the Schools Folklore Collection of 1936.

Moytura and Heapstown cairn

Some five kilometres east of the main group of cairns at Carrowkeel, on the opposite shore of Lough Arrow, lies Plain of Pillars or Magh Tuired, which is the mythical arena of the Second Battle of Moytura between the Túatha Dé Dannan and the Fomorians and many of the monuments and areas in Moytura have associated legends and placenames. The majority of these associations are linked to events in this cosmic proportioned saga and the actions of the gods of Ireland - the Túatha Dé Dannan (Moore 2000).

Two of the cairns, both possible passage tombs, at Seelewey in Barroe North townland and Heapstown Cairn, have strong associations with the mythical Battle of Moytura (Moore 2000; 2002). From Beranger's *Journal of a Tour in North Connaught* he writes about Heapstown cairn on June 27 1779 that "This carne said to be the Burial Place of Olioll [Ailill] King of Connaught in ye 4th century is situate in a plain near a village which got it from the name of Heapstown" (Ms4162:10; Harbison 2002:77). Heapstown Cairn was traditionally considered to be the grave of Ailill, brother of Niall of the Nine Hostages, who was the ruler of the area in the 4th century. Tirerill barony, where Heapstown is located, stems from *Tir Ailealla* which means 'Ailell's country'. A considerable number of other monuments are associated with the Battle of Moytura and were surveyed by Sligo's well known antiquarian Col. W.G. Wood-Martin (1884). He remarked that Heapstown cairn had nothing to do with the Second Battle of Moytura. He believed the legend that it was where Ailill was buried and therefore dated to the 4th century AD, hence, it could not be a prehistoric monument which was related to the Battle of Moytura. However, in the manuscript known RIA Ms 24 P 9, one of the two independent narrative versions of The Second Battle of Moytura is the following entry:

"The Fomoire had a warrior named Ochtriallach, the son of the Fomorian King Indech mac De Domnann. He suggested that every single man

they had should bring a stone from the shores of the River Drowes to cast into the well Slaine in Achad Abla to the west of Mag Tuired to the east of Lough Arrow. They went and every man put a stone into the well. For that reason the cairn is called Ochtriallach's Cairn". (Gray 1982)

This quotation shows the origin of Heapstown's name in Irish. The well Slaine, referred to in the passage, was created by Dian Cecht, the Túatha Dé Dannan's physician. The reason for the Fomoire blocking off the well was because wounded Dé Dannan warriors were bathed in the well, which cured them of all ailments meaning they could return to the battle. The Fomorians captures the well and the immense number of stones on the cairn was representative of their vast army. Seelewey (meaning 'Lugh's Seat) was where Lugh Lamhfhada, king of the Túatha Dé Dannan, surveyed the battle from. One of the two surviving independent narratives RIA Ms 24 P 9 containing *Cath Maige Tured* was written for the O'Flaherty's on Oileán Ruadh on Lough Mask in 1651 by David O'Duigenan, a famous professional scribe, who died in 1696. He lived, worked and is buried in the Moytura region. (Ó Cúiv 1945; Moore 2000). The other independent version is Harlein Ms 5280, which was written in the first part of the 16th century by Gilla Riabhach O'Cleirigh at a place called Corrlis, possibly located in Co. Leitrim (Flower 1926; Gray 1982).

The summit of Heapstown cairn is at 76 m OD, the surrounding ground level is 65 m OD. It is worth pointing out here that Newgrange is at 53 m OD. What makes Heapstown 'different' is its comparative topographical relationship. It does not occupy a dominant position in the landscape in comparison to the other focal monuments within the three other passage tomb complexes. However, it is the River Uinshin that appears to be an important element in the positioning of the cairn at Heapstown. The Uinshin lies 700 m west south west from the cairn. The cairn is clearly visible along a 1 km stretch of the river from where it exits the lake to a point below a long narrow drumlin ridge at Annagh., However, much of this stretch occupies a flood plain of the river with an approximate width of 200 m. This flood plain narrows in the vicinity of Ballyrush Bridge, the location of a important fording point across the Uinshin. The ford is identified as the 'Ford of Destruction' and the 'Ford of the Uinshin' – *Ath Admillte* and *Ath Unsen* in *Cath Maige Tuired* (Gray 1982, verse 85). This is where the Daghda meets the Morrigan, prior to the Battle of Moytura and has intercourse with her. He meets her later during the battle at the Ford where she gives him two handfuls of the blood of Indech De Mac Domnann, a Fomorian king. The ford is also mentioned in Tirechans Life of St Patrick where the trout of the lake form a bridge at the ford when the river was in flood to allow St Patrick to cross (Morris 1930). It is worth noting that the Daghda is also strongly associated with Newgrange as it was where he lived with Boann, another fertility goddess, before losing possession of the Brú to his son Óenghus (Ó hÓgain 1991; Swift 2001). The Daghda is also associated with the Eglone stone. This is one of many large glacial erratic that are located near Highwood village on the Moytura plateau, and these erratic, along with the megaliths here may have provided the name of the area – Magh Tuireadh – 'plain of pillars'. The Eglone is the largest of these erratic measuring 5.2 m in height. One local story says that while the Túatha Dé Dannan were waiting for the battle to begin and had a rock throwing contest to pass the time. The erratic were a result of this and the Daghda, a god of fertility, was the one who threw the Eglone (Moore 2000). One of the few locations within the Bricklieves that has any mythological association, and/or placename that relates to a mythical character, is linked to the Daghda. Just above a site known as the 'Stirring Rock', a Lughnasa assembly location, on the south end of the ridge which has cairn B on its northern end, is a large erratic boulder. This can be seen from a long distance. The boulder is called the *Budagh Dá* and according to John Garvin this means the Daghda's Penis'. (Garvin, 13-May-1944).

Lughnasa

The Bricklieves also feature as a gathering place for the Lughnasa Festival as a venue on Garland Sunday (the last Sunday of July) and Bilberry Sunday (the second last Sunday of July). Again, the focal point is Keshcorran Mountain. Traditionally it was a time of re-union, where extended families of people from the area came to visit along with large crowds from around Counties Sligo and Roscommon. Much of the activities took place at the base of the caves on the west side of the mountain but the majority of visitors and locals walked to the summit and cairn Q. The mountain was also climbed on the second last Sunday of July, Bilberry Sunday, when boys and girls went to collect bilberries (MacNeill 1982). On the same day the only recorded gathering for the eastern side of the Bricklieves is at Skein Hill and the Stirring Rock. This is an area to the south west end of the eastern side of the Bricklieve Mountains. On the west side of this hill is steep cliff edged valley containing an unclassified megalithic monument and a destroyed rocking stone, found in the townland of Carricknahorna West townland. These are both located approximately 350 m north northwest of cairn Y in the same townland. The rocking stone, or Stirring Rock, as it is known, was a large glacial erratic boulder that would move on its pedestal when pushed. Young couples went there in groups played music, danced and picked bilberries and would stay on Skein Hill until late in the evening. According to local tradition, the Stirring Rock was smashed up at the beginning of the 20th century by a local priest who wished to dissuade couples from visiting the site on Bilberry Sunday (MacNeill 1982:187-8). A cave on the south west end of Skein Hill has a tradition as being a shelter for a priest during the penal laws and was used as a shelter for cattle during the winter (Horan 2000-1:28).

School's Folklore Commission

The general area around Keshcorran Mountain contains many other legends and folklore, but do not deal directly with the hill or the caves, nor do any stories relate to the main cluster of monuments around Carrowkeel. The School's Folklore Commission manuscripts of 1937 contain various stories, many of them containing altered versions of stories that derive from early sources and local traditions, but again there seems to be an absence of any associations with the main cluster of cairns on the east side of the Bricklieves. A number of them relate to Keshcorran and one explains the construction of cairn Q as deriving from the burial place of a king's daughter and that anyone visiting the site left a stone in her memory, hence causing the construction of the cairn (School's Folklore Commission, 1937b:247). All the remaining National Schools in the area - Drumcormack, Cloghogue, Annagh, Anach, barely mention any of the cairns, although Gort an Locha NS in Ballinafad does provide a somewhat erroneous account of the 1911 excavations carried out by Macalister, Armstrong and Praegar (School's Folklore Commission, 1937a:646-50). Apart from that there are brief reports of 'Giant's Graves' covered by large heaps of stones and a story concerning the barrow at Sheerevagh townland where a battle took place in the field called *Thun na Fola* to the south of the barrow. A chieftain who died in the battle is apparently buried at the site. This barrow, like Heapstown cairn, is also mentioned as having a tradition of being the burial site of Ailill, brother of Niall of the Nine Hostages. (School's Folklore Commission, 1937b:298).

Carrowkeel: its lack of folklore

During Macalister's excavations he noted a number of placenames within the complex and complained in his report about the lack of information collected by the Ordnance Surveys in 1836 and 1885. Only one placename related to a cairn and that was cairn C, which the locals called 'the Leprechaun's House' (Macalister *et al* 1912). This is the only named cairn in the complex. According to Ó hOgáin leprechaun's and their popularity were a post-medieval development (1991). From an examination of existing early sources and later sources concerning the folklore, myths and legends of the Bricklieves, with particular reference to the cairns, it is clear that none of the cairns, apart from the on the summit of Keshcorran, get no attention whatsoever. On the eastern ridge of Carrowkeel is the plateau of Doonaveragh/Mullaghfarna, where there is an extensive early prehistoric enclosure and hut-site complex comprising at least 150 hut sites. This plateau receives some notice in a historic sense through being associated with a possible camp site of Red Hugh O'Donnell and subsequent battle of the Curlews in 1599 (O'Donovan 1848-51; Wood-Martin 1882:355). However, the cairn, the caves and mountain of Keshcorran feature considerably with a rich array of traditions. It is worth noting that Keshcorran is the highest of the hills within the Bricklieves and its cairn, although smaller than cairn F, appears to be the most visible from most directions The question remains why the eastern, dramatic and considerably visible cairns of Carrowkeel received virtually no attention. Out of all the other cairns it is Heapstown cairn that receives most attention but again this is considerably brief when compared to the folklore collection from the region that deals with fairyforts, churches, holy wells, mass rocks, castles etc.

On examination of the six inch to one mile 1st edition 1836 Ordnance Survey map of the Carrowkeel/ Keshcorran area (sheet 40), one immediately notes the large absence of features, predominantly due to the poor quality of the land in this upland area, described in 1633 as having " a great scope of mounteine and rockey ground" (Wood-Martin 1882-92, Vol. II:185). For the Ordnance Survey it was instructed that antiquities were to be mapped by the surveyors; both by Colby and the Placenames and Antiquities Department (Andrews 1997; 2001; Smith 2001). When dealing with Carrowkeel and Keshcorran the surveyors miss an enormous amount of antiquities. Of the cairns in the whole complex cairns Q on Keshcorran and F at Carrowkeel are sketched in as stone piles but are not indicated as 'cairn' or denoted as an antiquity. Cairns C, G, and H are denoted as 'cairn' and are drawn as piles of stone. The remaining eighteen cairns in the entire complex are not recorded in any way. What is unusual about this is that the surveyors actually used many of the cairns as trigonometric station, or had to walk past cairns to get to a vantage point in order to establish a station marker. Likewise, they failed to record the cairns as distinguishing features in the OS Namebooks (1837a). The caves of Pollnagaddy (the Thieves' Hole) and the School Cave are indicated on the map, yet the denuded passage tomb, cairn R, is omitted although it is a short distance from both caves. Both caves appear in the Name Books and the Teacher's cave, along with many of the tales relating to Keshcorran Mountain, appears in the OS Letters, but the monument is not mentioned. One interesting note about this lack of information on any of the cairns can be contrasted against the attention a single cashel gets in Carricknahorna East, to the south of the cairns. Cashelalan is discussed both in the OS Namebooks and OS Letters and is named as such on the map in Old English script used to denote antiquities. Some local placenames given in the name books do not appear on the final version of the 1st ed maps. 'Gull's Finger Stone', a large erratic in the south end of Carrickhawna townland (south of the Buddagh Dá stone) for example was used as trigonometric stations but was not named on the map - it is also remarked in the Namebooks that "before November, the old men used to assemble here to settle their little affairs for the ensuing half year". By having a name a particular space is given some importance, but this importance is ignored in many cases by the surveyors.

Discussion: Carrowkeel – a place apart

The location of Early Medieval and Later-Medieval ecclesiastical and important secular sites around or near the hill of Keschcorran - Toomour, Greenan, Templevanny, Drumrat, Ballinaglough and Ballymote – or those in the vicinity of Moytura – Killadoon, Ballindoon, Shancough and Kilronan - maybe partially indicative of the establishment and recording of elements of the legends, especially those associated with Cormac MacAirt. Likewise the traditions associated with the Moytura monuments, including Heapstown, may have strong associations with the redactors of the surviving narrative texts who were familiar with the region, such as David O'Duigenan, and Gilla Riabhach O'Cleirigh (Walsh 1947). The boundaries of both the baronies of Corran and Tirerrill and the parishes of Toomour and Aghanagh are divided by an approximate north to south line through the cairn on Keshcorran Mountain. These boundaries possibly date back to the early Christian period and the related stories concerning Keshcorran may relate somewhat to a socio-political group west of the mountain in Toomour parish.

Other than David, the O'Duignean family historiographers and scribes, whose chief patrons were the McDonagh of Ballindoon and the McDermotts of Moylurg were from Kilronan, just south east of Moytura. The 14th century Book of Ballymote was written at Ballymote Castle, the former seat of the McDonagh of Corran, under whose patronage the book would appear to have been made. It was written around the year 1392 and the principal scribes were Solam Ó Droma, Robertus Mac Sithigh and Magnus Ó Duibgennain (Another of the O'Duinean clan). It contains genealogical, topographical, biblical and hagiographical material, including Lebor Gabála (Book of the Invasions). This is a narrative concerning a number of invasions of Ireland by various divine or semi-divine groups, and the arrival of the first people in Ireland (the Sons of Mil). It is also worthy of note that Fergal O'Gara of Coolavin, 7 km south west of Keshcorran was a patron of the Annals of the Kingdom of Ireland which was compiled by the so-called Four Masters, led by the scribe Michael O'Clery between 1632 and 1636 (O'Donovan 1848-51; Walsh 1947; Slavin 2005). Perhaps it was the influence of these scribes and their patrons that aided the creation of a variety of tales associated with the areas of Keshcorran and Moytura.

A number of the passage tombs at Carrowkeel and Keshcorran show evidence of continuity of usage into the Bronze Age. Artefacts, cremations and inhumations were found in a secondary cist burial located on the west side of cairn V in Treanmacmurtagh (Rynne 1969:145-150; Waddell 1985:133; Ó Ríordáin & Waddell 1993:131). Very small secondary cist burials were also found in cairn B on the south-east side containing handfuls of bone dust and small fragments of pottery (Macalister *et al.* 1912; Waddell 1985:132). In cairn O during Macalister's excavations the irregular floor of the chamber contained heaped up discs of sandstone, burnt and unburnt bone and ashes with a secondary vase Food Vessel placed above these. (Macalister et al 1912; Ó Ríordáin & Waddell 1993:130). In cairn K Macalister found a secondary Food Vessel containing a small amount of bone dust on the floor of the corner formed by the central and right recess (*ibid.*). Other evidence of early prehistoric activity can be traced in areas around the Bricklieves. In the bog at Treanscrabbagh (between cairns E and F and cairn B) hearths of burnt stone and charcoal were found, although no archaeological objects were associated. One of these hearths was carbon dated to "around 4500 BP", putting them, which their level in an associated pollen diagram suggests, in the Early Bronze Age. It was suggested they may have been associated with a Fulachta Fiadh (Mitchell 1951:163; Göransson 1984:166-8). Mitchell does remark on a 'recent' discovery of a Bronze Age wrist bracer 15 cm above the base of the blanket bog there (*ibid*). This was a stray find of jasper wrist bracer found by peat cutters in the vicinity of Treanscrabbagh bog. Other Bronze Age finds include a bronze dagger found during peat cutting in the bog west of cairn R at Treanmore and a Late Bronze Age socketed and looped bronze spearhead found in peat at Treanmacmurtagh.

Iron Age dates come from human teeth, found in the Caves of Keshcorran. As part of the 'Cave Radiocarbon Programme', conducted by Peter Woodman and Marion Dowd, human teeth from two of the Keshcorran Caves – Coffey Cave and Plunkett Cave – were submitted for dating. The tooth from Coffey Cave was discovered at the cave entrance. It was the only human skeletal element found in the cave and may be the only indicator of Iron Age activity, though a number of undiagnostic artefacts were also found at the cave entrance including a whetstone, bone needles and bone points in addition to faunal remains. The radiocarbon date for this tooth was 210 BC to 60 AD. Four human teeth and a fragment of a left humerus were discovered scattered throughout Plunkett Cave. Two of the teeth belonged to the same individual, a young adult (Scharff et al. 1903:208), one of which was the tooth submitted for radiocarbon dating. The date obtained for the Plunkett Cave tooth falls between 530 AD and 680 AD, essentially towards the beginning of the Early Medieval period. However, in light of the Iron Age date obtained for the tooth that was found in the adjacent Coffey Cave, the tooth from Plunkett Cave was interpreted by Dowd as reflecting a continuation of Iron Age practises. Consequently, though the Plunkett tooth is not prehistoric in date. In the Coffey Cave instance, the human remains represent burials whereas the tooth from Plunkett Cave does not appear to have derived from an interment. None of the artefacts recovered from Plunkett Cave are readily diagnostic of the Iron Age. There is also a horse tooth dated from the Plunkett Cave to 260-480 AD. Horse and dog/wolf teeth have been found in other caves at Keshcorran (Dowd 2004). These all could be associated with certain symbolic significances with particular meaning and do not appear to be accidental. The Iron Age secondary deposition of human teeth and animal teeth at Carrowmore passage tomb 27 appears to reflect the possible ritual significance of this deposition (Burenhult 1984:64-7). The caves may have taken on special significance to people during the Iron Age. Prior to this the only prehistoric evidence from the caves was a find of a Neolithic polished stone axe (Scharff et al. 1903). The appearance, location and 'Otherworldly' aspects of these subterranean passage may have attracted Iron Age people to view the caves as a special place in the landscape, and this association may be reflected in some of the myths and legends, and the Lughnasa gatherings at them in later periods.

The passage tombs were most likely sealed by the Early Bronze Age, given the evidence from Macalister's excavations, and were also being partially enveloped in peat as the blanket bogs began forming in the Bricklieve Mountains c.2,600 BC (Göransson 2002). Scant evidence of artefacts shows activity throughout the Bronze Age with Iron Age activity being centred around the Caves of Keshcorran. It is entirely possible, but difficult to prove, that the passage tombs and access to the monuments and the landscape around them became taboo or restricted (Hirsch and O'Hanlon 1995; Carmichael et al. 1997).

Places had different meanings for the surveyors of the 1st edition Ordnance Survey and the local inhabitants, and these meanings are not mapped. Local knowledge and the cairns of Carrowkeel are not represented and the cairns are used as trigonometric stations. It appears that many of the locals living around the mountains are unfamiliar with the cairns and with the landscape around them; many see them from the lower ground and take them for granted. Even when the locals do visit them it is the outsiders, the visitors - archaeologists or non-archaeologists - who are most impressed with their scale and their dramatic location in the landscape. Today, some of the older local farmers tell stories of lights and music coming from 'fairy forts' or ringforts of the area, but no lore survives concerning the cairns and passage tombs. The cairns at Carrowkeel do not appear to offered the "conspicuous features in the landscape that provide tangible points of reference to which legends can be anchored" (Layton 1999:28), even though the cairns are visible from the lowlands. Bender (1993:252-75) demonstrated that the silence created around Stonehenge by the medieval Church which wished to create this silence to subdue the powerful attachment to this place and Smith suggests this kind of silence was imposed on Carrowkeel when the surveyors failed to represent the cairns on the 1837 map (2001:256). However, there is no evidence of this church imposed silence on many locales in the vicinity of the passage tombs at Carrowkeel considering the wealth of evidence of myths, legends and folklore that survive relating to Keshcorran and Moytura. Also there are a large number of holy wells and other possible pre-Christian sites or gathering sites near Carrowkeel that were possibly assimilated and acculturated by the arrival of Christianity (McGloin and Moore 1996a; 1996b).

The stories about Moytura and the caves of Keshcorran are still known today by many of the older people in the area, however, the lack of folkloric and mythical tradition within the passage tomb complex; the general current lack of local knowledge; and the absence of placenames from the Dinnsheanchas to the OS 1837 Name Books tend to show an absence of interest in or knowledge about the cairns. Some of the monuments at Moytura and the Caves of Keshcorran maintained a strong significance in the landscape as reflected in the folkloric traditions associated with these places. Local people were, and are, aware of the cairns at Carrowkeel; the OS field workers did stand on many of the cairns, but they are not recorded through local folk tradition or on the maps. Perhaps they were not seen as important - they are on hill-tops in out of the way places; they were a place apart from settlement; away from roads and productive land - places without much economic value. This absence of attention concerning the passage tombs and cairns continued beyond the production of the 1837 Ordnance Survey maps and, due in part to those who used the maps in later periods, failed to get any attention from antiquarians until seventy four years later. The complex's liminal place in the landscape was perhaps one of the reasons that attracted the passage tomb builders in the first place and an aspect this liminality meant it became a place apart, an almost forgotten cultural landscape that no one went to. Because megaliths appear to have acted as 'timemarks' in the landscape, ,they invite later peoples to rediscover, reinterpret and reuse them (Horltorf,1998:30: also see Hingley 1996). The evidence at Carrowkeel appears to suggest that its 'life history' was dormant for a considerable period of time, until Macalister's excavations in 1911. The 'biography', or the 'life history' of the passage tombs at Carrowkeel appear to erode or fade sometime in the latter part of the Early Bronze Age, while a cultural memory appears to remain at Keshcorran where both folklore and festive assemblies continue into present day.

Acknowledgements

Particular thanks are due to Dr Marion Dowd on information regarding the archaeology and manuscript material on the caves of Keshcorran. Thanks also to Dr Stefan Bergh of NUI Galway and to Ann-Britt Falk for their support.

References

Andrews, J.H. 1997. *Shapes of Ireland: Maps and Their Makers 1564-1839*, Geography Publications. Dublin.
Andrews, J.H. 2001. *A Paper Landscape: The Ordnance Survey in nineteenth-century Ireland.* Four Courts Press. Dublin.
Bender, B. 1993. 'Stonehenge: Contested Landscapes (medieval to present day)'. Bender, B (ed.)

Landscape: Politics and Perspectives. Berg. Oxford. 245-279.

Beranger, G. 1779. *Journal of a Tour in Connaught.* Ms4162, National Library of Ireland

Bergh, S. 1995. *Landscape of the Monuments: A study of the Passage Tombs in the Cuil Irra region, Co. Sligo.* Riksantikvarieämbet Arkeologska Undersöknigar. Stockholm

Bergh, S. 2000. 'Transforming Knocknarea - the archaeology of a mountain'. *Archaeology Ireland* Vol. 14 No 2. p.14-17

Bergh, S. 2002. 'Knocknarea: the ultimate mountain' in Chris Scarre (ed.) *Monuments and Landscape in Atlantic Europe.* Routledge. London.

Bhreathnach, E. (ed.) 2006. *The Kingship and landscape of Tara.* Four Courts Press for The Discovery programme. Dublin.

Bradley, R. 1993. *Altering the Earth.* Society of Antiquaries of Scotland, Monograph Series No. 8. Edinburgh.

Bradley, R. 2000. *An Archaeology of Natural Places.* Routledge. London.

Bradley, R. 2002. *The Past in Prehistoric Societies.* Routledge. London.

Breathnach, R.A. 1968. "Tóraigheacht Dhiarmada agus Ghráinne". Dillon, M. (ed.) *Irish Sagas.* Mercier Press. Dublin. 135-147.

Burenhult, G. 1984. *The Archaeology of Carrowmore: Environmental Archaeology and the Megalithic Tradition at Carrowmore, Co. Sligo, Ireland,* Theses and Papers in North-European Archaeology 14. Institute of Archaeology. University of Stockholm. Stockholm.

Carmichael, D., Hubert, J. & Reeves, B. (eds.) 1997.. *Sacred Sites, Sacred Places.* Routledge. London.

Champion, S. and Cooney, G. 1999. "Naming the Places, Naming the Stones". In Gazin-Schwartz, A. & Holtorf, C.J. (eds.), *Archaeology and Folklore,* Routledge. London. 196-213.

Chapman, J. 1997. 'Places as timemarks – the social construction of prehistoric landscapes in eastern Hungary'. Nash, G (ed.) *Semiotics of Landscape: Archaeology of the Mind.* British Archaeological Reports. International Series 661. BAR Publishing. Oxford. 31-45.

Condit, T. & Gibbons, M. 1991, 'A glimpse of Sligo's prehistory', *Archaeology Ireland,* Vol.5 No. 3, Issue 7, 7-10

Condit, T & Simpson, D. 1998, 'Irish Hengiform Enclosures and Related Monuments: A Review. Gibson A. and Simpson D. (eds.), *Prehistoric Ritual and Religion,* Sutton Publishing, Stroud, 45-61

Conwell, E.A. 1873. *Discovery of the Tomb of Ollamh Fodhla,* MacGlashan and Gill. Dublin.

Cooney, G. 1990. 'The Place of Megalithic Tomb Cemeteries in Ireland'. *Antiquity,* 64. 741-53.

Cooney, G. 1996. 'Building the Future on the Past: Archaeology and the Construction of National Identity in Ireland'. Diaz-Andreu, M. and Champion, T. (eds.) *Nationalism and Archaeology in Europe.* UCL Press. London. 146-163

Cooney, G. 2000. *Landscapes of Neolithic Ireland.* Routledge. London.

Corlett, C. 1997. Prehistoric Pilgrimage to Croagh Patrick. *Archaeology Ireland* 11 (2). 8-11.

Corlett, C. 1998. 'The Prehistoric Ritual Landscape of the Great Sugarloaf' Corlett, C. & O'Sullivan, A. (eds.) *Wicklow Archaeology and History* Vol. I. County Wicklow Archaeological Society. Greystones. 1-8

Corlett, C. 2001. *Antiquities of West Mayo.* Wordwell. Bray.

Dooley, A. & Roe, H. 1999. *Tales of the Elders of Ireland – Acallam na Senórach.* Oxford University Press. Oxford.

Dowd, M. 2004. *Caves: Sacred places on the Irish Landscape.* Unpublished PhD thesis, University College Cork. Cork.

Eogan, G. 1986. *Knowth and the Passage Tombs of Ireland.* Thames & Hudson. London.

Farrelly, J. & Keane, M. forthcoming. *A Classification for Barrows.*

Farrelly, J. & Keane, M. 2002. 'New barrow types in County Sligo'. Timoney, M.A. (ed.) *A Celebration of Sligo.* Sligo Field Club. Sligo. 97-102.

Flower, R. 1926. *Catalogue of Irish Manuscripts in the British Museum.* London.

Fredengren, C. 2002, *Crannógs,* Wordwell, Dublin

Garvin, J. 1943-6. "High Hollow Townlands" in *Roscommon Herald.*

Gazin-Schwartz, A. and Holtorf, C.J (eds.) 1999. *Archaeology and Folklore,* Routledge. London.

Gazin-Schwartz, A. and Holtorf, C.J. 1999. 'As long as ever I've known it . . .'. Gazin-Schwartz, A. and Holtorf, C.J. (eds.) *Archaeology and Folklore,* Routledge. London. 3-25.

Göransson, H. 1984, 'Pollen Analytical Investigations in the Sligo Area', Burenhult, G. *The Archaeology of Carrowmore: Environmental Archaeology and the Megalithic Tradition at Carrowmore, Co. Sligo, Ireland,* Theses and Papers in North-European Archaeology 14. Institute of Archaeology, University of Stockholm, Stockholm, 154-193.

Gray, E.A. (ed.) 1982. *Cath Maige Tuired: The Second Battle of Magh Tuired.* Irish Texts Society, Vol. LII. London.

Green, M. 1999. 'Back to the future: Resonances of the past in myth and material culture'. IGazin-Schwartz, A. and Holtorf, C.J. (eds.) *Archaeology and Folklore.* Routledge. London. 48-66.

Gregory, Lady, 1970, *Gods & Fighting Men.* Colin Smythe Ltd, Buckinghamshire (2nd Edition).

Gwynn, E. 1913. *The Metrical Dinsheanchas,* Vol. III. Hodges and Figgis. Dublin.

Gwynn, E. 1924. *The Metrical Dinsheanchas,* Vol. IV. Hodges and Figgis. Dublin.

Harbison, P. 2002. *'Our Treasure of Antiquities': Beranger and Bigari's antiquarian sketching tour of Connacht in 1779.* Wordwell. Bray.

Herity, M. 1974. *Irish Passage Graves: Neolithic Tomb Builders in Ireland and Britain 2500 BC.* Irish University Press. Dublin.

Hingley, R. 1996. Ancestors and identity in the later prehistory of Atlantic Scotland: the reuse and reinvention on Neolithic monuments and material culture. *World Archaeology,* Vol. 28 (2). 231-243.

Hirsch, E. & O'Hanlon, M. (eds.) 1995. *The Anthropology of Landscape: Perspectives on place and space.* Clarendon Press. Oxford.

Hogan, E. 1910. *Ononmasticon Goedelicum.* Dublin.

Horan, P. 2000/1. "The Stirring Rock"; *Corran Herald,* 33, Sligo.

Holtorf, C. 1998. 'Life histories of megaliths in Mecklenburg – Vorpommern (Germany)'. *World Archaeology* 30 (1). 23-38.

Ingold, T. 2000. *The Perception of the Environment.* Routledge. London.

Joyce, P. W. 1907. *Old Celtic Romances.* Talbot Press. Dublin.

Layton, R. 1999. 'Folklore and World View', Gazin-Schwartz, A. and Holtorf, C.j. (eds.) *Archaeology and Folklore.* Routledge. London: 26-34.

Macalister, R.A.S., Armstrong, and E.C.R., Praegar, R.L. 1912. 'Report on the Exploration of Bronze Age Cairns on Carrowkeel Mountain, County Sligo', *Proceedings of the Royal Irish Academy,* Vol. 29. Sect. C. 311-347.

MacNeill, M. 1982. *The Festival of Lughnasa,* Vols. I-III. Comhairle Bhéaloideas Éireann. Dublin.

McGloin, A. and Moore, S, (eds.) 1996a. *Aspects of Geevagh and Highwood, County Sligo.* Lough Arrow Research Project. Sligo.

McGloin, A. and Moore, S, (eds.) 1996b. *A Guide to the Carrowkeel/ Keshcorran Megalithic Complex.* Lough Arrow Research Project. Sligo.

McMann, J. 1991. *Loughcrew: Form, history and meaning in an Irish megalithic landscape.* Unpublished PhD Thesis, University of California, Berkeley.

Mitchell, F. 1951. 'Studies in Irish Quaternary Deposits: No. 7', *Proceedings of the Royal Irish Academy,* 53B, 111-206

Moore, S. (ed.) 2000. *The Moytura Record.* Highwood Resource Centre. Sligo.

Moore, S. 2002. 'Heapstown and Heapstown Cairn' Moore, S. (ed.) *Riverstown Vintage Day.* Sligo Folk Park. Sligo. 43-47.

Mount, C. 1995. 'Excavations at Rathdooney Beg, Co. Sligo'. *Emania,* 13. 79-88.

Mount, C. 1996. 'The Environmental Siting of Neolithic and Bronze Age Monuments in the Bricklieve and Moytirra Uplands, Co. Sligo'. *Journal of Irish Archaeology,* Vol. VII. 1-11.

Mount, C. 1998. 'Ritual, Landscape and Continuity in Prehistoric County Sligo', *Archaeology Ireland,* Vol. 12. No. 3. 18-21.

Mount, C. 1999. Excavation and environmental analysis of a Neolithic mound and Iron Age barrow cemetery at Rathdooney Beg, Co Sligo, Ireland. *Proceedings of the Prehistoric Society,* 65. 337-71.

Morris, H., 1930. *St Patrick in Co. Sligo.* Unpublished work, Sligo County Library.

Murphy, G. 1933. *Duanaire Finn 2.* Irish Texts Society Vol. XXVIII. London.

Newman, C. 1997 *Tara: an archaeological survey.* Discovery Programme Monograph 2. Royal Irish Academy, Dublin.

Ó Cathasaigh, T. 1977. *The Heroic Biography of Cormaic Mac Airt.* Dublin. Institute for Advanced Studies. Dublin.

Ó Cuív, B. 1945. *Cath Muighe Tuireadh.* Dublin Institute of Advanced Studies. Dublin.

O'Donovan, J. 1848-51. *The Annals of Ireland by the Four Masters.* De Burcas Books [1970 reprint.]. Dublin.

O'Grady, S.H. 1857. *Tóruigheacht Dhiarmuda agus Gráinne,* Ossianic Society. Dublin.

O Grady, S.H (ed.) 1892. *Silva Gadelica, ,* Vol. II. William and Norgate, London.

Ó hÓgáin, D. 1999. *The Sacred Isle: Belief and religion in pre-Christian Ireland.* The Collins Press. Cork.

Ó hÓgáin, D. 1991. *Myth, Legend and Romance: An encyclopaedia of the Irish folk tradition.* BCA. London.

Ó hÓgáin, D. 2001. "A Note on the Placename Ceis Chorainn".Higgins, J. & Timoney, M (eds.) *Keash and Culfadda: a local history,* Keash-Culfadda Local History Committee, Sligo. 218-19

O'Kelly, M. 1982. *Newgrange: archaeology, art and legend.* Thames & Hudson, London.

O'Rahilly, T. 1984. *Early Irish History and Mythology.* Dublin Institute for Advanced Studies. Dublin.

Ó Ríordáin, B. & Waddell, J. 1993. *The Funerary Bowls and Vases of the Irish Bronze Age,* University Press. Galway.

O'Rorke, T. 1886. *The History of Sligo: Town and County,* Vols. I-II. James Duffy & Co. Dublin.

Ordnance Survey of Ireland, 1837a. *Field Name Books, Co. Sligo,* Ordnance Survey of Ireland. Dublin.

Ordnance Survey of Ireland, 1837b. *Ordnance Survey Letters, Co. Sligo,* Ordnance Survey of Ireland. Dublin.

Praegar, R. L. 1934: *The Botanist in Ireland.* Hodges & Figgis. Dublin.

Ronayne, M. 2001. The Political Economy of Landscape: Conflict and Value in a Prehistoric Landscape in Ireland. Bender, B. and Winer, M. (eds.) *Contested Landscapes: Movement, Exile and Place.* Oxford and New York: Berg. 149-164.

Roymans, N. 1995. 'The cultural biography of urnfileds and the long-term history of a mythical landscape'. *Archaeological Dialogues: Dutch Perspectives on Current Issues in Archaeology,* 2 (1): 2-38.

Rynne, E. 1969. 'Cist Burial in a Cairn at Treanmacmurtagh, Co. Sligo'. *Journal of the Royal Irish Academy,* 99. 145-50.

Scharff, R.F., Coffey, G., Cole, G.A., Ussher, U. & Praegar, R.L. 1903 "Explorations of the Caves of

Keshcorran". *Transactions of the. Royal Irish Academy.* 32 (B). 171-244.

School's Folklore Commission, 1937a. Gort an Locha NS, *MS S-182,* Róinn Bhéaloideas Éireann. Dublin.

School's Folklore Commission, 1937b. Drumnagranshy NS; Clogogue NS, *MS S-186,* Róinn Bhéaloideas Éireann. Dublin.

Sharkey, P.A. 1930. *The Moytirra Record,* Dublin.

Slavin, M., 2005. *The Ancient Books of Ireland.* Wolfhound Press. Dublin.

Smith, A. 2001. *Mapping Cultural and Archaeological Meanings: representing landscapes and pasts in 19th century Ireland".* Unpublished PhD Thesis, University of Massachusetts. Boston.

Swift, C. 2001. The gods of Newgrange in Irish literature & Romano-Celtic tradition. Burenhult, G. (ed.) *Stones and Bones: Formal disposal of the dead in Atlantic Europe during the Mesolithic-Neolithic interface 6000-3000 BC.* BAR International Series 1201, BAR Publishing. Oxford. 53-64.

Taçon, P. 1999. 'Identifying Ancient Sacred Landscapes in Australia: From physical to social'. In W. Ashmore and A. B. Knapp (eds.) *Archaeologies of Landscape: Contemporary perspectives.* Blackwell. Oxford. 33-57.

Tilley, C. 1994, *A Phenomenology of Landscape,* Berg, Oxford.

Walsh, P. 1947. *Irish Men of Learning.* Three Candles Press. Dublin.

Waddell, J. 1985. *The Bronze age Burials of Ireland.* University Press. Galway.

Woodman, P. 1995. 'Who Possesses Tara? Politics in Archaeology in Ireland'. Ucko, P.J. (ed.) *Theory in Archaeology: A world perspective.* Routledge. London. 278-297.

Woodman, P. et al. 1997, "The Irish Quaternary Project", *Quaternary Science Reviews,* Vol. 16, 129-59..

Wood-Martin, W. G. 1882-92. *History of Sligo,* Vols., I-III. Hodges & Figgis. Dublin.

Wood-Martin, W.G. 1884. 'Antiquities of Sligo: on the battle ground and ancient monuments of Northern Moytirra'. *Journal of the Royal Historical and Archaeological Association of Ireland,* 60. 441-470.

Microhistory and ethnoarchaeology of a cultural landscape: the parish of San Pedro de Cereixa (Galicia, Spain)

Xurxo M. Ayán Vila[*]

William Blake, the English poet, once wrote "a poet is the person who sees the universe in a grain of sand". Tolstoi, more pragmatically, advised the emerging writer that if he wanted to sing the vast world, he would have to sing his homeland. This capacity to go from specific to universal and vice versa is just culture, the need to explain the world.

Xuan Bello (*Universal History of Paniceiros*)

Introduction[1]

Galicia is a small Atlantic region in the Northwest of the Iberian Peninsula (the *Finis Terrae of the Roman Empire*). From a geographical, cultural and landscape point of view, it is very similar to other Atlantic areas such as Brittany or Ireland. In this respect Galician history is characterized by great demographic pressure on the environment, a dispersed population and by a traditional and conservative rural society. The society is based on a survival economy and influenced by two fundamental phenomena: mass emigration to America since the mid nineteenth century and the failed industrialisation. Renewed industrialisation has taken place from the sixties onwards and only in cities.

As a result of this process, Galicia has preserved its traditional and rural landscape from the Prehistoric and Proto-historic times, and this is an advantage from an archaeological point of view. Furthermore, Galician society has preserved many traditions, customs and practices that agglutinate a group identity which has already disappeared in more industrialized and developed parts of Europe.

In order to maximize this ethnoarchaeological potential of the Galician rural landscape a new line of investigation has been implemented to examine the archaeological issues arising from the Iberian Northwest. A close link has been established between Rural Archaeology, Landscape Archaeology and Cultural Anthropology to develop co-operation and interdisciplinary approaches. This has resulted in a study about the genealogy and historical evolution of the traditional Galician rural landscape, with results that are usable by those three disciplines (Criado 1991, 1995; Criado and Ballesteros 2002).

In this sense, the study is the result of a line of work which, taking archaeology as a starting point carries out a study of the traditional rural landscape at a micro spatial, ethnoarchaelogical and interdisciplinary level. Our search strategy opens up at a crossroads where merge, on the one hand the Landscape Archaeology (Criado 1999) and on the other hand the Historical Anthropology, the History of the ideas and Micro-history. This has been consolidated during the last few decades in European historiography, as a result of the gradual merging of structural Anthropology and the so called third generation of the *Annales School* (Burke 1990; Barros 1993).

The theoretical-methodological framework

The starting point of our study is the concept of landscape as a socio-cultural product of the environment: in terms of space, of social action, both material and abstract conditions, and as a multidimensional reality: environmental, social, symbolic, and cultural perspectives (Criado 1999:5; Criado and Villoch 2000:64f).

Space is a social, imaginary construction, in continuous movement, deeply rooted in culture; therefore there is a close structural relationship in the space appropriation strategies between thoughts, social organization, survival and conception-use of the environment. (Criado 1993:42).

According to this theoretical and conceptual framework, we herewith are going to focus on the *Landscape Archaeology* of a parish located in Tierra de Lemos, called Cereixa. We approach it as a search strategy directed towards the study and reconstruction, using archaeology, of the space where the Cereixa community settles.

We first deal with archaeological bodies, silent remains of the material culture from which to get information of the social activities of past communities. The methodology used is the analysis of concrete material forms. This *formal analysis* of how every sociocultural formation settles in an area helps us to at least approach and understanding the structure of this landscape.

This archaeological deconstruction complements the study of the last evolutionary step of our parish micro history; that is, the organization of the traditional rural landscape. Regarding this subject, we are privileged by having not only historical documentation itself, but also the oral history of living members of this rural culture, at

---

[*] Archaeologist and researcher of the Laboratory of Archaeology, *Padre Sarmiento* Institute on Galician Studies, Santiago de Compostela (Spanish High Council for Scientific Research-Auntonomus Government of Galicia). phxurxo@usc.es
[1] This article is a corrected version of a homonymous paper presented at session coordinated by A-B Falk and D. M. Kyritz *Folk beliefs and practice in medieval lives*, 11th Annual Meeting. European Association of Archaeologists (Cork, 5-11 september 2005).

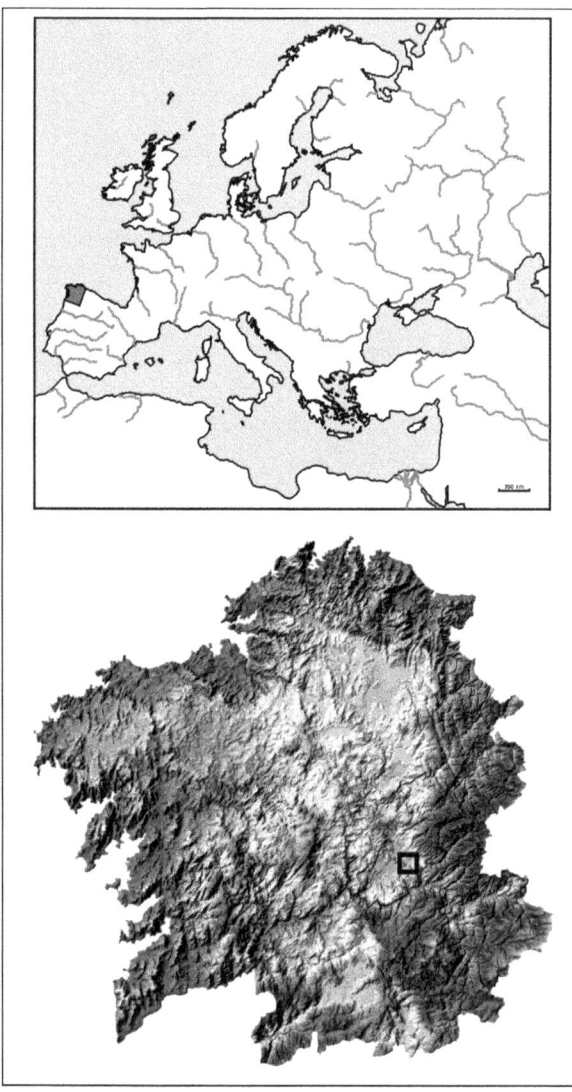

Figure 1. Situation of study area in Europe and Galicia.

the current time when the traditional culture is disappearing.

It is necessary to use *Historical Anthropology*, an approach that became quite popular in the seventies as an answer to the preponderance of structural History. This structural History focuses on social strata that have traditionally been marginalized by research, and pays attention to gesture analysis, sociability forms, religious beliefs, ideological discourse, everyday rituals, thoughts, behaviours that endure indefinitely in the heart of ancient minority cultural communities. (Le Goff 1985; Burke 1990a; Gurevich 1992; Burguière 1995).

In this regard, we admit the importance of *Micro-history*. This tendency tries to go into the symbolic dimensions of social action by means of a micro spatial approach (Le Roy Ladurie 1981; Ginzburg 2001:9ff). In order to do this, it uses a detailed analysis scale and also uses a *dense description* that maximizes the information coming from all type of sources and disciplines. (Geertz 1997:19ff).

Likewise we can tackle the study of the traditional rural society's material culture, and in our opinion it is essential to accept *Ethnoarchaeology* as a methodological tool. The hermeneutic, poststructuralist and historical points of view of the discipline provide the ideal setting for our approach to pre-industrial societies, in which living historic figures and *living* material culture can be found (González Ruibal 2003, 2003b). In this regard the material culture is full of meaning and is essential when rebuilding the rationality pattern of a society. It is a cultural product intended to communicate some information that is manipulated, whether intentionally or not, by the community. The material culture could be considered either a reflection or an active source of social behaviour. Therefore, it is necessary to analyze it as a living entity that plays an active role in the social make-up of reality. The social and symbolic background which lies behind this spatial model is well-defined by traditional rural society and can be tackled from this perspective (figure 1).

The time: historical approach to Cereixa Parish

Next we are going to deal with an archaeological-historical reconstruction of the occupation process of the area where the Cereixa parish settles, defining the different models of occupation in this environmental framework by the different sociocultural formations that happened from the Neolithic period up to the present moment. These models of space appropriation had to learn to adapt to and at the same time modify a defined physical environment marked by the river Saa low basin, a tributary of the river Cabe.

The environmental space: river Saa low basin

Before we talk about the physical geographical area, I would like to look at the parish description made by the liberal minister Pascual Madoz in the 1840's. From an economical, empirical and modern position, Madoz's characteristic position for that time,[2] is based on a bourgeois conception of the space as a framework for economic exploitation (Madoz 1845:307). Also, it will be an introduction to the spatial framework that is the object of our study:

St. Pedro de Cereija: parish in the province and diocese of Lugo (9 leagues) belonging to Quiroga administrative area and to the Puebla del Brollón town council. SITUATED in a hollow on the left bank of river Saa and right bank of Ramos stream. CLIMATE damp but quite healthy. It has about 70

---

[2] In 1833 the Spanish State starts the territorial distribution, which officially ends with the jurisdiction organization of the Ancien Régime. The French centralist model of Modern State is adopted, and the country is divided into regions, and every region is divided into different municipal districts (Town Councils). Therefore a contrived administrative organization is imposed; an organization with arbitrary limits, which in the Galician case, does not recognise the importance of the historic regions nor the legal existence of the parish as the centre of the Galician rural society.

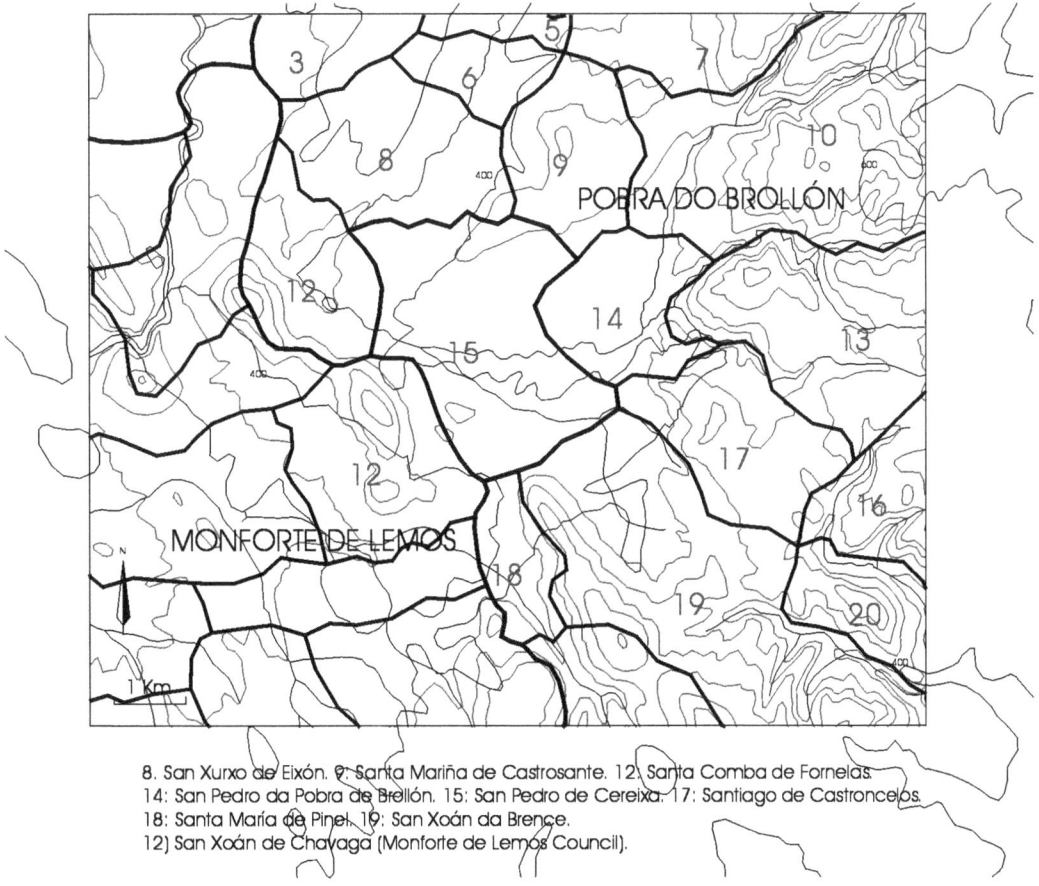

Figure 2. Parish organization in the study area. The limits prevail from high medieval period to nowadays.

medium-sized houses, arranged in the sites of Areas, Aquel-Cabo, Barrio- falcón, Cereija (town hall and church), Cima de Vila, Corbal, Giontiñas, Lende, Nogueiras, Puente, Rairos, Sierra and Zapateira. The parish church is capable and respectable. Its priest is of first order and of ecclesiastic and real patronage. The MUNICIPAL AREA stretches 1/8 leagues from N to S and ¼ from E to W. It borders to the N with Castrosante and Eijon; to the E. with Puebla and Castroncelos, to the S with Pinel and Chavaga and to the W with. Fornelas, including the mountains of Chá de Monte Mío, Lamas Boas, Penedos do Castro and Santa Bárbara. The SOIL is tough and clayey and in the summer it lacks of irrigation, although the said river Saa and the streams Regueiro and San Laurenceo water it, The ROADS are not in very good condition and on these roads we can find the Cereija and Nogueiras bridges and the Areas and Torrente pontoons. The MAIL delivery is made from Puebla del Brollón. PRODUCTION. Wheat, corn, potatoes, rye, legumes, chestnuts and wine; sheep, goats, cattle, pigs, hunting and fishing; mills, textile mills, tailors, shoemakers and some other trades. POPULATION. 63 inhabitants and 321 souls. CONTRIBUTE with the town council.

Broadly speaking the parish (350 m above sea level) settles in a well demarcated morphologic unit, the low basin of river Saa, related to the Lemos depression. Although from an orographic point of view, it is separated by a dorsal on the west, which is facing NorthWest-SouthEast, and which is defined by the Serra do Moncai (526 m), the Serra de Lamas (531 m) and A Costa (449 m). In the North some small hillocks can be found: Mompedroso (402 m), A Coroa/O Castro (416 m), A Lucenza, O Carpancedo and San Lourenzo (402 m). These small foothills are the pass between the river Saa plain and the Cha de Castrosante peniplain (420-440 m), which stretches between the rivers Cabe (W) and Saa (SE-E) (figure 2).

The weather is oceanic-continental, with moderate temperatures (14 degrees average), cold and frosty winters, and hot summers. Regarding vegetation, it consists mainly of pine forest and scrubland (brooms, ferns, onms and brumbles). In the valley there are still forests on the riverside of the Saa and near streams: (alder trees, black poplars, willows), some oak and chestnut woods, as well as fruit trees (apple trees, fig trees and cherry trees).

The soil in this small depression is *Pseudoglei* type, a matrix with tertiary clayey sediments. Its inner drainage

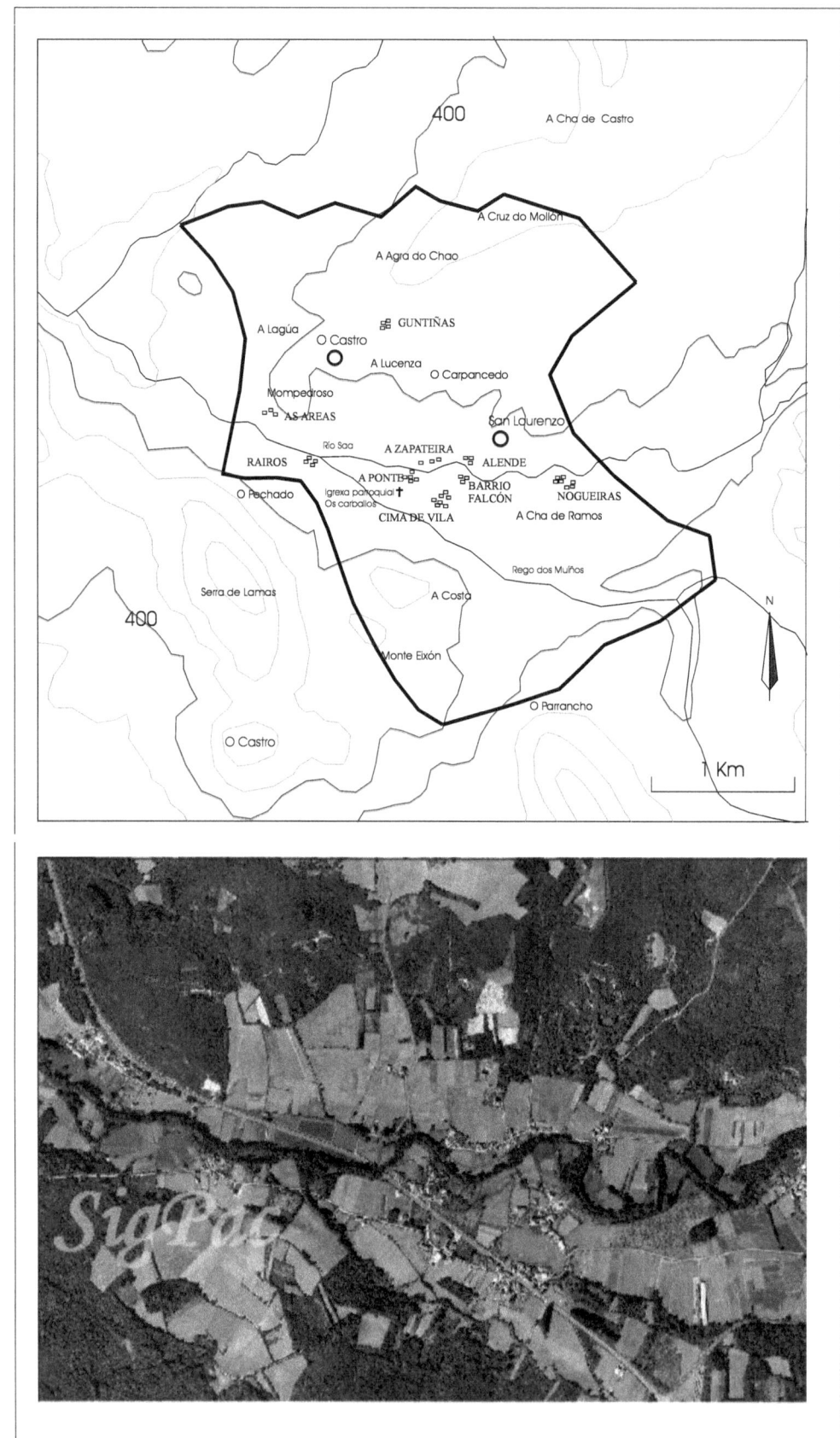

Figure 3. The parish of San Pedro de Cereixa.

is not good, and gravel and quartzite can be found within the first level (0-10 cm). In the deepest levels (60 cm) it changes into clayey and gravely sediments; reds and greens predominate (Guitián 1974). These characteristics determine to a great extent the evolution of the landscape in four main aspects:

- First, the tertiary clayey deposits of the river Saa basin underwent sedimentation processes in the Miocene period, creating alluvials or secondary deposits rich in gold. This explains their intensive exploitation by the Roman conquerors.
- On the other hand, these clayey lands made its drainage poor. Therefore it was necessary to build a complex architectural system (dams, channels etc...) to obtain proper irrigation and adaptation to intensively cultivate the deeper and more fertile lands of Saa valley.
- This geologic and pedologic framework has conditioned the local architecture from the Iron Age since the abundant quartzite boulders were used as building materials and clay was used as mortar in the construction of masonry walls. This can be seen in the place know as *As Pozas do Barro*, a place traditionally used for the extraction of clay.
- Finally, the quality of the clayey and sandy sediments of the land encouraged its intensive exploitation in the seventies by opening up quarries - that had been abandoned in the eighteeneighties - in the aforementioned northern hillocks. This mining activity caused serious damages in archaeological sites such as *A Coroa/O Castro* or *Castro da Lende/San Lourenzo* (figure 3).

A monumental landscape: the megalithic necropolis

There is no known information of the first settlement in this area, but there is some historical documentary evidence which demonstrates the existence of a Neolithic tumulus necropolis in the southeast natural boundary of the parish. At the macro spatial scale, the only evidence from the Neolithic period are some monuments or tumulus/burial mounds (known in the area as *modorras*) which are arranged into groups and can be seen in the high lands of the mountains, since the low lands are at that time covered with woods and are not very attractive for the Neolithic agricultural technology. (Criado and Fábregas 1989, 1994; Criado and Villoch 2000).

In this regard, the Ensenada Land Registry is ordered to be made by the Spanish Monarchy in the mid eighteenth century[3] and it is a historical source of inestimable value because it helps provide evidence for the existence of a necropolis, now disappeared, and that is symbolically reused for the definition of the parish boundaries. It is stated in the description included in *General Questioning* (year 1753):

> [...] *From here it goes up to the framework that is in the Alto dela Sierra de Cutarelos, and in the Highway that goes through the Zereixa reserve to Monforte village; from here and down the road to the framework of the 'Cruz do pechado', from here crosses and goes to the so called 'loureiro dobale'. That is in the road that goes from the Zereixa reserve itself to the frâ de Chavaga; then it climbs to the so called* **modorra da poza***, and then to the* **damodorra das fontes** *in the South bordering with the aforementioned parish of Chavaga and Pinel; From here crosses near the cortiña of the pedrerías de Pinel that is neighbouring Domingo de la Iglesia and frâ de Santa María de Pinel. From it, you can go up to the top of Vilarello hill called* **pena darca***. And then you can go down to the* **modorra named carballeiras de Vilarello***, and it continues down to the* **medorra dos rramos** *that is close to the Highway that goes from Cereixa to the parish of Santa María de quinta de lor.*

This documentary reference helps us to exactly locate the megalithic tumulus, which matches the stereotypical model of spatial settlement for the Northwest, and which also corresponds with studies made in neighbouring regions like Samos (Filgueiras and Rodríguez 1994). Then the *medorras* form a burial mound born by the application of the strategies of appropriation of the area where these communities settle (dorsals and peniplains). It is intimately related to natural roads in the mountains and the passes or hills used to overcome those orographic features. (Criado and Fábregas 1989; Villoch 2000).

Another interesting aspect to bear in mind is the territorial value of these tumuli as marks, or municipal area signposting, within the traditional rural space (Martinón Torres 2001). The megalithic prehistoric landscape, already lacking its functions, and what is more important, lacking its original meaning, is again interpreted by reference to other rural communities, different from the Neolithic community, but who had a clear idea of the area the community is living in and exploiting. There is another semantization process where the archaeological sites of an abandoned cultural and living area are used to demarcate a new cultural landscape.

The Iron Age settlements: The descent to the valley

We lack the archaeological registers to find data about Iron Age settlements in the area. Therefore we will focus on the conformation, during the first millennium B.C., of a new model of settlements characterized by the emergence of the first fortified settlements.

In this sense, the fort, the monumental milestone, built to see and be seen, symbolizes, (by means of fortifications, the location, and visibility), the territoriality of rural and

---

[3] Provincial Historical Archive in Lugo, Ensenada Land Registry, San Pedro de Cereija parish, General Questioning, Answer to Chapter 3º (year 1753).

warrior settlements during the Iron Age and the emergence of the domesticated landscape. (Parcero 2000; Parcero 2003; Parcero and Cobas 2004). The settlement pattern involves a descent to the low areas, the river valleys, the settlement in hillocks or hillsides between the current wood lands (extensive crops, forest exploitation) and arable lands (intensive agriculture, horticulture). Here is the clear precedent of the organization for the subsequent Galician traditional rural landscape (Criado Boado 1989).

In our opinion, in the area subject of study, a densely populated area at that moment, there is clear continuity from the Iron Age I with regards to the choice of the siting of the fortified settlements, and this is mainly because of the geographic influence of the Lemos depression which promoted the fortification of the most famous and most eminent hillocks, which encircle the valley (Ayán 1997).

As can be seen in figure 4, the forts of this area are usually located in the sides of foothills dorsals and in small hillocks preceding fluvial valleys, near important agricultural land and also near land appropriate for extensive exploitation. These fortified settlements form a visible network controlling rivers and natural road links to the Lemos Valley. *A Coroa* o *Castro*, located in our parish fits this pattern. *O Castro* is one of the fortified settlements occupied by the *Lemavos people*, mentioned in the classics and which in the old times gave its name to Terra de Lemos.

It is situated on a hillock with a great field of vision, controlling the low basin of river Saa as well as the peniplain of the Cha de Castro, and it has a clear and special relationship with other sites in the area that are probably contemporaneous (Castroncelos, Castrosante, Chavaga). It has an upper premise (*A Coroa*): its plan is elliptical; and on the West there is a joined terrace. It is covered with dense vegetation and its state of preservation is poor, mainly due to the changes it suffered during the sand extraction processes that took place in the seventies.

This is a good example of a settlement - the fortified settlement - which lasts almost a millennium, but which is greatly influenced by an exogenous factor: Romans arriving in the Northwest of the Iberian Peninsula.

The Romans and the establishment of a mining landscape

In the peninsular Northwest, the area consisting of the current town councils of Quiroga, Ribas de Sil, Pobra de Brollón, O Courel and Samos are one of the most important areas of gold mining during the Roman Empire after Augustus' conquer. The gold richness in the region creates an intensive exploitation system during the first and second centuries A. D. and this factor modifies totally the landscape and historical evolution of the native communities living there at that moment.

In the last two decades a new research line about the gold exploitations in the basins of rivers Sil, Lor and Cabe has been carried out, which is based on a systematic archaeological study of the area that allows the characterization of the archaeological elements related to this process: mining forts, mines and roads (Luzón et al.. 1980; López González 1993). This is a mining landscape, partly fossilized, which has not undergone many modifications since the roman mines were abandoned (López González 1993, Ayán 1997).

In this context, the model of roman occupation is based on a double dynamic: on one side, the selective

Figure 4. A Coroa: *example of Iron Age hillfort in Galicia.*

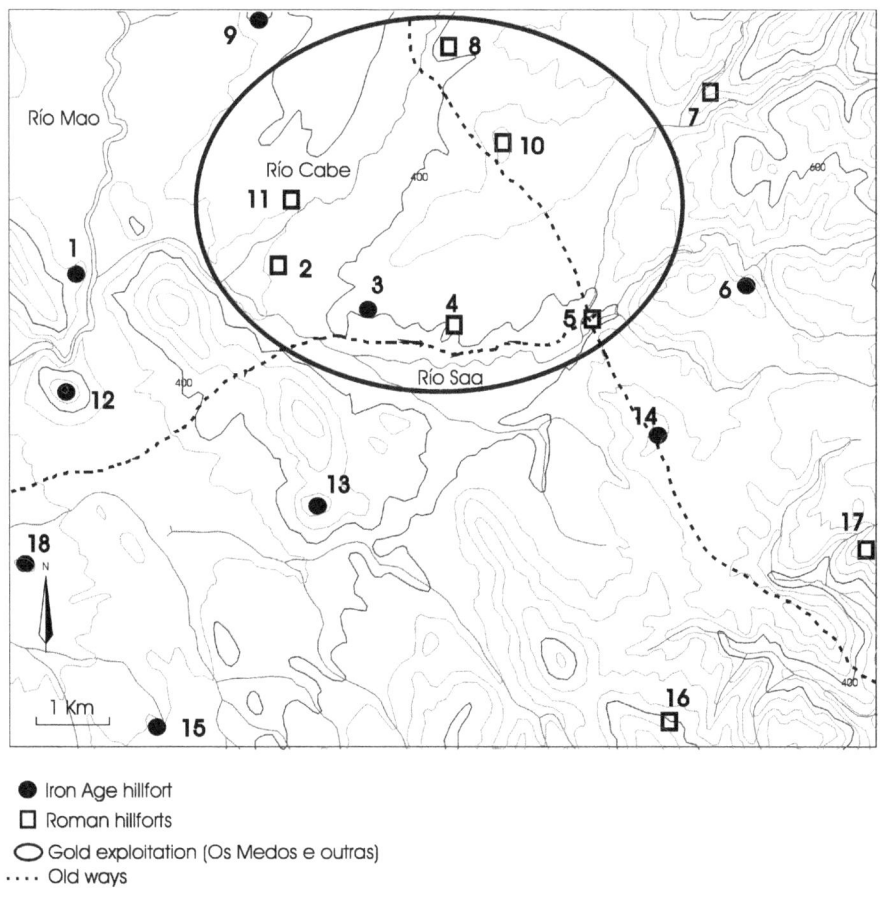

Figure 5. Settlement pattern of Iron Age and the imposition of a mining landscape in Roman period (1-2 centuries A.D.).

exploitation of previous fortified settlements, depending on strategic economic characteristics and relationship with other settlements, and on the other hand, the establishment of a new forum as a way to impose a new demographic and territorial distribution.

The establishment of this new model of settlement is clear in our area when carrying out a special analysis of fort sites at a regional scale. During the first century A.D. a series of *ex novo* settlements are built near the mines themselves and the rivers, creating a visible network that takes up the whole territory.

Castro da Lende or *San Lourenzo* is one of the most paradigmatic sites of this type. We do not know if the old fortified settlement of *A Coroa/O Castro* from the Iron Age is abandoned or if it is still occupied when this new strongly architecturalized settlement arrives, it is in a privileged place that allows control of the spectacular gold mine of Os *Medos*, as well as the natural communication East-West along the river Saa and the road that comes from the South, and from the river Lor, that goes deep into the Belesar curves of the river Miño.

The settlement consists of an elliptical shaped premise surrounded by a stone wall made of quartzite and slate pebbles. The defensive system is reinforced by a double line of parapets and a defensive ditch on the Northeast-Southwest; the most accessible part coming from the plains of *Agra de Castro*.

The ethnographic survey ads some data regarding the existence of small gold mines around the fort (reflected in the gold microtoponym *As Grovias*) and also regarding the existence of a plot of land near the lot called Nogueiras, next to the river Saa. This plot of land is known as *O Escourial*.[4] In this place several iron slag heaps have been found spread throughout the ground, indicating those settlements use technology to process the mineral: reducing furnaces with slag tapping, brought to the Northwest by the Romans (figure 5).

---

[4] The Age of this micro toponym and the existance of the slag heap itself are shown in Ensenada Land Registry when it refers to the limits of A Pobra parish: [...] *going down the river Zereixa and crossing through the place called hescourial is Rañoa located in the Highway*. AHPL, Ensenada Land Registry, San Pedro village of Puebla del Brollón, General Questioning, Answer to Chapter 3 (year 1753).

Hillfort	Chapel onto the hillfort	Church onto the hillfort	Church at the foot of the hillfort	Parish onto the hillfort	Parish at the foot of the hillfort
1			Santa María		A Parte
3					Guntiñas
4	San Lourenzo				
5		San Pedro		A Pobra	
9		Santa María		*Burgum Pinu*	
10		Santa Mariña		Castrosante	
13			San Xoán		O Alto/Pacios
14			Santiago	Castroncelos	
15			Santa Baia		Eirexa

Chart 1. Christianization and habitat continuity in the hillforts of study area.

This convergence of data allows us to consider the hypothesis that o Castro da Lende could have been populated by a metallurgical settlement specialized in the extraction and production of iron, within the system of systematic exploitation of the land developed by the Romans.

The site, therefore, becomes part of the new model of territorial distribution, based mainly on economic interests, and as a consequence of the political climate. We say climate because, according to the current research, the total abandonment of this mining system and of the related settlements dates from the beginning of the third century A.D. (Rodríguez Fernández 1994:172).

Therefore, the river Saa basin is in a marginal and outlying area that becomes slightly important as a mine only during the high empire period and also because it is near a road that is built to get to Lemos from the river Sil basin. The survival of the substratum, of the farming model and of the native cultural pattern explains the continuity of this type of environment., Although some forts are abandoned quite late, most of them (none of them Roman mining forts) are the future settlement for high medieval villages (chart 1).

The organization of the land in the high medieval period: from the fort to the village

After the Romans abandon the gold mines in the third century AD a new sociocultural reality arises in the region: a new model of settlement with open villages without defensive features. This new sociocultural landscape, disapproved of by Christian ideology, has in our area of study two sides: firstly, there is an intensive occupation of the low areas of the valley, and secondly, the old forts are settled to a great extent.

The seeds of this ambivalent process can be found in the political and territorial organization of the Swabians during the fifth and sixth centuries. In this period some important forts are still populated and also there is a scattered environment of open villages that include in their toponymy Germanic *possessors*. In this concrete case, there is documental verification that the neighbouring fort of *Zavaga* (Chavaga) forms part of the *'paramiense'* county (David 1947) and also, there is evidence of the existence of Guntiñas within the parish - the only village with a clear Germanic toponymy (situated on high ground, on a plain by *O Castro/A Coroa*). Therefore we can say there is settlement continuity between the old fortified fort and the new open village.

This territorial distribution process becomes important during the eighth and tenth centuries, when the low part of the valley of the river Saa basin is occupied following a common pattern in Galicia at that time. In this sense - the macro spatial scale - this period marks a clearly defined regional organization of the land that takes as a demarcation reference mainly rivers, mountains and evidences of fortified settlements; still noticeable by the high medieval rural society (Ayán 2005, figure 6).

In our area of study we have the demarcation line of the Benedictine monastery reserve of Saint Vicenzo do Pino, thanks to the preservation of a document dated 847. This document helps us to imagine the distribution of the old Lemos land during the ninth century (Ferreira Priegue 1988:225):

et feret in rivolum Chave ad illa villa que dicent Purcis, et vadit quomodo venit Chave usque ad Fornellas, et vadit per illum rivolum que dicent Cerosia usque feret et item per illum portum de Ferraria et vadit in directum per illa aqua de Cerosia usque in portum qui vocitam Portoesia, et feret in illa semita antiqua que venit de Castrosancto et concludet inde per illa semita antiqua que vadit sub illa villa de Pignario totum per illa semita antiqua usque circa Lupos, et item pergit de alia parte Lor usque ad cacumen montium que vocitant Vilar Planu et concludet per verticem montem, et pervenit ad illas traavesas inter Lor et Caricoca, per castro de Arias, et desecendit ad flumen Syle.

As we can see, the settlements are organized in *villae* situated in valleys of the rivers *Chave* (Cabe) and *Cerosia* (the present river Saa). It also explains how the Lemos,

Figure 6: Areal photograph of the Roman hillfort of Alende.

Lor and Quiroga territories are defined, territories also referred to in a document of Celanova monastery dated 886 (Baliñas 1992:348):

Donamus vobis villas que dicunt Salzeto, Villaplana, Dominici, et sunt ipsas villas territorio Lemaos secus rivulo Laure.

From a micro spatial scale, the *villa*, according to the Galician medieval research (Baliñas 1992:194ff; Andrade 1996; Portela and Pallares 1998) can be defined as a small village in a very well defined and demarcated territory (by a river or neighbouring villas) and with human activities related to the dwelling and exploitation of land during the ninth and tenth centuries. It appears as the basic cell of land occupation, (a very well established structure), that is based on the distinction between dwelling groups, areas of farmland and uncultivated lands. It is characterized by great flexibility to allow its adaptation to changing social conditions.

These villages, within a territory delimited by marks of physical references, as well as archaeological ruins with megalithic monuments or roman militaries (Andrade 1996:279ff) would turn into the present Galician parishes. This seems to be the case of Cereixa parish, its origin being a primitive settlement villa type from which the name of the village is recorded and which is situated in a higher level than the area where the high medieval primitive church would be situated. The territory of this village, encircled by the neighbouring villages of *Fornellas, Castro Sancto* and *Braulione*, seems to match point by point the limits described in the Ensenada Land Registry.

Therefore, we are dealing with a very long process of land distribution which means a historical continuity up to the present moment of a steady environment, by the rural people living in a concrete territory that stays the same up to now (Portela and Pallares 1998:42f).

The rural communities settled by the river Saa form a scattered environment in small villages; the source of a land distribution system that would end up being subsumed by the protofeudalization process encouraged by the pressure of the monastic powers. Therefore, the rich and fertile Terra de Lemos is the land where the monasteries, like Samos and Celanova, promoted by the Asturian monarchy, are responsible for defining the population pattern and start to slowly occupy wide territories, where the rural population does not have free use of their fields. This process is consolidated in the eleventh century, as stated in the donations made to Samos monastery by several villages in Lemos:

> *Et III^a villa in Lemabus, que fuit de Luliano et ipsa villa vocabulo Ceresia,* (Santa María de Saa) *et habuimus ipsa villa per suum pretium subtus basílica sancte Marie, discurrente rivulo Cerasia, et est per termino de Laurenti, et inde per termino de sancto Petro, et inde per Braulione, et inde per Castro Sancti, et inde per Ferrarios.* (Document dated 1050 and included in Lucas Álvarez 1980:286f).
> *Et est ipsa villa Ferrerua iuxta aula sancti Martini per terminos de monte Aguto et inde per aqua de Cerasia et inde per Castro Sancti et inde per Sancta Eulalia de Rege et inde aqua in festo de Cabi ubi dicent Palatio.* (Document dated 1074 and included in Lucas Álvarez 1980:468).

The middle medieval rural environment is fully constituted, characterized by the power of the monastic nobles and the classification of the rural class within a spatial structure, a structure that is more and more parish (Andrade 1996:290, figure 7).

The middle medieval parish in A Pobra de Brollón jurisdiction

The documentation from the twelfth and thirteenth centuries defines clearly the parish organization system: It refers to *Cerosia Rivolum* as the spatial axis and then there is express reference to population groups as a parish

Figure 7: The parish of Cereixa is a good example of galician peasant traditional landscape. General view from the top of A Coroa *hillfort.*

church; for instance the references to *San Pedro de Cereija* (documents from Lugo Cathedral dated 1st April 1235), *Eijion Ecclesia* (San Xurxo de Eixón*), Ecclesia Pinu Sancta María* (St. Mary Of Piño) or *Abrenze* in Lemos (San Xoán da Brence) (Rielo Carballo 1975).

The road from Sil valley to Pobra de Brollón plays an important role in the parish configuration. This road following the river Saa course, goes through Cereixa, crosses the hill, and from there it goes to Monforte de Lemos. This natural route, of roman origin, would still be considered a main road in the medieval period, as proved by the fact that the same road would stay as a model when it comes down to face the orographic conditionings.

This route to Galicia, used as a pilgrim route to Santiago, becomes quite popular as a commercial route and helps the emergence of A Pobra de Brollón in the twelfth century, a Crown jurisdiction, dependent directly on the Crown and therefore exempt from paying the feudal charges imposed by the nobility and/or the ecclesiastics. In fact, there are some documents with complaints of the Council reported to the Catholic Monarchs in 1494 regarding the extra jurisdictional abuses imposed by the Lemos Count on the people who live in A Pobra (García Oro 1987).

A Pobra de Brollón becomes the core of the jurisdictional land Cereixa parish joins. However, San Pedro de Cerixa's reserve and parish depend directly on Lugo diocese by the last third of fourteenth century. From that moment and up to the beginning of nineteenth century, Cereixa is an exception in the group of parishes of A Pobra de Brollón jurisdiction, since it is the only parish yielded to Abadengo rule. It is represented by the Bishop of Lugo, who rules a hundred parishes, although most of them in the capital's jurisdiction. The parish is referred to in the *General Questioning of Ensenada Land Registry* as:

The reserve and Parish of San Pedro de Zereixa is and belongs to the Episcopate of the City of Lugo and on behalf of the His Grace the Bishop to whom we pay the Letuosa, the best of the oxes that survives after every neighbours' pass away, without concurrence of any other thing for dominion or vassalage reasons.[5]

The parish in the Ancien Régime

Data given by the said historical source of Ensenada Land Registry, although they refer to a specific and temporary period, (year 1753) they depict very well the socioeconomic structure of the parish during the Ancien Régime. So the *General Questioning* tells about a cereal-producing, rural survival economy based on extensive monoculture of rye en *régimen de año y vez* (lands lied fallow during 14 months, from harvest time to the following autumn); this cereal is cultivated in second or third quality lands, whereas first quality lands *produce*

---

[5] Provincial Historical Archive in Lugo, Ensenada Land Registry, Reserve and Parish of San Pedro de Cereija, General Questioning. Answer to 1st Chapter (Year 1753).

wheat without pause and the following year more wheat alternately.[6]

On the other hand, the *Personal Book of Legos* tells us about the size, typology and structure of the domestic organizations that made up San Pedro de Cereixa's parish in 1753. There is an average of 5.07 people/homes and therefore it coincides with one of the characteristics of this area of Lugo that differentiates it from the rest of Galicia: the large size of the rural families.

Almost a century later, according to the reference supplied by P. Madoz, Cereixa has in the 1840's, about *63 inhabitants and 321 souls*. Therefore it may be deducted a rate inhabitant/homes of 5,09, that is, an almost identical number to year 1753. This proves that that demographic reality shown by Ensenada Land Property is not temporal at all.

Low production yields, communitarian restrictions to extension of cultivated land, and work requirements of an extensive agriculture-cattle raising based on rye farming *en régimen de año y vez*, and great exploitation of scrublands demanded a large labour force, and therefore, larger work units – work domestic groups.

In short, Cereixa parish meets the general characteristics of a rural family in central-Eastern Galicia: high percentage of complex domestic groups, many children, important role of co-residents and not much significant presence of servants. This variable forms a cultural pattern of main familiar organization clearly conditioned by a specific and limited ruling agrarian system.

This farming, demographic and familiar structure develops under a feudal noble system and burdens the peasants with taxes like the *luctuosa*. That is, when the head of the family dies, the family has to give their Lords an animal; this payment in kind, although it is paid from time to time, has a great impact on rural economies, as well as the tithes, the solemn vows to Santiago, or the *alcabala viexa* paid to the Lemos Countess from time immemorial.

The space: an approach at micro scale

The parish land is defined first of all as a farming landscape that creates a particular spatial model, as shown in chart 2.

Cereixa parish matches the farming landscape of the small open valleys of Galicia, shaping a closed physiographic unit that is situated around a river, limited by its divisions and that shows all the natural possibilities the traditional farming system demands. (Ballesteros 2002:13f). So **a gradual system of land exploitation** is formulated; a system where the land close to the houses is used as gardens for pulses, vegetables and other fruit

---

[6] Answer to Chapter 4.

Agrarian exploitation system: A Veiga, Trigais, A Cha de Nogueiras, A Cha de Castro, A Cha de Ramos, A Agra de Arriba, O Chao, O Chao das Cortiñas, o Agro, Cenoira, Cortiña de Alende, A Aira, A Viña Vella, A Viña Longa, Os Currais, Chouselas, O Covallo.

Scrub and forest: A Devesa, A Castañeira, O Souto, Carballedo, O Carpancedo, O Amieiro, Punxedo, A Carqueixa, O Toxal, A Xesteira, O Cachón, A Costa, A Serra, Moncai, Monteixón, Mompedroso, Penelas de Vilarello.

Wetlands and pastures: A Lama, A Lamela, Lamasboas, Os Lameiros, O Sobrado, Entrerríos, A Ínsua, Foncerbeiras, Bourallos, O Gorgorelo, o Rego de Amieiros, Caldelas, A Torrente.

Land divided: O Cerrado, O Pechado, a Cancela, O Canceleiro, O Igrexario, Muradella.

Mining extraction: As Areas, As Forgas, O Barredo, A Pedreira, As Grovias, O Escourial, O Pozo do Lago, As Pozas do Barro.

Other activities: O Limpadoiro, O Moíño, Albariza, O Pozo dos Cabalos, O Liñar, o Pombar,

Traditional ways: o camiño da Serra, Rairos, a Retorta, a Calzada, a Ponte Vella, O Lombao, A Cabarca, a rúa da Fonte, As Cadeiras

Archaeological remains: San Lourenzo, O Castro da Lende, A Coroa (O Castro)

Symbolic borders of the parish: A Cruz, a Cruz do Mollón

Abandoned compounds: Lamas, Cavagares, O Corbal.

Other place names: A Lucenza, O Cazapedro, Vilarello, A Rañoá, A Raposa, Mioqueira, O Belido, As Lampazas, O Piteiro.

Chart 2. Microtoponymy of Cereixa parish (from ethnographical inquiry and Ensenada Land Registry, 1753).

trees, and in the vicinity, in a lower level, arable lands (*agras*, *chas* and *chaos*). The pasture lands are in the lower part of the hill and in the damp parts of the banks of the rivers and tributaries. The wood and mountains are above the houses.

Also, the division system of the area of farmland and the rent paid for it arises from a great demographic pressure on the space dedicated to own mixed farming of a familiar survival economy, with no commercial potential or intention. The existent agrarian structure in Cereixa in middle eighteenth century, based on gardens, meadows, cortiñas, agras, and scrublands survives until 1960, guaranteed by cereal harvest (agras and municipal scrubland) necessary for survival. Meadows and cortiñas increase the food and fodder production for cattle in intensive stabling.

Mythical Structure of the parish

In the second part of this work we are going to prove the existence of a mythical structure that over imposes the existing agricultural space as a result of a semantization process of the space; a symbolic appropriation of the medium by the traditional rural community. In this sense, the parish limits are ritualized following a common

Figure 8. The symbolic centre of the parish is conformed by two spatial references. Os Carballos (The Oaks) – nowadays the party field of the parish - and the new church which was built in 1802.

practice in rural Galicia (Llinares and Vázquez Varela 1990) by the reutilization of *modorras* as monument frames or the raising of stone crosses, which besides frames are also symbols for the community when facing overseas enemies. This boundary limits a micro space where the axis is the river Saa. This river divides (and links) the parish in two areas where most villages are situated by the river and by the fords that cross it. The original centre of population is situated where the neighbourhood A Ponte now stands, at the site of the primitive church. The church is the symbolic centre of the parish around which the population settles. This explains the microtoponomy of Alende (on the other side of the river related to this symbolic centre) and Cima de Vila. This church of A Ponte, probably Romanesque, is always quoted in *Pastoral Visits* to stress its terrible state of repair:

> *We have to admit how deteriorated it is and its bad state of preservation, and we order it to be moved to a better place and for this, the priest must charge the amount from the Church and brotherhood of the Holy Sacrament, leaving only some amount to defray his expenses. Parishioners must understand their obligation to pay and help, and to look for a skilled person to carry out the building Works, planning it in advance with our approval before drawing up the deeds.*[7]

This situation is governed by the parish jurisdictional Lord patronage, the bishop of Lugo, during that year (1802) *Pastoral Visits* states:

> *On 11th March 1802 stones were brought and broken to start the building of the new church of San Pedro de Cereyxa and these works finished by the end of August of the same year; Domingo Antº Arca was the builder and it cost twenty thousands, thirteen thousand were given by Felipe Fozara and Lord of Lugo, Josef Benito Pérez from that region and at that moment priest of San Salvador de Villauje, gave one thousand reals. The Factory contributed five thousands and the brotherhood of the Holy Sacrament contributed another thousand and the parishioners made the carts, and the 2nd September was blessed by the priest and he offered mass with other Lord Priests who joined the Solemnity and so that this may be officially recorded I the priest sign on 6th September 1802.*[8]

The support of the bishop of Lugo and his role as a symbol of power is undoubtedly crucial regarding the quality and capacity of this building that contrasts with the rest of churches in this region (figure 8).

What is more surprising from this foundation *ex novo* is the selection of the site, in a central position in Cereixa geography, at a crossroads, near a hundred-year-old oak grove known as ***Os Carballos***. It is a communal area used

---

[7] Diocesan Archive in Lugo, San Pedro de Cereixa, Factory, Book I (years 1715-1941). Pastoral visit in 1802.

[8] Diocesan Archive in Lugo, San Pedro de Cereixa, Factory, Book I (years 1715-1941). Personal note of the priest. Year 1802.

as a secular festival field; a natural ritual space to celebrate fire festivities like the *The night of the logs* the day before St. Blaise. This new site is probably chosen for the *genius loci* of a space, sanctioned by the rural tradition that needs to be Christianized according to the official religion. Anyway, this dual, conflicting and complementary space, made up by the sacred architecture of the parish church – its portico, a communal space for meetings of neighbours – and by the natural and ritual space of Os Carballos (true *wild monument*), is in fact the symbolic centre of this mythical structure, the axis of the domestic world, that contrasted with the outlying natural mountain areas, where old times ruins inhabited by mythical beings still remain: the *moors* (equivalent to the *gnomes* and Celt-Germanics *kobolds* from Northern Europe legends or the Breton *Corrigans*).

A Coroa/O Castro and the Lende Fort/San Lourenzo: spaces of the collective imagination

In this undomesticated area, surrounding the parish we must underline the role played by these two protohistoric monuments as symbolic stages. The forts, after their abandonment, become important in the traditional rural landscape and hence a significant economic resource. However, its role as a referent of a pagan past does not go unnoticed in the traditional society, the church or during the early Christianization process in Galicia. This explains the construction of chapels on top of forts, and the celebration of festivities, processions and religious services on those protohistoric settlements (Ayán and Arizaga 2005).

The fort is, not a place of worship or adoration but a symbolic support; a meeting point between the sacred and secular worlds; a privileged centre for the interaction of human and supernatural beings. (Mandianes 1984:71f). In this regard, the fort is perfectly demarcated in the parish, and is usually used as a neighbourhood, ritual, pragmatic, symbolic and representative area, that stresses the community unity (Fernández de Rota 1984:152ff).

These archaeological ruins are related to the mythical universe of the *mouros* - their ancestors and legends. This aspect is shown in the legends we have collected in the last few years, and that are very similar to folk references coming from neighbouring villages like O Incio (González Reboredo 1971) and O Courel (Alonso del Real 1983).

O Castro/A Coroa
From the hill road there is a gold chain and a bucket used by the Moor to pick up water from Areas River.
Snakes have been seen in the Fort suckling the teats of a cow.

O Castro da Lende/San Lourenzo
It is said Moors lived in San Lourenzo.
The fort was an old fortification, Romans and Celts used the fort and in those times, from there they communicated with Morse code with Salcedo, with Chavaga, with Castrosante... The fort is entrenched because the hills are very sharp and they dug to make it more difficult to reach; in those times, war was made with sticks and bayonet.

Moors are Moors; there was a time when Moors reined here and of course, those people dwelled places like the forts, with many woods because they were used to living in woods... There was a Moor war and many other wars because for several generations they fought each other; there came Celts, Celt Iberians, Goths, Visigoths and Romans; but they were all thrown out. This is a long story...

I heard the Moors had a chain and a golden bucket that go from the fort to the river and it picked up water for the fort and this water was put in a well that there was in the fort called the Moor Hole.

It is said the gold chain went down to the river and at night the pulley wheel roared.

The legend says the Moors killed a girl that was lost in the fort; her parents were looking for her and called out her name ¡Mariquiña, Mariquiña! And a Moor woman said:
¡Ni que Mariquiña ni que Maricuela,
que tu Mariquiña está en mi cazuela!

It is said there were in the fort some chicks that appeared and disappeared. One day one girl followed the chicks and disappeared too; they looked for her and shouted ¡Mariquiña, Mariquiña!, and a voice said:
¡Que Mariquiña, ni que Maricuela,
por ser lengoreta está en la cazuela!

On the road to the fort it was said to be some clothes hanging out on the blackberry bushes and a hen with the chicks and a Moor woman combing her hair. Her hair was as black as tar and very long; and in the twinkling of an eye woman and hens disappeared.

The elders also told the story of a man hidden in the hole of a chestnut tree and then he disappeared, and they said it was the Moors. These are things from the old times, when people had nothing to do, when there was no television, and what were they supposed to do but to tell stories and make up tales and legends.

When we were young we were told that in the Grovias ditch there was Noah's Ark during the Flood.

O Castro de Chavaga
There are many legends of the Fort; it was said there was a gold chain between the Fort and Sindrán and that could be found by the sheep legs because it was not very deep.
There is a gold chain from the Fort to A Meda, and it will be found by the sheep legs.
There are two beams under the ground in the Fort, a golden one and poison one; if the poison one was found first everything would explode.
In the Coroa it could be seen silk bedspreads put out in the sun to dry, and when getting there, they disappeared because they were from the Moors who lived there under the ground in the Fort.

Figure 9. Aerial photograph of the hillfort of Chavaga.

In the Fort Moors hung out clothes and when the people from Chavaga arrived they disappeared because they were enchanted.
My father believed in Moors; he used to tell me that 'Moors exist, they live under the ground; sometimes, on the way home from Monforte market you travelled with a man who was a moor and suddenly he disappeared when entering the Fort'.
Moors lived there under the ground; people believed it, of course, mainly because some vases were found buried in Coroa and that proved they lived under the ground.
When I was young, an elder woman told me some Moorish tales; one was the story of the Refoxo fountain. They say there was a girl who went to pick up some water from the fountain, where water gushed from earth like boiling. When she got to the fountain a Moor woman turned up and gave her a bag on condition that she did not open it before she arrived home. The girl took the bag and left; but of course, she was very curious and opened the bag. There was some coal inside and she threw the bag away. However, when she got home she found some coal in the pleat of her clothes but it was no coal but a gold ounce. The following day she went back again to the fountain to try to find the rest of the gold and the moor woman turned out and said:
You have not done as I told you and you will stay under the ground boiling.
And that is why the fountain water gushes from earth like boiling.

We are not going to deal with a background of these legends, since nowadays Anthropology has explained very well their function and sense (see the works of Criado Boado 1986, Llinares García 1990; Aparicio Casado 1999 or Ayán and Ameixeiras 2002). However, we must highlight the fact that our informants' conception of the fort settlements' organization in the landscape is very clear, and that they are aware of their visibility and their functions of control and power of the area. Therefore, the popular culture, when explaining the fort as a historical phenomenon, fully coincides in this regard with the conclusions made by spatial and landscape Archaeology. Villagers think this coincidence of forts in the area is due to their military and strategic function, in a cyclical historical perception based on the series of different warlike races (figure 9).

Rationality standard: official religion and popular culture

In this last section of this work we are trying, by means of a detailed description, to find the rationality standard used by the traditional rural society and which gives sense to the mythology aforementioned.

To achieve this aim we develop an approach that maximizes the overall contributions of different disciplines (Rural History, Historical Anthropology, History of Mentalities) with the use of several methodological tools (like literary analysis, the ethnographic survey, the iconographic analysis and Oral History).

This rationality standard is not a static model, but a view of the world historically defined, where breaking-offs and continuities, popular culture and interventions of the ecclesiastical power-knowledge system go together. The documents we have, for instance, the Pastoral vistis to the parish during the second half of the eighteenth century, corroborate the results obtained by the Galician modernist research about the mind universe of the Galician in the Ancien Régime (Dubert 1994; Saavedra 1994:275ff). Then we find a rural parish where the governing clergyman plays an important role, displaying attitudes close to the peasants, who are opposed to customs and the civilization promoted by the ecclesiastical authorities since the Ecumenical Council of Trent.

Consecutive visits show a *shocking and remarkable disobedience*[9] by the priest who does not pay the necessary attention to the fight against pagan beliefs neither in the population nor to the deep rift between them. For instance, the requirements of the archpriest of Santalla de Rei, representing the Bishop of Lugo, during his pastoral visits to Cereixa parish:

The Holy Communion is renewed at least every eight days. Confession must under no circumstance take place outside Church, and confession must not be heard to women with portable confessionals but with fixed confessionals and closed with a thick screen. Visitors are received in the confessionals to avoid simony or avarice, and given a warning of severe

---
[9] ADL, San Pedro de Cereija, Factory, Book I (Years 1715-1941). Pastoral visit in 1794.

*Figure 10. Main altarpiece of the Cereixa parish church.
From left to right: Saint Laurence, Jesus, Saint Peter, Saint Joseph and Saint Anthony of Padua.*

punishment to the Unrepentant. This redeemer priest must inform about them and also about the Clergymen that with no reason at all, go to festivals and fairs, and about those that go to fairs without the proper adornment and respectably dressed, against whom we will proceed with the utmost severity.[10]

The said priest is commissioned to study the village women and midwives of his parish, and to instruct them in Holy water cases and to examine in Christian doctrine the young people. We hope this redeemer priest's religious zeal could be seen in the cleanliness and decency of his church.[11]

We are told the Holy Sacrament is taken out in some churches of the Bishopric, and it is ordered that under no circumstance is it taken out again, but in the Corpus Christi procession.. 'Take care the parishioners do not work in holidays because it is forbidden, only in cases of extreme necessity and with the corresponding license.[12]

This official fight in favour of the inculcation of orthodox Christianity with regard to popular beliefs and devotions has undoubtedly a bearing on the peasants' cosmic vision. But in some ways it is a complete failure due to the religious syncretism of the peasants who kept some rituals until the twentieth century and some others are still alive today.

In order to deepen the micro history of this mental universe, complex and floating in time, we use iconographic analysis of the religious statues in the main altarpiece of Cereixa parish church, a religious pantheon that helps us to understand the cosmic vision of the Christian peasants.

The religious pantheon of the parish

The main altarpiece of the Cereixa parish church is neoclassical style, with wall paintings on the heading from the nineteenth century; also statues of St. Laurence, Jesus, St. Peter, St. Joseph and St. Anthony of Padua. The iconographic collection of the church (dated eighteenth century) is rounded off with another two minor altarpieces of characteristic of differing artistic styles through history in popular art; the altarpiece on the right, Solomon style, has statues of St. Sebastian, St. Blaise, Saint James, St. Roque and St. Jerome, while the left altarpiece shows a set of women saints, with statues of St. Barbara, Our Lady of Rosario, the Virgin Mary and St. Theresa of the child Jesus (figure 10).

This mixture of statues, apparently chaotic, represents the process undergone since the sixteenth century in Galician rural parishes regarding religious saints, and it can be seen as a double process: On the one hand new worship styles are imposed (Our Lady of Rosario or St. Theresa of the child Jesus) and on the other hand, very deeply-rooted ancient traditions are observed since the Middle Ages. In fact, we know the strategy followed by post-tridentine clergy regarding religious art in order to bring peasants

---

[10] Ibíd. Pastoral visit in 1771.
[11] Ibíd. Pastoral visit 6th August, 1772.
[12] Ibíd. Pastoral visit in 1782.

closer to the dogma established by Trent. In those times iconographies of very popular saints (the real catechism for peasants) are used again and these saints are given some virtues not seen before; like St. Barbara, advocate of good death, or St. Sebastian, a shield against plagues (Saavedra 1994:306).

It is true the ecclesiastic authorities promote most of these popular devotions, but local traditional and deeply-rooted worships also play an important role. (Saavedra 1994:352).

In this regard, the so called *religious pantheon* of Cereixa shows in a very significant way the convergence of this triple dynamics. First of all, St. Peter as the patron saint of the parish from its origin, one of the oldest saints in Hispanic worship (sixth century) and the most common patron saint in Galician parishes, after The Virgin, and he is also the most represented in baroque altarpieces. Despite his central position in the main altarpiece, in this particular case he is not the centre of devotion. On the contrary, the Counter-Reformation offensive has a greater impact, with the imposition of worship of Our Lady of Rosario by the end of sixteenth century. Nowadays she is the official patron saint of the parish, and the patron saint's day is celebrated in her honour at the beginning of October.

In parallel with this official religiousness a traditional popular religion exists side by side, centred on devotion to St. Blaise and St. Laurence with a very interesting historical and anthropological background, so much so that it gives sense to the mythical landscape we identified before.

Next we are going to analyze in detail this dual process where official religiousness and peasant Christians exist side by side.

The Counter-Reformation character. Our Lady of Rosario and the brotherhoods

San Pedro de Cereixa's parish, under the Bishop of Lugo's authority, is a paradigmatic example of the application of the Counter-reformation religious agenda. Its focus is the Eucharistic worship (Holy Sacrament), to encourage devotion to The Virgin and to promote the brotherhoods as the ideal tool to control the religious associations in both urban and rural communities. (González Lopo 1997).

In this context is the devotion to Our Lady of Rosario, spread thanks to Dominican preaching in their fight against the Protestants and the political interests of the Papacy (this festival is celebrated 7th October in commemoration of the Battle of Lepanto in 1571). In Galicia this worship is successfully promoted by the ecclesiastical authorities as is shown by the following: there are not any brotherhoods in Galicia devoted to this worship during 1547-48 but by the year 1750 it rises to 398 (66,8 % of total) (González Lopo 1997:300f).

Therefore, this is an *ex novo* worship, backed by the church, and that bursts in upon the religiousness standard of the inhabitants of the parish. But it does not start from an old tradition, unlike St. Blaise who does enjoy mass fervour. This fact makes the Bishop of Lugo organize St. Blaise brotherhood in order to channel this old worship, as is stated in *Constitutions, Stipulated by Mr. Joseph Taboada y Camba. Although it was tolerated till now because of the custom entered by its members and that the Bishops authorized, having done it His Grace Juan Saenz de Buruaga Bishop and Lord of this Diocese.*[13]

These constitutions, dated from mid eighteenth century, are an attempt to regulate this ancient religious association (there are some records explaining its existence already in 1689), regulating their behaviour, their gestures and rituals within the sacred building, according to the official religious practice.

However, this initiative of the church conflicts with the popular devotion and religiousness because they have their own expression channels, for instance the *noite dos Cepos* (the night of logs) a ritual festival still celebrate in today.

'St. Blaise': the festival of the elders

St. Blaise, bishop of Sebaste in fourth century Armenia, who was martyred during the Diocletian persecution, and who is believed to have miracle-working powers (especially versus throat infection and ears pains), is a very popular saint in Galicia. This is because of the popularity of Early Christian martyrs in the northwest of Spain (St. Marina, St. Laurence, St. Lucy, St. Christopher etc.) who were used by the church to christianize some pre-roman worship. (Castro Pérez 2001).

This devotion is very popular in Terra de Lemos (together with St. Barbara, also in one of the altarpieces of the parish), backed up by Lemos Count and Countess during the sixteenth century because some relics of the saint are brought from Italy. This religious dedication in Cereixa parish can be considered as the most representative devotion within the peasants' cosmo vision. In *Memorial of members of the Brotherhood*[14] we find the geographical origin of the devotion of the saint from several parishes of the zone, and therefore we must say there is great local worship punished by popular tradition.

---

[13] Diocesan Archives in Lugo, St. Pedro de Cereija, Brotherhoods, St. Blaise Brotherhood, Book nº I (Years 1689-1791), *Cosntitutions of St. Blaise Brotherhood* (18th January, 1765).

[14] Some individuals are registered of the following parishes of Fornelas, Brence, Castroncelos, Castrosante, Eixón, Santalla de Rei, Saa, Pinel, Chavaga, A Parte, Sindrán, Lamaigrexa, Veiga, and Ribas Pequenas. (Diocesan Archives in Lugo, St. Pedro de Cereija, Brotherhoods, San Blas, Book nº 2, years 1736-1762).

Figure 11. Celebration of the traditional Oak logs Party in Os Carballos (February, 2004).

It is considered to be *an elder people feast, a tradition which dates from time immemorial, much before the Our Lady of Rosario*. Like a 90 years old parishioner tells us:

> St. Blaise was their feast, he has been the patron saint since time immemorial. When I was young they stopped celebrating this feast. It was a very popular feast, and the faithful came with offers even from other parishes. It was the custom to burn dry oak logs in Os Carballos, the night before. Logs were picked up by men with carts in Pinel, and Brence, and on their way they collected root vegetables and other things. A big rice casserole was prepared and the feast was started. It was a very funny feast, because we used to eat the pork products from slaughter. But in Rosario feast everything was brought from other places outside the parish. I still remember the stanza dedicated to the patron saint:
> My patron saint St. Blaise of Viana,
> Made of alder tree,
> Brother of my clogs,
> Brought up in my stream.

Although it is remarkable for its importance in the liturgical calendar since it is leading up to Lent (hence the saying *Let's go girls, to St. Blaise, 'cos there are not any other festivals*), much more remarkable is the fact it is a milestone in the agricultural calendar of the community. At the height of winter, when life is centred around the house and the family (in contrast to summer time, the high point of communitarian jobs) and when the animals are slaughtered, basic activity in their survival economy, St Blaise festival (also called *festa das cacholas* –festival of pig heads-) strengthens the bonds of the community - ritualized the previous night in the so called *Noite dos Cepos* (the night of logs, figure 11).

It is a fire festival that transfers us to the so-called *folións de véspera*, with bonfires the night before the saint festivity, or with visits with torches to ritual places like the forts (Ayán and Ameixeiras 2002). This is a very common practice in Galicia (Taboada 1980; Bouza Brey 1982) and in this particular area becomes important. The *folións* in Ribeira Sacra of Miño River, currently preserved only in the parishes of Castelo (Taboada) and Vilelos (O Saviñao), and the procession of St. Sebastian in Castro Caldelas (Ourense) (Vázquez Rodríguez 1996-1997).

During the *Night of Logs* (*Noite dos Cepos*) celebration, which the church could do nothing to eradicate despite the control through the Saint Blaise brotherhood, fire merges in a purifying and propitiatory ritual, collective act, symbol of the self-affirmation of the parish as community (the different parts of the parish take turns to organize the festival according to a pre-established order) and the symbolic core of the parish; *Os Carballos* is clearly ritualized. This core is the current field of the festival and until the 1980s it is covered with a hundred-year-old oak wood.

Finally, it is important to say that this feast is thought to be the Christianization of old Pre-Roman feasts, such as in Celtic culture with the feast of *Imbolc*, which means the transition to the second half of winter when days are longer. Popular sayings refer to this: *when St. Blaise*

Figure 12. Our Lady of Rosario and Saint Blaise, after the religious procession around the church. Saint Blaise has miracle-working powers, especially versus throat infection and ears pains.

comes, put some bread and some wine in your saddlebag, 'cos days are longer or *'cos St. Blaise day is two hours longer'* and it is replaced in the Christian calendar with the Mullein and St. Blaise (García Quintela and Santos Estévez 2004; García Quintela 2005).

This popular feast is given up before the civil war period 1936-1939, but it is started again at the beginning of the seventies, and at the same time as keeping the traditional mass with procession in the church vestibule (patrons are Our Lady of Rosario and St. Blaise), the exhibition of the saint and the offer of pink and blue ribbons by the devotees as well as the food and candles blessing (figure 12).

Vicissitudes of a 'hidroforos' saint: St. Laurence, from the fort to the river and from the river to church

Devotion to St. Blaise continues till now. A different case is the devotion to St. Laurence. A devotion that was very important in the cultural landscape of Cereixa parish in the past. In fact, in the main altarpiece of the church there is still a statue of this saint and it is said it came from a chapel, now in ruins, situated on the Lende fort and hence his naming as St. Laurence. I myself have heard this saint's story from the mouth of my grandfather:

St. Laurence was brought by those priests, from the fort for the church, but the saint left and went back to the fort, he wanted to stay there, and that is why a chapel was built in the fort. My grandmother used to tell me the rogations made in drought periods; one year it did not rain at all and they went in procession from the fort to the river and as they bathed the saint in the river it started raining and the harvest survived. I cannot remember the chapel, but some walls remain. Its stones were taken for the houses of Alende.

As was said before, St. Laurence, a martyr in third century Rome, is one of the oldest saints in the Hispanic liturgical calendar (fifth century) and one of the saints with a great tradition in Galicia. Seventythree parishes are named after him and several chapels, most of them situated on forts. He is an early Christian martyr who, as

Figure 13. Saint Laurence image that originally was venerated into the chapel of Alende *hillfort.*

In Cereixa, the ethnographic survey helps us to rebuild this old tradition that ritualizes the importance of water in this valley of river Saa, like the Moor legends. On the other hand, the archaeological analysis provides us not only with documentation of a Christianized fort but also helps us to recuperate the original purpose of an essential monument in the mythical life of the parish. This is an example of the symbolic appropriation of these protohistoric settlements by the peasants. A process that is positively sanctioned by the ecclesiastic authorities, that authorize the building of some chapels devoted to Early Christian martyrs (St. Cyprian, St. Marina, St. Christina, St. Laurence) on these sites (Aparicio Casado 2002:81f).

The age of the devotion can be demonstrated by the presence of the micro-toponomy S*an Lourenzo*, referring to Lende fort, in the Ensenada Land Registry. On the top of this S*an Lourenzo* site there are still some remains of the chapel that originally was of rectangular plant with an arcade in its façade. The reveal and the lintel of the chapel were reused in a house in Lende neighbourhood. In the lintel there is still an inscription that refers to the nineteenth-century improvements of the chapel: AVE MARIA/ESTE CORPO LO HIZO (a cross figure) D JOSE BR EN 1876.

F. Bouza Brey shows in two splendid works (Bouza Brey 1963, 1982a), is reinterpreted by the peasant Christians as a *hidroforos* saint, considered as a *water carrier* (according the hagiographic tradition that describes his martyrdom burnt alive in a grill), replacing old pre-Roman divinities (Bouza Brey 1982a:236ff).

This popular relationship of the saint with the fire leads him to be named by the communities in prays and rituals calling on rain during the summer (the festival is celebrated 10th August) and in many places and occasions the statue of the saint is put under the water, like in Ferreiros parish (Cuntis) or in San Lourenzo de Ouzande (A Estrada) (Bouza Brey 1963:131f).

And this is the end of our journey. The archaeological-historical and anthropological analysis at micro spatial scale made in this work results in a better understanding of an environment space, the low basin of river Saa, and the change of this natural space into a cultural space, finally modelled by the traditional rural society. This community gives sense to its social space, according to a rationality standard that we interpret in detail, so much so that we can identify the mythical structure inherent in it, and moves to everyday life, the agricultural calendar and the liturgical calendar - a concrete symbolic appropriation of the space and the configuration of the religious pantheon, based on the syncretism of the peasants' Christianity.

In the following chart we explain very briefly the mythical structure, now almost non-existent.

Dedication	Antiquity of Cult	Date	Space	Spatial category	Community	Origin of Cult	Force	Animal
St. Blaise	Paleochristian martyr	3rd February	*Os Carballos*	Natural/Central	peasants	Iron Age (¿)	Fire	cow
St. Peter	Apostle	29th June	Church	Religious/central	christians	high medieval	Corpus Christi	------
St. Laurence	Paleochristian martyr	10th August	*Alende* hillfort	Mythical/peripherical	*mouros*	High medieval	water	snake
Lady of Rosario	Counter-Reformist dedication	7th October	Church	Religious/central	catholics	XVI c.	Rosario	-------

Chart 3. Mythical structure of Cereixa parish.

Figure 14. Architectural remains of the chapel of Saint Laurence which were reused in the walls of a vernacular house. The door is decorated with an announcement of Our Lady of Rosario Party (October, 2005).

Consequences

Our first aim is to make an archaeological-historical reconstruction of the genealogy and structure process of a cultural landscape on a local scale, developing interdisciplinary research strategies that start from landscape archaeology as a theoretical-methodological frame. Based on these assumptions we explain the different special patterns that take place in the course of history in the low basin of the river Saa, shaping a landscape that shows not only a survival pattern but also the rationality standard of these societies.

This archaeological reconstruction is also applied to the study of the last period of that process, which gives some meaning to the traditional rural landscape. From an interdisciplinary approach we bring closer to the rationality standard, a chronological contextualization – usually not easy at all - of the popular beliefs to the collective imagination of the peasants, that determine not only the population model but the agricultural structure or the organization of the symbolic and ritual spaces.

To learn, even from a distance, the meaning of this cultural landscape, is the *raison d'être* of this micro historical study, that also tries to link the local and apparently insignificant, to the socioeconomic and cultural superstructure of every historical period of the rural Galician world. But, like any other discursive practice, this is a discussion text, and it has a triple aim. First, regardless of the results of the investigation, that may be satisfactory or not for the reader, we believe it is necessary to use archaeological analysis as an essential tool to carry out diachronic studies about the cultural

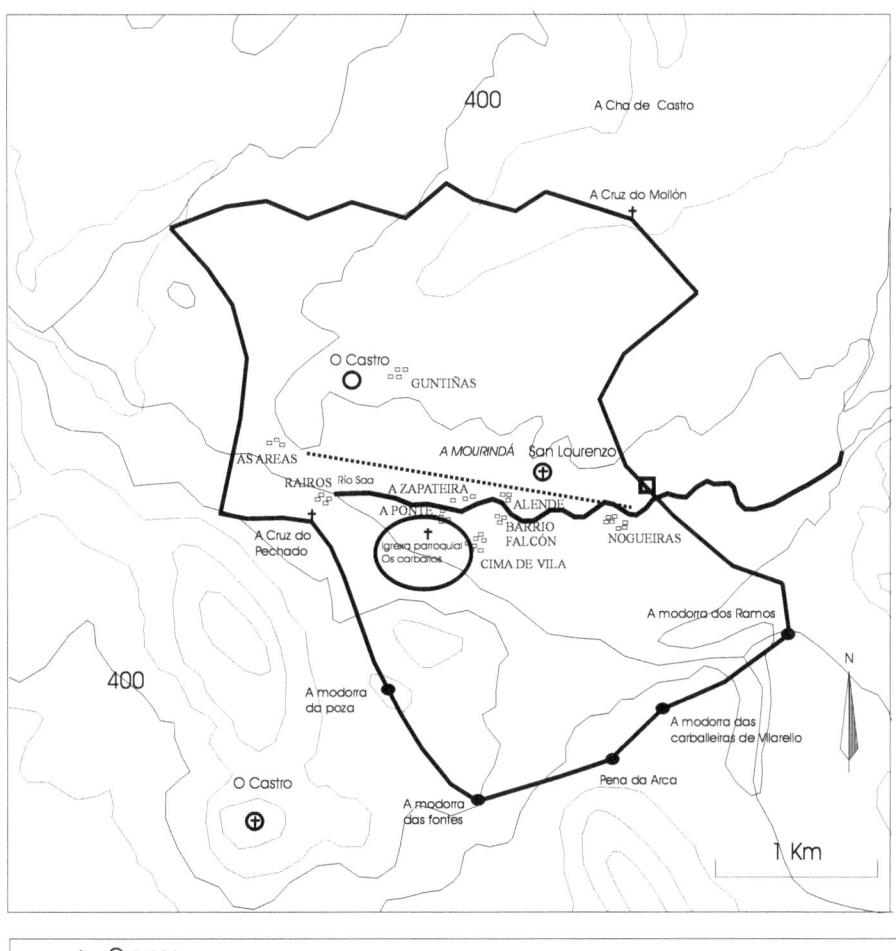

Figure 15. Symbolic markings of the parish limits and mythical cartography identified in Cereixa.

concrete shapes of the ancient cultural landscapes (Criado et al. 1991, Rodríguez Fernández 1994; Parcero et al. 1998; Fernández Mier 1999).

Being part of these research strategies, we have tried to launch a similar project, on detailed analysis scale. When getting close to the purpose of our study, that is, how landscape changes and understanding it as a sociocultural product in time, we delimit the space where this process of social construction of reality is expressed. We are aware that a study about the Iron Age, for instance, cannot be based only on the register of only one fort. However, the *zoom* effect gives a view that allows us to investigate carefully the processes that form the discourse of the great general synthesis, that is, the problem of the space-temporal categories, the breaks and continuities, the cultural dichotomy popular-culture of the elites, tradition and innovation, etc...

Our second aim is within this context: to demand micro historical studies, not making naïve, idealistic and parochial pretensions. Then, for example, the micro spatial study of two high-medieval Galician villages (Portela and Pallares 1998) gives excellent information to help us to understand better this period historically speaking, to understand the relationships of the medieval community with the environment, the organization of the land, the spatial pattern and the configuration of the social space. This is a legitimate perspective that complements the information obtained from the transcription of hundreds of chartularies and monastic records or quantitative studies of the demographic or socioeconomic kind.

Likewise, we pledge our firm commitment to a, more than ever, necessary ethnoarchaeology of the Galician traditional rural landscape. Rigoberta Menchú said she did not see herself as an anthropologist of her own people, because she could not see her people as the subject of a study. It is probably true. We ourselves, as archaeologists, try to be silent witnesses, looking for an approach, starting from material culture, to the symbology and the rationality standard of ancient communities. In the space of a few years we won't be able to be anthropologists of our own people because of the lack of people who know the visual and symbolic code of the social landscape built by the traditional society. There will only be a fossilized cultural landscape, like the landscape studied in the first chapters of this work.

The space model we have built in our work, that mythical structure, that cosmic vision, is only kept in the mind of a small number of peasants aged more than 80 years old. If all this collective imagination was not recorded, in a short period of time we would not be able to know about archaeological ruins, like the ruined chapel of San Laurenceo, and would not understand the true meaning of that cultural expression. To be honest, I'd rather be an anthropologist than an archaeologist of our identity.

References

Alonso del Real, C. 1983. Notas etnográficas de O Courel. *Boletín do Museo Provincial de Lugo*. T. 1: 131-140.

Andrade Cernadas, J. M. 1996. Las Villae en la Galicia de la mutación feudal: el caso de Celanova. En *A guerra en Galicia. O rural e o urbano na historia de Galicia*: 277-290. Santiago de Compostela: Asociación Galega de Historiadores.

Aparicio Casado, B. 1999. *Mouras, serpientes, tesoros y otros encantos. Mitología popular gallega*. Cadernos do Seminario de Sargadelos, 80. Sada: Ediciós do Castro.

Aparicio Casado, B. 2002. *A sociedade campesiña na mitoloxía popular galega*. Biblioteca de divulgación. Serie Galicia, nº 27. Santiago: Universidade de Santiago de Compostela.

Ayán Vila, X. M. 1997. *Aproximación á cultura castrexa e á romanización no concello de A Pobra de Brollón (Lugo)*. Traballo Academicamente Dirixido. Universidade de Santiago.

Ayán Vila, X. M. 2005. Os castros despois dos castros: un espazo simbólico na pasiaxe rural tradicional galega. En P. Ballesteros Arias (coord.): *Encontros coa Etnografía*: 63-136. Editorial Toxosoutos.

Ayán Vila, X. M. and Ameixeiras, F. 2002. Mámoas, castros e tesouros: a Mourindá nas terras de Cuntis. En Ayán Vila, X. M. (Coord.): *Pasado e futuro de Castrolandín (Cuntis, Pontevedra). Unha proposta de recuperación e revalorización*. TAPA (Traballos en Arqueoloxía da Paisaxe) 29: 143-68. Santiago: IEGPS (CSIC-XuGa).

Ayán Vila, X. M. and Arizaga Castro, Á. 2005. Os Castros de Neixón como espazo simbólico na paisaxe rural tradicional (notas etnográficas e reflexións sociais). En Ayán Vila, X. M. 2005. *Os Castros de Neixón (Boiro, A Coruña)*: 291-327. Serie Keltia 30. Noia: Edición Toxosoutos.

Baliñas Pérez, C. 1992. *Do Mito á Realidade. A definición social e territorial de Galicia na Alta Idade Media (Séculos VIII e IX)*. Coordenadas Monografías, 18. Santiago de Compostela: Fundación Universitaria de Cultura.

Ballesteros Arias, P. 2002. *A paisaxe agraria de Elviña: os elementos e as formas*. CAPA (*Cadernos de Arqueoloxía e Patrimonio*), 15. Sntiago. IEGPS (CSIC-XuGa).

Barros, C. 1993. La contribución de los Terceros Annales y la Historia de las mentalidades: 1969-1989. En González Mínguez, C. (Ed.). *La otra historia: sociedad, cultura y mentalidades*: 87-118. Bilbao: Univ. de Bilbao.

Bouza Brey, F. 1963. Ritos impetratorios da choiva en Galiza: a inmersión dos sacra e os vellos cultos hídricos. En *Actas do primeiro Congresso de Etnografia e Folklore* (promovido pola Câmara Municipal de Braga, 22-25 de Junho de 1956). Vol. I: 125-38. Lisboa: Biblioteca Social e Corporativa.

Bouza Brey, F. 1982. El espíritu de la tierra en Galicia y las ceremonias ígnicas lustrales del campo gallego. En Bouza Brey, F.: *Etnografía e Folklore de Galicia*. Vol 2: 105-10. Vigo: Edicións Xerais de Galicia.

Bouza Brey, F. 1982a. Los mitos del agua en el Noroeste hispánico. En Bouza Brey, F.: *Etnografía e Folklore de Galicia*. Vol 2: 219-39. Vigo: Edicións Xerais de Galicia.

Burguiére, A. 1995. L'anthropologie historique et L'École des Annales. En Barros, C. (Ed.): *Historia a Debate*, III: 127-37. Santiago: Historia a Debate D.L.

Burke, P. 1990. *The French historical revolution: the Annales School: 1929-1989*. Oxford: Polity Press.

Burke, P. 1990a. *La cultura popular en la Europa moderna*. Madrid: Alianza.

Castro Pérez, L. 2001. *Sondeos en la arqueología de la religión en Galicia y norte de Portugal. Trocado de Bande y el culto jacobeo*. Vigo: Servicio de Publicacións da Universidade de Vigo.

Criado Boado, F. 1986. Serpientes gallegas: madres contra rameras. En Bermejo Barrera, J. C.: *Mitología y Mitos de la Hispania prerromana*, 2: 241-74. Madrid: Akal.

Criado Boado, F. 1989. Asentamiento megalítico y asentamiento castreño: una propuesta de síntesis. *Gallaecia*, 11: 109-37. Sada: Ediciós do Castro.

Criado Boado, F. (dir.). 1991. *La Arqueología del Paisaje en Galicia. El área Bocelo-Furelos entre los tiempos paleolíticos y medievales. (Campañas de 1987, 1988 y 1989)*. Arqueoloxía/Investigación, 6. Santiago: Xunta de Galicia.

Criado Boado, F. 1993. Galician rural landscape and its archaeological genealogy. In *1st Symposium on Galician Studies (Oxford, april 1991)*: 43-57. Santiago de Compostela: Xunta de Galicia.

Criado Boado, F. 1995. The visibility of the archaeological record and the interpretation of social reality. In Hodder, I.; Shanks, M. *et al.* (ed.): *Interpreting Archaeology. Finding meaning in the past*: 194-204. Oxford: Routledge.

Criado Boado, F. 1999. *Del Terreno al Espacio: Planteamientos y Perspectivas para la Arqueología del Paisaje*. CAPA (Criterios y Convenciones en Arqueología del Paisaje), 6. Santiago: Grupo de Investigación en Arqueoloxía da Paisaxe.

Criado Boado, F. and Ballesteros Arias, P. 2002. La Arqueología rural: contribución al estudio de la génesis y evolución del paisaje tradicional. En *Congreso de Ingeniería Civil, Territorio y Medio Ambiente* (1º. 2002. Madrid, 13,14 y 15 de febrero de 2002): 461-479. Colegio de Ingenieros de Caminos, Canales y Puertos, Comisión de Medio Ambiente. Madrid: Colegio de Ingenieros de Caminos, Canales y Puertos.

Criado Boado, F. and Fábregas Valcarce, R. 1989: The megalithic phenomenon of northwest Spain: main trends. *Antiquity*, 63 (December 1989):682-96.

Criado Boado, F. and Fábregas Valcarce, R. 1994. Regional patterning among the megaliths of Galicia (NW Spain). *Oxford Journal of Archaeology*, 13(1): 33-47. Oxford and Cambridge.

Criado Boado, F. and Villoch Vázquez, V. 2000. Monumentalizing landscape: from present perception to the past meaning of Galician megalithism (North-West Iberian Peninsula). *European Journal of Archaeology*. Vol. 3(2): 188-216. London, Thousand Oaks, CA and New Delhi.

David, P. 1947. *Etudes historiques sur la Galice et le Portugal du 6è au 12è siècle*. Paris-Lisboa: Institute Français au Portugal.

Dubert García, I. 1994. A Cultura popular na Galicia rural do Antigo Réxime, 1500-1830: Ofensivas e resistencias. *Grial*, t. 32, n. 122 (abr.-xuño 1994): 235-54.

Fernández Mier, M. 1999. *Génesis del territorio en la Edad Media: arqueología del paisaje y evolución histórica en la montaña asturiana: el valle del río Cigüeña*. Oviedo: Universidad de Oviedo.

Fernández de Rota, J. A. 1984. *Antropología de un viejo paisaje gallego*. Madrid: CIS, Siglo XXI.

Ferreira Priegue, E. 1988. *Los caminos medievales de Galicia*. Anexo nº 9 del Boletín Auriense. Ourense.

Filgueiras Rey, A. and Rodríguez Fernández, T. 1994. Túmulos y petroglifos. La construcción de un espacio funerario. Aproximación a sus implicaciones simbólicas. Estudio de la Galicia Centro-Oriental: Samos y Sarria. *Espacio, Tiempo y Forma*, 7: 211-253. Madrid: UNED.

García Quintela, M. V. and Santos Estévez, M. 2004. From Rock Carvings to Weltanschauung in A Ferradura: Sanctuary of the Hillfort Cultura in NW Spain. *The Journal of Indo-european Studies*, 2 (3-4): 319-36. Washington: Institute for the Study of Man.

García Quintela, M. V. 2005. Celtic Elements in Northwest Preroman Spain. In Alberro, M. and Arnold, B. (eds.): *The Celts in the Iberian Peninsula*.

Journal of Interdisciplinary Celtic Studies, e-Keltoi, 6: 497-569. Milwaukee: Milwaukee University.

García Oro, J. 1987. *Galicia en los siglos XIV y XV*. Galicia Histórica. A Coruña: Fundación Barrié de la Maza.

Geertz, C. 1997. *La interpretación de las culturas*. Barcelona: Gedisa.

Ginzburg, C. 2001. *El queso y los gusanos. El cosmos según un molinero del siglo XVI*. Barcelona: Ediciones Península.

González Lopo, D. L. 1997. As devocións relixiosas da Galicia moderna (séculos XVI-XVIII). En *Galicia terra única. Galicia renace*: 290-303. Santiago: Xunta de Galicia, Deputación de A Coruña.

González Reboredo, X. M. 1971. Folklore dos castros do Incio. *Grial*, 31: 21-29 Vigo.

González Ruibal, A. 2003. *Etnoarqueología de la Emigración. El fin del mundo preindustrial en Terra de Montes (Galicia)*. Pontevedra: Servicio de Publicacións da Deputación de Pontevedra.

González Ruibal, A. 2003a. *La experiencia del Otro. Una introducción a la Etnoarqueología*. Akal Arqueología, 3. Madrid: Ediciones Akal.

Guitián Ojea, F. 1974. *Itinerario de los suelos de Galicia*. Santiago de Compostela: Servicio de Publicacións da Universidade de Santiago de Compostela.

Gurevich, A. 1992. *Historical anthropology of the Middle Ages*. Ed. by Jana Howlett. Cambridge: Cambridge Polity Press.

Le Goff, J. 1985. *Lo maravilloso y lo cotidiano en el Occidente medieval*. Barcelona: Gedisa.

Le Roy Ladurie, E. 1981. *Montaillou aldea occitana de 1294-1324*. Taurus.

López González, L. F. 1993. *Caurel-Valle de Quiroga. Estructura social y territorio*. Tesis de Licenciatura inédita. Madrid: Universidad Complutense.

Lucas Álvarez, M. 1980. *El tumbo de San Julián de Samos*. Santiago: Obra Social Caixa Galicia.

Luzón Nogué, J. M. et alii. 1980. *El Courel*. Excavaciones Arqueológicas en España. nº 110. Madrid.

Llinares García, Mª. 1990. *Os Mouros no Imaxinario popular galego*. Santiago: USC.

Llinares García, Mª 1990a. *Mouros, ánimas, demonios*. Madrid: Akal.

Llinares García, Mª. M. and Vázquez Varela, J. M. 1990. Señalización simbólica del territorio: la acción de los seres imaginarios. En *Actas del Simposio Internacional de Antropoloxía Identidade e Territorio:* 97 e ss. Santiago: Consello da Cultura Galega.

Madoz, P. (Ed.) 1845-1850. *Atlas de España y sus posesiones de Ultramar: notas estadísticas e históricas*. Madrid.

Mandianes Castro, M. 1984. *Loureses. Antropoloxía dunha parroquia galega*. Vigo: Galaxia.

Martinón Torres, M. 2001. Los megalitos de término. Crónica del valor territorial de los monumentos megalíticos a partir de las fuentes escritas. *Trabajos de Prehistoria* 58 (1): 95-108. Madrid: CSIC.

Parcero Oubiña, C. 2000. Tres para dos. Las formas del poblamiento en la Edad del Hierro del Noroeste ibérico. *Trabajos de Prehistoria*, 57: 75-95. Madrid: CSIC.

Parcero Oubiña, C. 2003. Looking forward in anger: social and political transformations in the Iron Age of the north-western Iberian Peninsula. *European Journal of Archaeology*, 6(3): 267-99. London, Thousand Oaks, CA and New Delhi.

Parcero Oubiña, C. and Cobas Fernández, I. 2004. Iron Age Archaeology of the Northwest Iberian Peninsula. *The Celts in the Iberian Peninsula. Journal of Interdisciplinary Celtic Studies, e-Keltoi*, 6: 1-45. Milwaukee: Milwaukee University

Parcero Oubiña, C; Criado Boado, F. and Santos Estévez, M. 1998. Rewriting landscape: incorporating sacred landscapes into cultural traditions. *World Archaeology* 30 (1): 159-176.

Portela, E. and Pallares, Mª. C. 1998. La villa, por dentro. Testimonios galaicos de los siglos X y XI. *Studia Historica, Hª Medieval, 16*: 13-43. Salamanca: Ediciones Universidad de Salamanca.

Rielo Carballo, N. 1975. Voz *Cereixa* en Valiña Sampedro, E. et al. *Inventario Artístico de Lugo y su provincia*. Vol. 2. Madrid: Ministerio de Educación y Cultura.

Rodríguez Fernández, T. 1994. El fin del mundo fortificado y la aparición de las aldeas abiertas. La evidencia del Centro-Oriente de Lugo (Samos y Sarria). *Espacio, Tiempo y Forma*, 7: 153-189. Madrid.

Saavedra Fernández, P. 1994. *La vida cotidiana en la Galicia del Antiguo Régimen*. Barcelona: Crítica.

Taboada Chivite, X. 1972. *Etnografía galega. Cultura espiritual*. Vigo: Galaxia.

Taboada Chivite, X. 1980. *Ritos y creencias gallegas*. A Coruña: Sálvora.

Vázquez Rodríguez, X. M. 1997-98. Cerimonias de véspera. Os folións na Ribeira Sacra. *Boletín do Museo Provincial de Lugo*, VIII. Vol. 1: 215-308. Lugo

Villoch Vázquez, V. 2000. *La Configuración social del espacio en las sociedades constructoras de túmulos en Galicia: estudios de emplazamiento tumular*. Teses de Doutoramento da Universidade de Santiago de Compostela: Disco 2 (Humanidades e Ciencias Sociais).

Traditions of the Milesian invasion from the medieval Irish text *An Lebor Gabála*; the context of their survival in connection with archaeological monuments and topographic features on the south-west coast of Ireland

Simon Ó Faoláin

It is the intention of this paper to briefly explore the relationship between the medieval Irish mythological chronicle *An Lebor Gabála* and folk traditions relating to a number of archaeological sites and topographical features on the Atlantic seaboard of Counties Kerry and Cork in south-western Ireland (Figure 1). We will be discussing the nature of these traditions, as well as outlining the archaeological character of the monuments in question. In conclusion, the folk traditions will be critically assessed in the light of the oral and literary records.

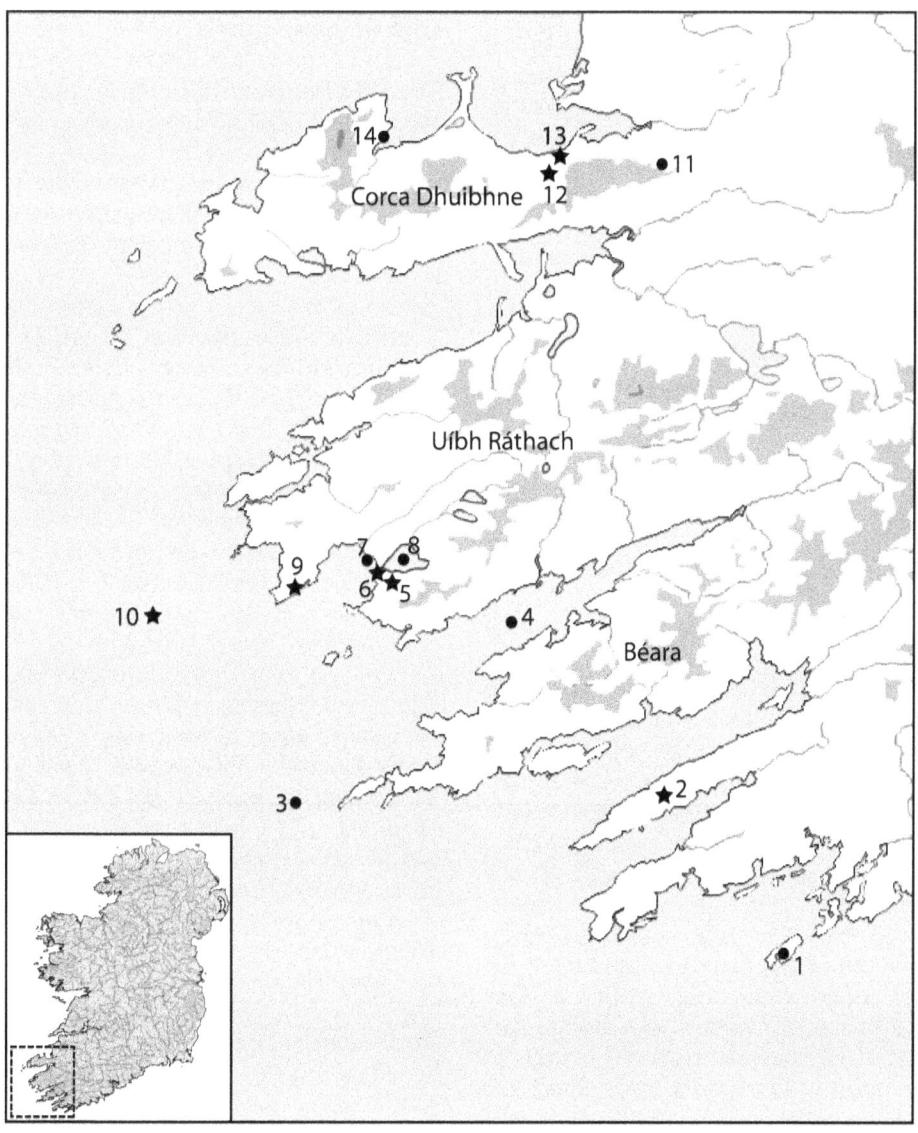

Figure 1: Map of coastal south-western Ireland showing locations with Milesian associations mentioned in the text. Stars indicate archaeological monuments/complexes. Circles indicate associations not directly linked with an archaeological monument.
1 Cléire (Clear Island), 2 Rath Aimheirghin (Raferigeen), 3 Inis Baoi (Bull Rock), 4 Inbhear Scéine (Kenmare 'River'), 5 Íochtar Cua, 6 Baile Breac, 7 Carraig Éanna, 8 Loch Luighdeach, 9 Cill Rialaig, 10 Sceilg Mhichíl, 11 Uaigh Scotia (Scotias Grave), 12 Cill Eiltín (Killelton), 13 Gleann Fais, 14 Baile Dhuinn.

The *Lebor Gabála*

The *Lebor Gabála* (Modern Irish *Leabhar Gabhála*), is most commonly translated into English as the 'Book of Invasions', but a more correct rendering would be 'The Book of Capturings'. It appears in its earliest surviving written form in the compendium known as *An Leabhar Laighneach,* 'the Book of Leinster', which is generally regarded to have been written around the year AD1160. Its content is fairly well known within Ireland and amongst scholars of early Celtic literature, consisting of a mythical account of a series of six invasions by different ethnic groups culminating in the arrival of the Gaelic Milesians, who wrested the lordship of Ireland from the penultimate group of invaders, the Tuatha Dé Danann (Tribes of the Goddess Danú) in a short but bloody conflict. The work may contain some elements of historical truth, but these remain impossible to discern against the fictional core of the story. In particular, an attempt is made to fuse Gaelic mythology and genealogy on the one hand with Old Testament biblical events on the other. Referring to the *Lebor Gabála,* one modern authority calls it 'a masterpiece of muddled medieval miscellany' (McKillop 1998:259), a description which, if somewhat flippant, is nonetheless apt. This should not, however, lead one to dismiss the ideological importance of the *Lebor Gabála*:

> With its elaborate portrayal of the evolution of Gaelic ascendancy, it constituted the central historiographical component of bardic ideology
>
> Caball 1998:4.

Up until the 17th century the *Lebor Gabála* was generally accepted unquestioningly as historical fact (O'Rahilly 1946:263-4). A good example of this is Geoffrey Keating's pioneering 17th century history of Ireland *Foras Feasa ar Éireann*, which makes extensive use of the *Lebor Gabála* as a source (Dinneen 1908). The *Lebor Gabála* has been the object of much academic and some not-so-academic debate, particularly in the nascent period of serious Celtic Studies in the late 19th and early 20th centuries. At that time much of the work was still accepted by some scholars as perhaps not strictly historical, but at least inspired by actual historical events. This is an appraisal which would be accepted by few serious scholars today, although popular writers, especially those of a 'New Age' bent, continue to display an uncritical, ill-informed and fatuous acceptance of the *Lebor Gabála* as historical fact (e.g. Abalos & May 2004). The value of this text is now seen by scholars primarily in terms of literature and secondly in terms of sociology; as an opus which reveals much about the cosmology and *weltanschauung* of the medieval Irish if approached in a critical manner.

One aspect of the text is certainly historical in terms of the motivation behind it. This is the strong element of medieval political propaganda present, dating from a time in the later 1st millennium AD when the northern Irish dynasty of the Uí Néill were attempting to create a high-kingship of all Ireland centred on the existing prehistoric ceremonial site at Tara, Co. Meath. The dispute in the narrative of *An Lebor Gabála* between two Milesian princes – Éremón and Éber – and the eventual accession of Éremón, lord of the northern part of the country, to the high-kingship of all Ireland, is the most blatant example of such propaganda. This was obviously intended to legitimize the claims of the Uí Néill, traditional lords of the northern part of Ireland, to be rightful overlords of the kings of the Eóganacht dynasty who held power in the south.

The *Lebor Gabála* is a vast text, and so only the relevant parts will be outlined here.

The Milesian landing & late megalithic monuments in Uíbh Ráthach

The Milesians derive their eponym from their patriarchal figure Míl Espáine, whose name is derived from Latin and roughly translates as 'Spanish soldier', averring to the fact that the Milesians were said to have dwelt in Spain for a period during their extended odyssey from the Levant, where they were portrayed as one of the lost tribes of Israel.

According to the narrative of the *Lebor Gabála*, the invading Milesians came ashore at the south-western peninsula of Uíbh Ráthach in present day County Kerry, having fought their way in through a magical storm created by the Tuatha Dé Danann. Many of the Milesians were drowned in the storm episode and several of Míl's offspring were amongst the dead. As we proceed, it will be seen that almost every member of Míl's family who dies during the landing account is associated with some aspect of the landscape in the Baile na Scealg (Ballinskelligs) area of Uíbh Ráthach.

The first of these unfortunates is Érannán, said to have been the youngest of Míls sons. It is related that he was posted lookout at the masthead of one of the ships when he fell from his eminence and died as a result (Macalister 1956, vol. v:71). According to several sources Érannán was buried under a megalithic stone row at Cill Rialaig on the south-western side of Ceann Bólus (Bolus Head) (Barrington 1976:277; O'Sullivan & Sheehan 1996:52). This row consists of four free-standing monoliths which now form part of a wall (plate 1).

Another member of Mil's family is said to have been buried under a megalithic row in the Baile na Scealg area. This is Scéine, the wife of Mil's son, the poet and brehon (judge) Ameirgin Glúingeal. The *Lebor Gabála* omits to tell us the cause of Scéine's sudden demise, but notes that it is she who gives her name to Inbhear Scéine, now Kenmare Bay, on the southern side of Uíbh Ráthach. Local tradition records that she is buried beneath the stone row at Íochtar Cua (plate 2), on a ridge that runs between Loch Coireáin and Bá na Scealg (Barrington

Plate 1: View of stone alignment at Cill Rialaig, Uíbh Ráthach, Co. Kerry, looking north-west.

Plate 2: View of stone alignment at Íochtar Cua, Uíbh Ráthach, Co. Kerry, looking east. The southern shore of Loch Luighdeach is just visible at left.

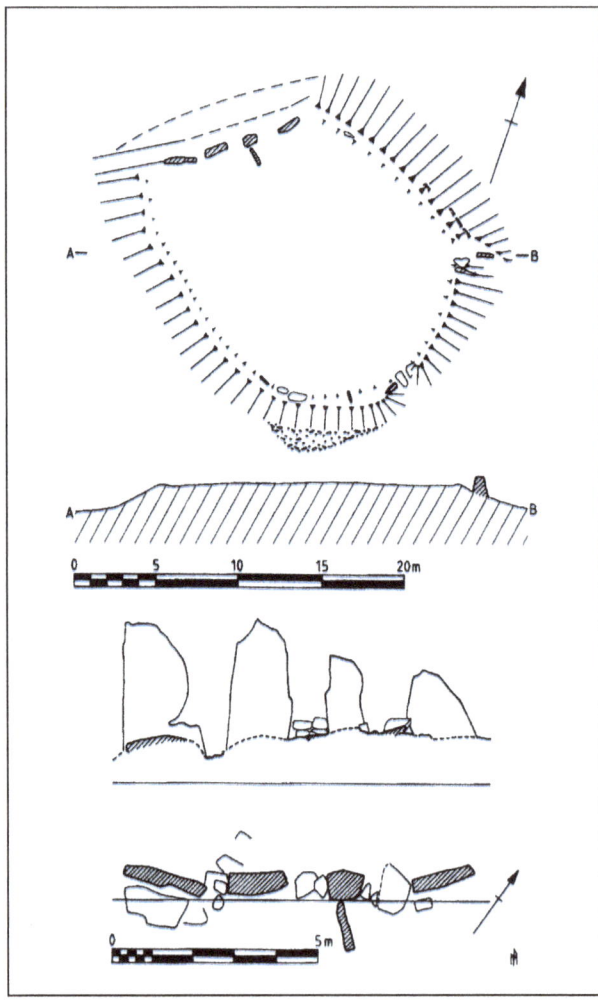

Figure 2: Top: General plan and profile of enclosure at Íochtar Cua, Uíbh Ráthach, Co. Kerry, with stone alignment at north-west. Upper Centre: Profile of enclosure. Lower Centre: Profile of stone alignment. Bottom: Plan of stone alignment (after O'Sullivan & Sheehan 1996).

1976:284; O'Sullivan & Sheehan 1996:51). These megaliths now form part of an enclosure (figure 2). The rest of the enclosure consists of a low earthen bank, the whole forming an oval shape in plan. The stone row is probably earlier than the enclosure as, if the whole had been constructed as a unit one would expected that the megaliths should be the central focus within the enclosure, rather than forming part of the boundary. Strengthening the latter point is the fact that such stone rows are often found to have alignments of astronomical significance, as outlined below.

Archaeologically speaking, our state of knowledge regarding these stone rows is still quite rudimentary. Over 70 examples are known from Counties Kerry and Cork, where they form part of a late prehistoric megalithic assemblage incorporating other monument types such as stone circles and boulder burials.

It is clear from the work of a number of scholars that the stone rows frequently have alignments of astronomical significance (Lynch 1981; Ó Nualláin 1988; Ruggles 1999). Though these studies are frequently not in agreement regarding their exact findings, they all agree in demonstrating that the builders of these monuments possessed an exact, accurate understanding of the regular movements of the sun and moon. For example, the stone row at Íochtar Cua has been found to be aligned on the azimuth of sunset at the winter solstice (21st of December). Other stone rows in south-western Ireland show solar alignments on the solstices of summer and winter. It has further been found that the row at Cill Rialaig mentioned previously is aligned on the northern major lunar limit, i.e. the most northerly point which the moon reaches within its 18.6 year long cycle (Lynch 1981:26). That lunar events should be the subject of the focus of some of these stone rows is not so surprising as it first appears. As previously mentioned, in south-western Ireland stone rows are closely associated with a further type of megalithic monument, the stone circle, and a group of these monuments in Scotland has been found in recent work to bear a closer relation to lunar movements than to those of the sun (Ruggles 1999: 97-9). Absolute dating evidence for stone rows remains poor, but the limited evidence suggests some of them at least were constructed in the Early or Middle Bronze Age (c. 1700 – 1400 BC).

To move again from archaeology to myth, in the narrative of the *Lebor Gabála* the next fatality to occur is Fial, one of Míl's daughters. By this stage the magical storm of the Tuatha Dé Danann had abated and the Milesians, having landed, appear to have been taking a much-needed break. The story relates the somewhat bizarre incident of how Fial was bathing in Loch Coireáin when she encountered her husband Luighdeach. They were both naked and Fial died of shame. Her husband (apparently a man without a whit of common decency) shamelessly failed to die however, and it is reputedly from him that the lake gets the local name by which it is commonly referred to in Irish; Loch Luighdeach.

The prudish Fial is said in the locality to be buried beneath a megalithic tomb at Baile Breac (plate 3), a short distance from the Íochtair Cua stone row (Barrington 1976:284; O'Sullivan & Sheehan 1996:41). The Baile Breac tomb consists of several large stone slabs laid one atop the other, with smaller stones assembled around its base. Archaeologically, it is difficult to classify and does not fit into any of the convenient categories of megalithic tomb, a fact reflected in its unclassified listing in the *Iveragh Archaeological Survey*. Nonetheless, it seems to have affinities with two types of burial monument used during the Irish Bronze Age: wedge tombs and, to a greater extent, boulder burials. The wedge tombs are conventionally regarded as the final tomb-type in the sequence of the great Neolithic megalithic tradition of Ireland, although their use and re-use period extends into the first half of the 2nd

Plate 3: View of unclassified megalithic tomb at Baile Breac, Uíbh Ráthach, Co. Kerry, looking south-east. Note overlapping slab construction and small boulders acting as basal supports.

millennium BC (Waddell 1998:92-9). The similarity of their basic construction method – rows of recumbent slabs laid on twin supporting side walls of orthostats – has been noted as similar to that of the Allées Couvértes tombs of north-western France, though a direct evolutionary relationship between the two types is currently deemed unlikely. It is the overlapping slabs of the Baile Breac tomb which suggest a possible relationship with the wedge tombs. The other similarity noted is with the boulder burials which form part of the aforementioned late megalithic assemblage of south-west Ireland, along with the stone rows and circles (O'Brien 1992). Such tombs are relatively modest in form, generally comprising a single large boulder or slab supported upon several smaller rocks. The large number of such supports under the Baile Breac tomb suggest a relationship, which is unsurprising given that a number of boulder burials exist nearby in the surrounding area. Limited evidence for the dating of boulder burials suggests they were in use in the middle and latter half of the 2nd millennium BC. The Baile Breac tomb might be tentatively suggested as an intermediate type between wedge tombs and boulder burials in terms of form and perhaps also date.

The Battle of Sliabh Mis & Early Medieval monuments in Corca Dhuibhne

To continue with our discussion it is necessary to move to Corca Dhuibhne, the peninsula lying to northwards of Uíbh Ráthach. Here there are a further two archaeological sites associated with the Milesians, although there is a difference. The monuments associated with this tradition in Uíbh Ráthach are all Chalcolithic or Bronze Age in date, whereas the examples here are early medieval. As the samples are very small in both cases this is probably not significant, but is worth noting.

Events in the *Lebor Gabála* continue with the Milesians moving north-east to the Sliabh Mis mountains, where a major battle is fought against the Tuatha Dé Danann. The Milesians are triumphant, but at great cost. Amongst the slain are Scotia, the widow of Míl himself, and their daughter-in-law Fais.

Tradition records that Fais is buried at a site in the valley to which she gives her name, Gleann Fais, on the western side of the Sliabh Mis. The site itself, known as Faisi's Grave, is a large recumbent ogham stone (plate 4). As well as ogham and uncial inscriptions, there is a small cross incised into the monolith. The ogham script reads

Plate 4: View of recumbent ogham stone at Camp, Corca Dhuibhne, Co. Kerry, looking north-west. The oghan inscription is visible on the near upper arras, running from upper left to lower right.

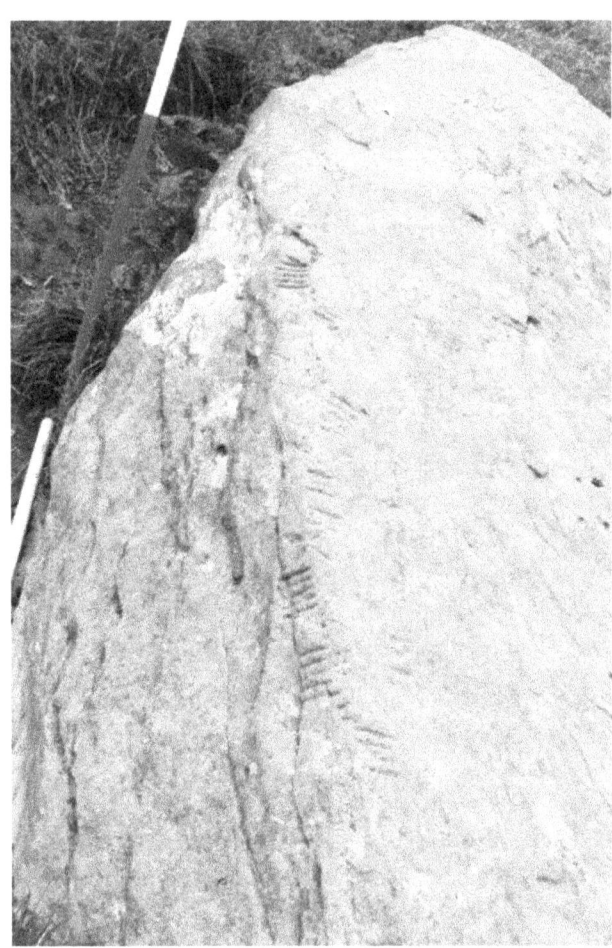

Plate 5: Close up view of ogham inscription on stone at Camp, Corca Dhuibhne, Co. Kerry, looking west. The inscription reads CONUNETT MAQI CON(U)R(I).

CONUNETT MAQI CON(U)R(I) and the uncials FECT CUNORI (Cuppage et al. 1986:254). The ogham (plate 5) is important and exceptional, being one of only a bare handful which can be shown to refer to a mythological or quasi-mythological character. Strangely, this is not Fais, who is supposedly buried here, nor indeed any other individual from the *Lebor Gabála*, but the mysterious hero Cúraoi Mac Dáiri, an important figure in *An Rúraíocht;* the Ulster Cycle; at times a friend to the main protagonist Cú Chulainn, at other times an adversary (see for example Hellmuth 1998). The uncial script also refers to this character although reservations have been expressed regarding its antiquity. An impressive promontory fort, Cathair Chon Raoi (Cuppage et al 1986:81-2), lying on and giving its name to the mountain peak directly overlooking the site of the ogham stone, is also closely associated with Cú Raoi in local folklore.

Confusing the tradition, another site in this area is also claimed to be the grave of Fais. This is the early medieval ecclesiastical site of Cill Eiltín, which consists of an oratory and post-medieval Cillín or children's burial ground which may mark the position of the early medieval graveyard (plate 6). The antiquary John Windele visited this site in 1840 and was told by a local informant that Fais was buried here and that the early Christian oratory was built over her grave (Ó Súilleabhán 1931:123). Another source claims that the oratory is built on a mound surrounded by a kerb of slabs (Barrington 1976:237). However, no trace of such can be identified today and none was identified during surveying in the 1980s (Cuppage et al. 1986:304-5). During limited excavation accompanying restorative work on the oratory, a small underground chamber was discovered in the floor of the building. Possibly the local people were aware of this feature and associated it with the grave of Fais.

Milesian associations in Toponyms and personal names

The number of archaeological sites in Kerry identified as having links in folk tradition with the Milesian invasion is small – just five are known – although there may possibly have been a considerable number more, the knowledge of which was lost as oral tradition broke down

Plate 6: View of remains of early medieval oratory at Cill Eiltín, Corca Dhuibhne, Co. Kerry, looking east.

in the 19th and 20th centuries. What is true for the possible loss of folk associations with regard to archaeological sites is similarly true for toponyms, especially microtoponyms. As the majority of people now no longer interact with the rural landscape in an intimate and regular fashion it is these microtoponyms – names of rocks, fields, lesser coastal headlands and inlets etc. – which have been overwhelmingly forgotten. Nonetheless, this small body of monuments is accompanied by a slightly greater number of topographical features linked with the Milesians. We have already seen how Loch Luighdeach in Uíbh Ráthach is reputedly named after the skinny-dipping hero of that name. It has also already been noted that Scéine, who is reputedly interred under the stone row at Íochtair Cua, gives her name to Inbhear Scéine (Kenmare Bay). The other examples are discussed briefly hereunder.

Near the shoreline in Bá na Scealg is a reef named Carraig Éanna, the rock of Éanna. Éanna is referred to in local tradition as another chief of the Milesians who died after being wrecked on the shore (e.g. An Seabhac 1954:48). He seems to be a purely local character not mentioned in the *Lebor Gabála,* although some would regard him as a regional variant of Érannán (P. Bushe, pers. comm.). It is also of possible significance that Éanna was the only Milesian given by name in an extremely brief oral version of the story of the Milesians recorded from the noted seanachaí (i.e. keeper of Gaelic oral tradition) Seán Ó Conaill. He notes that Éanna is said to have been buried in a tomb on the island monastery of Sceilg Mhichíl (Ó Duilearga 1977:267-8), and it is possible that it is one of the early medieval tombs of the monastery that he has in mind. There is also a reference to Éanna in the work of a local 17th century poet, also named Seán Ó Conaill, of Cathair Bearneach on the shores of Loch Coireáin:

I gconntae Chiarraí in iarthar Éireann
de ghlacadar caladh ag Inbhear Scéine.
Atá ag bun Choirreáin fós gan traocha
an charraig ler cailleadh go seachmhallach Éanna.

(in county Kerry in western Ireland
they took their port at Inbhear Scéine.
There is below Coireáin yet unwearied
the rock on which Éanna waywardly perished.)
O'Rahilly 1977:65.

This extract from the long poem *Tuireamh na hÉireann* ('the Dirge of Ireland'), the subject of which is the historical woes of Ireland, appears to be the only surviving literary reference to Éanna, supporting his interpretation as a purely local mythological figure. However, it is worth pointing out that Érannán is the only one of Míl's sons not mentioned in the poem, and this absence coupled with the exceptional presence of Éanna might support the abovementioned view that the two are actually one and the same. In terms of the reference to his burial on Sceilg Mhichíl, the *Lebor Gabála* mentions this same island monastic retreat as the resting place of Ír, another son of Míl killed during the landing attempt (Hayward 1946:199; Smith 1756:63). In this regard the local tradition mentions only Éanna and the *Lebor Gabála* only Ír. Although Ó Conaill refers vaguely to a tomb in the case of Éanna, neither he nor Ír is recorded as being associated with a particular monument on the island, although there is no shortage of suitable candidates amongst the surviving Early Medieval remains.

Donn, the eldest of the sons of Mil likewise never made the mainland alive in the *Lebor Gabála* narrative, his ship being wrecked at a place called *Dumhacha* meaning 'dunes' (Macalister 1956, vol. V:71; MacAirt 1951:36). This henceforth became the location of Teach Dhoinn ('the House of Donn') which features as a type of early Irish otherworld or land of the dead in the mythological and Fenian cycles, Donn assuming an Osiris-type role as lord of this realm after his shipwreck and death. In the medieval compendium of versified place-name lore, the *Dindshenchas*, Donn's brother Ameirgin foresees the role of Teach Dhoinn:

> *'Ticfad a munnter an maighin sin' ol Amhirghen. Is aire sin adellad na hanmanda peccacha co teach nDuind ria techt a n-ifearn, do reir na ngennti*
> ('His people will come to this place', said Ameirgin. That is why the souls of sinners go to Teach Dhoinn before going to hell, according to the pagans).
> Gwynn 1991, vol. iv:310.

Teach Dhoinn was also used as an expression of the westernmost extreme of Ireland, which was at that time the western limit of the known world, as demonstrated in the first quote below, which refers to the geographic extent of the lordship of mythic hero Fionn mac Cumhaill.

> *On tsruth ar baisdeadh Críosd do theigh a chíos go Toigh in Duinn*
> (from the stream where Christ was born his tribute extended to Teach Dhoinn).
> Murphy 1933:208.

The second example is from the Dalcassian propaganda tract *Cogadh Gáel re Gallaib* ('the War of the Irish against the Foreigners') and refers to the social situation which pertained in Ireland following the victories of Brian Ború over the Vikings.

> *'ná rabí cáthlech ó Beind Édair co Tech Duind iar nÉrind gan Gall i ndáirí fair'*
> (there was not a winnowing sheet of any kiln from Howth to Teach Dhoinn in the west of Ireland without a Norse slave to work it).
> quoted in Meyer 1910:87.

Two locations on the south-western coast have been linked with Teach Dhoinn in the popular imagination. These are Baile Uí Dhuinn, a small coastal townland in northern Corca Dhuibhne and Inis Baoi, or the Bull Rock, off the coast of the Béara peninsula in western county Cork.

The equation of Bull Rock with Teach Dhuinn is far more widely known and attested (e.g. O'Donovan 1841:148; Gwynn 1991, vol. v:203). Indeed, the Bull Rock, and its accompanying Cow and Calf Rocks, are visible from Bá na Scealg, the folkloric focus of the Milesian landing, as outlined above. There is an arched cavern which extends through the rock from one side to the other and this was reportedly regarded in Béara folklore as the doorway through to the underworld; Donn's kingdom (O'Brien 1991:115). The tradition of Donn in west Cork must certainly extend back into the prehistoric period and has been suggested to have a connection with the reinterpretation and use of megalithic tombs by the inhabitants of this area in the Iron Age (O'Brien 2002).

Baile Uí Dhuinn in Corca Dhuibhne, on the other hand, is not widely associated with Teach Dhoinn. The connection can only be traced to the words of a local priest. In a letter of 1849 addressed to Richard Hitchcock, father John Casey wrote:

> The tigh-Dhuinn of ancient Irish history is at present called Ballyduin. Contiguous thereto a graveyard was discovered a few years back, covered, as I was informed, by the spring tides.
> Ó Súilleabhán 1931:481.

And speaking to Hitchcock in the same year he had this to say:

> This graveyard was on the strand near Brandon quay between two sand banks. The spring tides often covered part of it. There is now nothing to be seen but a few stones stuck up here and there. Father Harrington twenty-eight years ago (1821) found human skulls and bones of the largest description and fragments of coffins
> Ó Súilleabhán 1931:481

It seems possible that Casey, accepting literally the tale of the Milesian invasion, associated these burials with those of the crew of Donn's ship. The archaeological constraint maps for the Record of Monuments and Places does show two burial grounds near to the beach (KE026-015 and 016), but neither of these are close enough to the tidal zone to be the site in question. However, local information places the 19th century burials at a part of the upper tidal zone known as Clais na Marbh (the trench of the dead) the given location for which might suggest it was a seaward extension of burial ground KE026-015 (Cuppage et al. 1986:349). Several hundred metres east of the latter site is the rock outcrop of Carraig na Cille, which in English translates as 'the rock of the church/graveyard', and this might be a further option for the location of the burials referred to by Casey. Sitings of medieval churches in such dune-head locations are known throughout the western coast and the structural and human remains of one such site in Corca Dhuibhne have been eroding out of dunes at Cathair Caoin over the last decade in a similar manner to what Casey describes above (Bennett et al. 2005). Why he was apparently so certain of the link with Teach Dhoinn, as suggested in the first quote, is hard to explain, as research for this article unearthed no other source linking Baile Uí Dhuinn with the Milesians. Some sources give the name of the townland as Baile Uí Dhuibhne, implying a derivation unconnected with Donn and possibly having a similar root to the peninsula of Corca Dhuibhne itself or alternatively derived from the surname Ó Duibhne. However, as pointed out by An Seabhac (1939:221), that surname is not common in the area and the pronunciation of the townland name in both Irish and English is not in agreement with such a derivation.

The final associated toponym is in Gleann Scoithín in the eastern Sliabh Mis. A rock outcrop in this mountain glen is reputed to be Uaigh Scotia, the grave of Scotia, wife of Míl Espáine, who is said to have died in the Battle at Sliabh Mis. Although at least one author refers to this site as a megalithic tomb (O'Brien 1991:115), such terminology is misleading as the site referred to is clearly a natural protrusion of the sandstone bedrock. An alternative, local version of Scotia's demise recounts how it was her habit to jump her horse across this glen and that one day, as a result of her being heavily pregnant, her horse failed to reach the far side of the glen and they fell to their death. The rock outcrop features many names deeply engraved into it and seems to have been a focus of exceptional public interest for the last two centuries at least. There is reputedly a piece of ogham engraved on the rock reading 'leacht Scotia', the grave of Scotia, but this is generally regarded as a modern fake and could not, in any case, be located by the author or other archaeologists in recent years.

Turning finally and briefly to the matter of personal names, those of the Milesian Princes Éber and Éremón were used on the Gaeltacht island of Cléire (Cape Clear) in south-west Cork into the 20th century (for examples see Lankford 1999:116,125; Lankford 2003:30). Furthermore their use goes back at least as far as the 18th century and probably further, clearly predating and unrelated to the late 19th century Gaelic Revival. Both these names were in limited use in other parts of Ireland until relatively recently (see Ó Corráin & Maguire 1981:82,89; Wolfe 1923:17), a fact probably reflecting the final vestiges of the medieval genealogies adopted by major Gaelic septs which supposedly traced their ancestry to the first Milesian kings in Ireland. However, in the case of Cléire the particular significance of the names Éber (local dialect *Éabhair*) and Éremón (local dialect *Éiremháin*) on Cléire could be seen as lying in the fact that both are found in use together on this quite small island. This might suggest a common familiarity on the island with the story from the *Lebor Gabála*, or some variant of same. Indeed, O'Rahilly speculates that in the earliest versions of the story, now lost, Míl had only two sons, Éber and Éremón (1946:195). One writer does record that:

> It is thought that [the Milesians] landed either on the coast of Cork or Kerry, though old tales, particularly among the island people, say that they landed first on Clear Island.
> Roberts 1988:9.

The above author gives no reference to his source as regards this statement and it must be admitted that one noted book of Cléire folklore (Ó Síocháin 1940) and several other more general collections of West Cork folklore (Verling 1996;1999, Ó Cróinín 1985) make no reference to the Milesians. Nonetheless, there seems no obvious reason to doubt the truth of Roberts' statement. Roberts also refers to the townland of Raferigeen on the Sheep's Head peninsula in West Cork (Roberts 1988: entry no. 64), stating that it takes its name from a ringfort named after Míl's son, Ameirgin the *file* (i.e. poet/seer). Again, no source is given, but the linguistic derivation seems to be accurate, with the Irish *Rath Aimheirghin*, Ameirgin's Fort, anglicised to Raferigeen. An archaeological inventory of this townland lists one ringfort which may be that in question (Power et al. 1992:201). However, in the current absence of a definite link with a specific archaeological monument this must be regarded as a toponym only.

The nature of the Milesian tradition on the south-western seaboard

A consideration of all the above associations gives rise to many questions regarding the authenticity, origins and age of the Milesian tradition in the south-west. However, this is a subject too complex and multi-faceted for full consideration here. It would be desirable that discussion here be confined to a consideration of the origins and means of transmission of the Milesian traditions attached to the archaeological monuments in Uíbh Ráthach and Corca Dhuibhne. Nonetheless, it is obviously the case that related toponyms adhering to natural features result from the same sources and processes, so that any attempt to make a strict division in the evidence would be false.

From whence came the folkloric tradition of the Milesians on these peninsulas and how far back does this tradition stretch? Is it a tradition attributable mainly to the educated, literate classes or an oral tradition of the 'common people'?

In the case of Corca Dhuibhne and West Cork the evidence is currently too fragmentary to attempt any answers to these questions and more research will be needed.

On the other hand, western Uíbh Ráthach has the greatest concentration of evidence, in terms of places connected with the Milesians, and also a certain limited amount of written material relevant to our understanding of the Milesian tradition in the area. From this material we can make a tentative comparison between the oral and literary traditions here.

A native of Baile na Scealg parish, the seanachaí Seán Ó Conaill, mentioned above, was lauded as perhaps the foremost surviving proponent of the Gaelic oral tradition in Ireland in the early 20th century. We would reasonably expect that if a coherent account of the Milesian invasion existed in the local folklore that such would be well known to him. Ó Conaill's apparent ignorance of the details of the story is therefore telling. In his vast compendium of story and tradition, the account of the Milesian invasion occupies only a bare page and, in contrast with most of his stories, is decidedly vague and lifeless in tone. Though speaking in Irish, Ó Conaill refers to the protagonists as 'Milesians' rather than Mílísigh, using an English plural suggesting an English language background for his source, and therefore one not likely to be local. Further, with regard to the supposed tradition that the Milesian prince Érannán is buried beneath the stone row at Cill Rialaig, Ó Conaill makes no reference to either Érannán or his place of rest, despite the fact that Ó Conaill lived in Cill Rialaig all his life. Indeed, the only individual Ó Conaill gives by name is Éanna who, as discussed above, is a local figure not mentioned in the *Lebor Gabála*. Also of relevance here is a short account of the origins of Carraig Éanna from the Schools Folklore Collection of the 1930s. This account, collected by a pupil of Imleach Droighneach National School from Donnchadh na Leamhna of Rinn Ruadh, maintains the rock is a vessel which was turned into stone by magical means and which changes back into a ship every Bealtaine (May Day) morning. What is interesting is that the tenuous link between the Milesians and Éanna is not made here, indeed the Milesians are not mentioned at all in any of the folklore collected in the 1930s through any of the schools in the locality. This is a fact which has obvious implications for the hypothesis that the Milesian landing forms part of a local oral tradition.

It is noted by the author that assessment of the oral tradition through literary evidence, even if the sources were oral, is somewhat self-contradictory as a concept, even if there is no alternative method available. Nonetheless, the above evidence from the work of Ó Conaill, supported by the negative evidence of the Schools Folklore Collection, suggests that the Milesian invasion was not an established element of local oral tradition in Uíbh Ráthach. Furthermore, it should be pointed out that most of the authors who make reference to a Milesian traditions in the area – Barrington, Hayward, Smith – were not from the area and none gave their supposedly local sources explicitly by name.

What, then, of the literary tradition in Uíbh Ráthach? In this regard knowledge of the *Lebor Gabála* and familiarity with its Milesian associations can certainly be traced back some centuries amongst the Gaelic learned classes. The celebrated Uíbh Ráthach poet of the early 19th century, Tomás Rua Ó Súilleabháin, was clearly quite familiar with the story (Bushe 1991). Writing poetry in praise of his patrons, the O'Connell family of Derrynane, Ó Súilleabháin describes his contemporary, the famed politician Daniel O'Connell as:

Ó Conaill geal de phór Mhíléisis
(shining O'Connell of the seed of Miletus).
Dubh 1914:79.

In a marriage celebration poem, Daniel's brother is similarly described as:

De scothaibh Chlanna Míle agus fíor Chonaill cóir
(Of the great Clan of Míl and a true, just O'Connell).
Dubh 1914:61.

At first glance this might seem particularly telling. However, the greater Gaelic families were always keen to stress their Milesian ancestry, regardless of whether or not the part of Ireland they inhabited was associated with the story of the Milesian invasion (for an amusing mid 18th century account illustrating this tendency amongst the Gaelic aristocracy see the account by blind harper Arthur O'Neill in Durrell & Kelly 2000:30-1).

On the other hand, lengthy references in Ó Súilleabháin's song *Sighle Ní Ghadhra*, written as an aid to teaching early Irish history, makes it very clear that he was familiar with the *Lebor Gabála*. The probable source of this can be quickly identified. Ó Súilleabháin was a noted scholar with an impressive collection of handwritten manuscripts. In his lament *Amhrán na Leabhar* (the song of the books), he describes his collection of priceless tomes which were lost when the boat carrying them foundered on a rock in Derrynane harbour. Amongst the many tracts, literary, mathematical, theological and philosophical, is listed a copy of the Book of Leinster (*'Leabhar na Laighneach beannuighthe ba bhreaghtha fé'n spéir'*) where, as mentioned above, the *Lebor Gabála* appears in its earliest surviving written form. He also lists Keating's *Foras Feasa ar Éireann* (*'Céitinn, leabhar an tseanchais'*), large parts of which are derived from the *Lebor Gabála*.

One fact which is very relevant here is that in *Sighle Ní Ghadhra* Ó Súilleabháin suggests the Milesians landed not in Uíbh Ráthach, but near the town of An Daingean on the more northerly peninsula of Corca Dhuibhne (*'do dheineadar talamh 'san Daingean nó lámh leis'*). This implies that the tradition of the Milesians landing in Bá na Scealg was either not in existence in the earlier 19th century or was unknown to the poet. As the latter seems unlikely, it is suggested that traditions attached to archaeological sites in the Baile na Scealg area associated with the story of the Milesian landing and its concomitant deaths are later 19th century or 20th century in date.

As we know from the work of the poet Seán Ó Conaill, the literary tradition of the Milesians in the area stretches back to the 17th century at least and may well be unbroken from medieval times. This does not seem unlikely when one bears in mind the importance of the Milesians to Gaelic clan genealogy. The division between literary and oral traditions is seldom clear-cut and is certainly not so for the west of Ireland. The strong inclination towards learning recorded by Smith amongst the 'common people' of Uíbh Ráthach in the mid-18th century is relevant here (1756:60), as it probably reflects a long and venerable tradition. He noted that both Latin and Greek were known by many of the non-English speaking inhabitants, and recounts how he visited a hovel in the west of the peninsula where young boys were learning Homer. What we seem to be encountering is probably more a case of the primarily literary entity of the Milesians occasionally permeating into the realm of folk belief, but in a weak, short lived and unconvincing fashion.

References

Abalos, J. & May, C. 2004. *The Dingle Diamond*. Banton Press. Arran.

Barrington, T. 1976 *Discovering Kerry: its History, Heritage and Topography*. Blackwater Press. Dublin.

Bennett, I., Gapert, R., Scanlan, E. & Parrott, K. 2005. Teampall Bán – The Erosion of the Past. Connolly, M. (ed.) *Past Kingdoms: Recent Archaeological Research, Survey and Excavation in County Kerry*, 65-79. Kerry County Council. Tralee.

Bushe, P. 1991. A Resonant Tradition: some Gaelic poetry of Uíbh Ráthach. O'Connell, M. (ed.) *Daniel O'Connell: Political Pioneer*. Institute of Public Administration. Dublin.

Caball, M. 1998. *Poets and Politcs: Reaction and Continuity in Irish Poetry 1558-1625*. Cork University Press. Cork.

Cuppage, J. et al. 1986. *Archaeological Survey of the Dingle Peninsula*. Oidhreacht Chorca Dhuibhne. Baile an Fheirtéaraigh.

Dinneen, P. (ed. & trans.) 1908. *Foras Feasa ar Éireann le Seathrún Céitinn*. Irish Texts Society. London.

Dubh, S. 1914. (ed.) *The songs of Tomas Ruadh O'Sullivan : the Iveragh poet (1785-1848)*. Gill. Dublin.

Durrell, P. & Kelly, C. (eds.) 2000. *The Grand Tour of Beara*. Cailleach Books. Allihies.

Gwynn, E. (ed. & trans.) 1991. *The Metrical Dindshenchas*. Dublin Institute for Advanced Studies. Dublin.

Hayward, R. 1946. *In the Kingdom of Kerry*. Tempest Press. Dundalk.

Hellmuth, P. 1998 'A Giant Among Kings and Heroes: Some preliminary thoughts on the character Cú Roí mac Dáire in medieval Irish literature'. *Emania: Bulletin of the Navan Research Group* 17. 5-11.

Lankford, E. 1999. *Cape Clear Island: its People and Landscape*. Cape Clear Museum Society. Cork.

Lankford, E. 2003. *Cape Clear Island Heritage Trail*. Comharchumainn Chléire.

Lynch, A. 1981. Astronomical alignment or megalithic muddle? Ó Corráin, D. (ed.) *Irish Antiquity*, 23-7, Cork Irish Texts Society. London.

Mac Airt, S. (ed. & trans.) 1951. *The Annals of Inisfallen*. Dublin Institute for Advanced Studies. Dublin.

Macalister, R. (ed. & trans.) 1956. *Lebor Gabála Éireann*. Irish Texts Society. London.

Meyer, K. (ed. & trans.) 1910. *Fianaigecht: being a collection of hitherto inedited Irish poems and tales*. Hodges Figgis. Dublin.

McKillop, J. 1998. *Dictionary of Celtic Mythology*. Oxford University Press. Oxford.

Murphy, G. (ed. & trans.) 1933. *Duanaire Finn: the book of the Lays of Finn*. Irish Texts Society. London.

O'Brien, D. 1991. *Beara: a journey through history*. Beara Historical Society. Midleton.

O'Brien, W. 1992. Boulder-burials: a Later Bronze Age megalith tradition in south-west Ireland. *Journal of the Cork Historical and Archaeological Society* 97. 11-35.

O'Brien, W. 2002. Megaliths in a mythologised landscape. Scarre, C. (ed.) *Monuments and landscape in Atlantic Europe: perception and society during the Neolithic and Early Bronze Age*, 152-76, Routledge. London.

Ó Corráin, D. & Maguire, F. 1981. *Irish Names*. Lilliput Press. Dublin.

Ó Cróinín, S. 1985. *Seanchas o Chairbre: tógtha síos o Séan Ó hAo*. Irish Folklore Commission. Dublin.

O'Donovan, J. 1841. *The Antiquities of the County of Kerry*. Royal Carbery. Cork.

Ó Duilearga (ed.) 1977. *Leabhar Sheáin Uí Chonaill*. Irish Folklore Commission. Dublin.

Ó Nualláin, S. 1988. Stone Rows in the south of Ireland. *Proceedings of the Royal Irish Academy*, 88C. 179-256.

O'Rahilly, C. 1977. *Five Seventeenth Century Political Poems*. Dublin Institute for Advanced Studies. Dublin.

O'Rahilly, T. 1946. *Early Irish History and Mythology*. Dublin Institute for Advanced Studies. Dublin.

Ó Síocháin, C. 1940. *Seanchas Chléire*. Government Publications Office. Dublin.

Ó Súilleabhán, T. 1931. *Romantic Hidden Kerry*. Tralee.

O'Sullivan, A. & Sheehan, J. 1996. *The Iveragh Penensula: An Archaeological Survey of South Kerry*. Cork University Press. Cork.

Power, D., Byrne, E., Egan, U., Lane, S. & Sleeman, M. 1992. *Archaeological Inventory of County Cork, Volume 1: West Cork*. Government Publications Office. Dublin.

Roberts, J. 1988. *Exploring West Cork: the guide to discovering the ancient, sacred and historic sites of West Cork*. Key books. Clonakilty.

Ruggles, C. 1999. *Astronomy in Prehistoric Britain and Ireland.* Yale University Press. Yale.

Seabhac, An (P. Ó Siochfhrada) 1939. *Triocha-Céad Chorca Dhuibhne.* Dublin.

Seabhac, An (P. Ó Siochfhrada) 1954. *Uíbh Ráthach.* Dublin.

Smith, C. 1756. *The Ancient and Present State of the County of Kerry.* Mercier Press. Dublin.

Verling, M. (ed.) 1996. *Gort Broc: scéalta agus seanchas ó Bhéarra bailithe ó Phádraig Ó Murchú.* Coiscéim. Dublin.

Verling, M. (ed.) 1999. *Béarrach mná ag caint : seanchas Mháiréad Ni Mhionacháin.* Cló Iar-Chonnachta. Indreabhán.

Waddell, J. 1998. *The Prehistoric Archaeology of Ireland.* Galway University Press. Galway.

Wolfe, P. 1923. *Irish Names for Children.* Gill and Macmillan. Dublin.

The Power of Tradition

Ann-Britt Falk

Archaeology interprets the material remains from past societies and tries to explain how and why they were left for us to find. These remains are traits of human activity, one can postulate that it is the remains of something that did happen. When working with archaeological records from the Middle Ages, there is a possibility of using written sources as analogies. When it comes to the study of ritual expressions there are a lot of written sources about Christian liturgy, devotion and heresy. They are politically and religiously coloured, presenting what was forbidden to do and what was recommended to do. Driving this supposition to its extreme one might say that written sources represents how people were supposed to behave and archaeological material represents what really did happen.

Sometimes there are no written sources to use as analogies when studying a certain phenomenon. In this article I am dealing with Scandinavian building offerings. I have not found a single word or notion in the medieval sources about a tradition that archaeologically have been proved to be a widely practiced custom in the Middle Ages. This fact implies that building offerings was not looked upon as Christian liturgy neither as heresy. The failing written sources also implicates the need for another theoretical approach.

Background

This article is an outline of a study on building offerings in the Scandinavian Middle Ages (Falk 2007). Offerings in relation to buildings are known from ethnographic sources as the custom of depositing a gift in the foundation of the house as means of gaining fortune to the household. The custom is identified from different times and different cultures. Depositions categorised as building offerings is known of from the Stone Age and forth in Scandinavian archaeological records (Karsten 1994; Carlie 2004). In Scandinavia the phenomenon has been studied in Iron Age records as a pre-Christian fertility ritual, connected to agricultural development. The depositions from Medieval times which might be categorised as "building offerings" has not been studied as a single topic before and the material has been collected and analysed by the author.

As mentioned above there are no medieval sources concerning this practise except from the archaeological evidence. Obviously, this custom was neither part of a Christian liturgy nor mentioned as a heretical tradition practised by the people. This fact leaves us with the unanswered question about how this tradition was looked upon in the Christian medieval society. The traits in the archaeological record show an unbroken chain of similar material expressions, from pre-Christian time to modern time. What kind of (religious) beliefs is expressed in this ritual? Is this a pre-Christian reminiscence in medieval society or something in between Christian and pagan? As stated above these depositions are the remains from some kind of human practice, but do they represent the same connotation in different times?

While there are a lot of interesting aspects to this topic, this article primarily deals with a methodological attempt to implement ritual theory on archaeology. Building offerings have been studied in pre-Christian contexts and to some extent as a 19th century folk belief. The works done on pre-Christian material often uses a structural point of view trying to explain the symbolic connotations of the deposited artefacts in the light of socio-political order (Andersson 1999; Renck 2000; Carlie 2004). Building offerings is categorised as a *rite-de-passage*, where the house and its inhabitants is reborn in a new unit (van Gennep 1960; Siech & Berggren 2002:138; Carlie 2004:28f). Ritual is seen as a way to appropriate social order and explain cosmology. Even though ritual is regarded as a social activity connected to and dependent of the social arena, ritual it is also closely connected to religion and a sacral sphere.[1]

When the theoretical approach is of hermeneutic or phenomenological art the deposited object is seen as an "offering", mediating between man and God (Paulsson 1993; Carlie 2004). This view implies that the deposition is a gift from man to God, and the ritual a way of pleasing supernatural forces. The deposition can also be regarded as made for magical purposes. In the case of a magical deposition, the ritual is performed not as a gift but in order to manipulate supernatural forces or beings (Paulsson 1993; Siech & Berggren 2002; Carlie 2004). In the more outspoken structuralist tradition, the deposition, is viewed as a transformand, where the symbolic connotations of the deposited object refers to f. ex. an objects transformation from functional to symbolic, or the man made transformation of nature to culture. This transformed symbolic meaning could also be a metaphor for the existing or requisite state of society (Andersson 1999; Renck 2000:215ff; Siech 2002:138f). In either case, the deposited object is seen as crucial for the interpretation of the ritual. The form and function of the deposited object is reflecting the wish of the actor. As such the object has gained focus for categorising the character of the offering (e.g. Paulsson 1993; Andersson 1999; Renck 2000; Siech & Berggren 2002; Carlie 2004). The categories that have been used are e.g. votive offerings, guardian offerings, offering of amendments, communion sacrifice and fertility offering; these categorisations are founded in the Old Testament of the Bible and from research on the ancient Greek and Roman

---

[1] In this article I am only referring to those studies on building offerings where the theoretical approach have been outspoken.

cultures (Henninger 1987; Carlie 2004). Are these categories of relevance for a Scandinavian medieval record?

The study of building offerings has been focused on the deposited object and its symbolic connotations. Ritual has been seen as a static reflection of society. Building offering rituals have been used as a key to culture, for revealing religious thoughts expressed in deposited objects. The analogies applied to uncover these symbolic are almost always borrowed from the Icelandic sagas (Kitzler 2000; Carlie 2004:30ff). The Sagas are primarily used to illustrate a background to the offerings, possible receivers and intentions. I am not going to dwell on the problems in using the Icelandic sagas as analogies for pre-Christian times or medieval times, but rest my case on the fact that the Icelandic sagas might be seen as a source to explain how the medieval authors imagined pre-Christian society (Clunies Ross 1998; 2002; Habbe 2006).

Beside the sagas ethnographic sources have been used as analogies in order to categorise the intention of the offering (Paulsson 1993; 1997). This analogy might cause an obvious problem though the categories are also used by the researchers that have been collecting the ethnographic material. There is an apparent risk of arguing in a circle (e.g. Hauge 1965). The ethnographic records have served to establish a link between the pre-Christian depositions and the ones from early modern time. The connection is based on the prerequisites in pre-industrial agrarian society (Paulsson 1993; 1997). I find this analogy more fruitful than the former.

To some extent the concept of ritual have in these studies become both a method of analysis and an object for analysis (Bell 1992:14). Building offerings have been analysed as a fixed ritual, categorised into pre-existing intention-based types. The kind of deposited object and its position have been critical for the interpretation of the ritual. I do believe that these two characteristics are of great importance for the interpretation, but I find the existing model for what ritual is, constraining and to objectivistic. In this article, I would like to introduce a new way of studying building offerings as rituals. My attempt here is to try to explain why this ritual was practiced, and especially why it was continuously being practised. I would like to move focus from the deposited objects symbolic connotations to the activity of depositing objects. I am going to analyse the pattern of position and variation in objects, not in terms of their specific intention or symbolic value, but rather concerning their variations and regularities.

Early modern building offerings and ethnographic evidence

Before moving on to the archaeological records and my theoretical attempt I am going to make a short remark about the early modern evidence of building offerings, which are of importance for the understanding of my hypothesis.

The ethnographic sources that I have used were recorded in the late 19th and early 20th century in southern Scandinavia. These records contain information from questionnaires about "deposited horse skulls" (Egardt 1950) and scattered documentation about household rituals/traditions (Paulsson 1993; 1997). The records are in most case brief, the subject is touched upon when dealing with something else. The informants are conscious about the fact that folk practice in the early 20th century was looked upon as superstitious, and that is probably one reason why the records are so brief. Folk belief records from the 19th and 20th century in Scandinavia recognises the practice as quite common in the pre-industrial society. It is said that when a new house was being built it was custom to deposit a gift in the foundation to bring good fortune to the family living there. The gift was a way to please or bribe the genius living in the surroundings. Sometimes it is said that one had to buy the ground free from the gnomes. The gift could be a coin, some food or a vessel. Depositing small animals or parts of animals was also common. It remains unclear however, whether this also could be seen as a gift or if it was seen as a guardian.

There are two basic ideas. The first is that you could by the ground free from the little people, and the second is that if an animal were deposited alive it would guard the house for its expected lifetime (Paulsson 1993; 1997; Hauge 1965). It is not looked upon as magic or supernatural, certanely not explained as such. It was simply a custom you were supposed to follow. The ritual is closely bonded to the household and its happiness. It is considered as a natural part of peasant cosmology. The informants are unwilling to acknowledge any deeper significance to the practice.

There are findings from house-foundations from the 18th and 19th century matching this information. The same traits are found in the archaeological record back to pre-Christian time. How should we then interpret these older findings: as "meaningless" ritual praxis or as remains of a ritual with deeper significance? Ritual doesn't have to be a religious action, but it is a significant action. The ethnographic sources indicate that building offerings were an insignificant action, mentioned by chance. But still we have archaeological traits showing that this ritual has been practised for hundreds of years. This practice must have been very significant indeed; otherwise it wouldn't have survived through hundreds of years. We know that it is not part of the Christian liturgy *per se* but it was of major importance in the Middle Ages and afterwards.

Theoretical approach

Ritual studies have become a school of its own, involving scholars from sociology, anthropology and history of religion. The notion of *ritual* has achieved some autonomy, bridging hierarchical notions like liturgy versus magic and becoming an essential conception on the study of ritual expressions (Bell 1992:3ff). The notion of ritual is constituted on the dichotomy of thought and action, grounded in the objectivistic schools of Durkheim and Levi-Strauss, where humans are considered to be structured by external forces. It might be a little odd mentioning Durkheim and Levi-Strauss as the originators of the same concept. That is of course not my intention, but the history of the notion of ritual is far too extensive to cope with in this article. My point is that ritual has been an autonomous topic for decades, and the theoretical discussions have focused on the origins and functions of rituals, not on ritual as a concept.

Catherine Bell addresses the problems connected with ritual in *Ritual Theory, Ritual Practice* (1992). Her main critique of ritual is that it has become both a method of analysis and an object for analysis, and her aim is to recapitulate the notion of ritual (Bell 1992:14ff). She doesn't reject the concept but she wants to modulate and create an awareness of what "ritual" implies. Her way of solving or bypass these is to relocate focus to ritualization.

Bell applies a theory derived from practice theory, and she is inspired by Bourdieu and Foucault, but not totally uncritical to them. Her aim is not to formulate a theory of society but solely to focus on the problems of ritual. Her theoretical standpoint is therefore concerned with practice theory as useful when analysing rituals. In this article I am going to apply her theory of ritualization on building offerings, but first I would like to add a basic assumption of my own theoretical standpoint.

Practice theory is about giving meaning to human activity, trying to bridge the gap between mind and body. The most famous practitioner of this aspect is Pierre Bourdieu (1977), and his notions of Habitus as a way of transcend the thought and action. Shortly after the introduction of Bourdieus *An outline of theory of practice*, Anthony Giddens formulated his *Theory of structuration* (1984). There is in a way an ocean between their personal standpoints and theoretical backgrounds, but it is also possible to see what they have in common. The notion of Habitus and the duality of structure both aim at explaining the constraining and mediating factors in human behaviour. Habitus is related to the individual but working both inside and outside of the human being (Bourdieu 1977:78ff; 1995:149ff). Giddens structure is not a pattern of social relations or phenomena, but an intersection of presence and absence, structures are recursively instantiated when actors draw on it. (Giddens 1984:16f). These two basic concepts of explaining human behaviour are in a way complementing each other when trying to explain social relations (Mouselis 1995:100ff). The reason for me to make this statement is that I want to add an aspect of materiality to Bell's theory, an aspect that is based on Gidden's theory of structuration.

John Barrett (2002) has formulated a theory of the importance of materiality as a structurating object. Based on the concept of *duality of structure* he pinpoints the fact that objects as well as structures are both facilitating and constraining human thought and act. Barrett states that materiality has an important role in regionalising the room, structuring the field in time and space, creating framing devices and focal points (Barrett 2002:159). In this way materiality becomes critical for the application of the structuration theory onto archaeological evidence. One might actually talk about the duality of materiality. Converted to Bourdian terms, materialities are principles constituting Habitus. Habitus is a product of inherited and socialised dispositions; the dispositions are the results of principles ordering the social life. Materiality as a principle affecting Habitus underlines the importance of materiality in interpreting human behaviour. Materiality in human environment affects the individual position and possible movement. The material remains in a deposition are not only a reflection or a result of human interaction but also a media and prerequisite for human behaviour. This gives the deposited object not only a value as evidence of symbolic connotations, but it becomes a media for and result of human interaction.

Ritualization

In 1992 Catherine Bell reinvented the concept of *ritualization* and gave it a new meaning. Her point was to shed light on the question why are some practices being ritualized? What makes them special? Instead of only studying the actual ritual and its performance it might be more fruitful to investigate why this action becomes a ritual. Her basic assumption is that practice, that is action, is creating relations. Ritual is actions constructing privileged relations (Bell 1992:89ff).

She moves focus from ritual to ritualization. As noted before one of her points is that the notion of ritual has become both an object for and a method of analysis (Bell 1992:14). Another critical aspect of hers is that the concept of ritual invites us to view the actor as a non thinking object performing instrumental activity (Bell 1992:28). From a "practice theory point of view" ritual is meaning in the making. The actors are conscious partakers in a meaningful practice.

Studying ritualization instead of ritual makes it possible to understand why the ritual is being practiced. Bell denies that the concept of ritual should have any essence. Rituals are actions that can be more or less ritual-like. The clue is not to define ritual as a specific kind of action but to establish that ritual is a significant action. Ritualization is a strategy that makes a specific action important and superior to other "normal" actions. The relations constructed through this "superior action", is relations superior to other relations. Ritual constructs power-relations or privileged relations. Through investigating why an action has been ritualized it is possible to understand why it has been practiced (Bell 1992:88ff).

Rituals have often been studied as a one way action, where the ritual empowers those who control the rite. Bell emphasizes that ritual activity is not only restraining, the concept of ritualization also involves acceptance and resistance. By focusing on the ritual activity instead of the "ritual", it is easier to study it as a social act, and try to understand the reason for this activity.

Bell has proposed four perspectives that could be useful in ritual studies.

1. how ritualization empowers those who more or less control the rite,
2. how their power is also limited and constrained,
3. how ritualization dominates those involved as participants,
4. how this domination involves a negotiated participation and resistance that also empowers them (Bell 1992:197ff, Nordström 1997:53).

How can we use these four perspectives when working with an archaeological material? Without written sources about a phenomenon and without knowledge about its function and place in society?

The first perspective is the one that usually has been discussed in archaeology. It is a frequently used power-relation perspective. It is of course important but also a little bit tricky when you don't know that much about the performance and the actors of the rite. In archaeological material we only have the "left over" from the ritual activities. But we should keep in mind that ritual activity is about constructing, and usually somebody does get empowered by the rite.

The three other perspectives all talk about the limited power of the initiator and the possibility of the part-taker to influence the actual performance and the meaning of the ritual. Important is also to emphasize that a ritual activity is under perpetual negotiation, and that ritual activity is dynamic. These three perspectives modulate the former power-relation perspectives on ritual by shedding light on the assumption that power is not only a one way communication. Ritual as social control (power-relation regulating social relations) has to be a two way communication, were power-relations to some extent are individually appropriated by the partakers in order to make ritualization an efficient strategy of gaining social control (Bell 1992:222f).

The first conclusions that one can draw from this is that when handling such a long living tradition like building offerings, it is most likely that a lot of things in performance and meaning have changed during 2000 years. But still there has been a need for continuously performing this social activity and re-establish the relations and structures that the ritual has embodied. As noted above building offerings in early modern times are not seen as a significant action. Rather than a ritual it is performed like a tradition. The power of tradition is immense and it could be used as a strategy of making an action important (Bell 1992:118ff). Turning back to empirical matters I am going to epitomise the use of Bell´s theory by examine two examples of variation in the material pattern. I will analyse these material residues as media for and results of human interaction.

Archaeological material

The archaeological material is collected from the southern part of Scandinavia, especially Scania and Denmark. I have not only looked for evidence from the Middle Ages but also from Iron Age and post-medieval contexts as references. In this article I won't account for the material to its full extent, instead I am referring to previous articles on the topic (Falk 2003; 2006; 2007). Though it is possible to trace back the vestige of building offerings to the Stone Age (Karsten 1994), I have restricted my study to the last part of Iron Age in order to collect a reference material to the Middle Ages.

Archaeologically I'd like to define these remains from building offerings as: *artefacts deposited in or under a building, where the deposition is sealed with the continuing construction.* The type of artefact is not specifying the definition in order to collect all the sealed artefacts, to avoid being caught in traditional thinking.

This rather strict definition of a building offering has the disadvantage of not including other means of evil aversion connected to the house and the household. But on the other hand it has the advantage of pinpointing the depositions connected to the building or rebuilding of a house, which could be seen as the foundation of a new household.

Despite the strict definition, the material shows both continuity and discontinuity in its sequential display. To make a short review of the material, two critical aspects are going to be displayed: the character of the deposited artefacts, and its spatial context.

Aspect 1

The deposited artefacts have been divided into 12 groups according to character and function. The artefacts represented consist of household utensils, tools and animal bones etc. Some artefacts are so characteristic or prevalent that they form groups of their own, e. g. coins, ceramics and gold foil figures. The most obvious thing in the sequential display of the occurring artefacts is that there are more labels present around the time of Christianisation than both before and after. The variety of deposited artefacts is increasing drastically in late Iron Age. The variety persists throughout the Middle Ages but comes to a sudden end in post medieval time. Another distinct feature in the chronological display of the

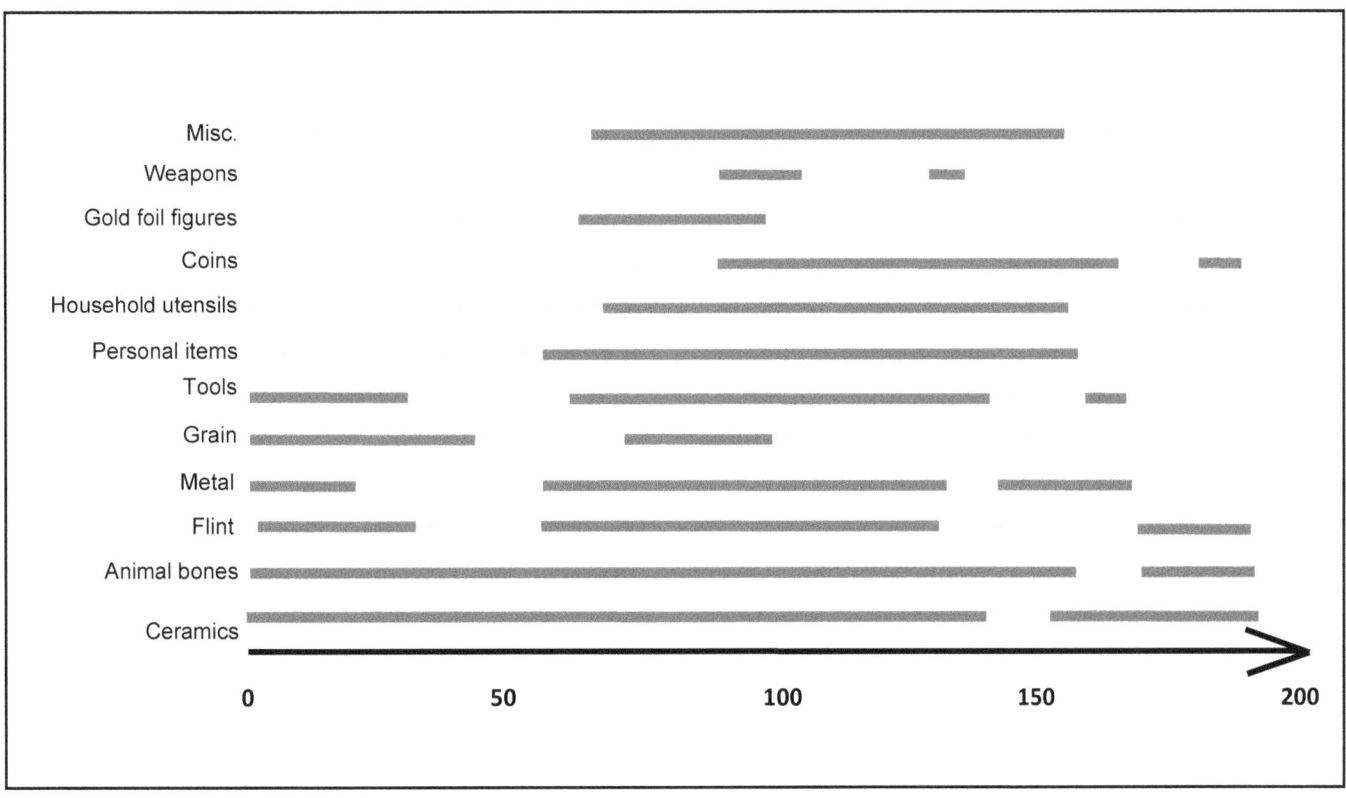

Figure 1. Different artefacts occurring as building offerings over time. The table is based on the catalogued material presented in Falk 2007.

deposited artefacts is the depots of remarkable findings in pre-Christian times. These depots are found in the houses belonging to the upper class, the so called "hall-buildings". This trait of the Iron Age findings has no counterpart in the Middle Ages or post-medieval time. In the later eras there is no difference in the characteristics between findings from houses from different social strata.

Aspect 2

The second aspect concern the spatial context, which denotes where in the house the object has been deposited. Construction details concerned are mainly postholes, floor remains, sills and remains from hearths. Because of the different construction technologies that have been used, it is not possible to compare the different contexts through time. I have therefore chosen to look at the symbolic value of the position in the house. The most obvious symbolic positions are findings from "inside" the house and findings from the borderline of the house. The grouping of the contexts in these categories displayed some striking results. The pre-Christian era gave a mixed picture with findings from both the border-line and the internal parts. In medieval time there was a clear tendency of depositing the artefact in the outer/external parts of the house. This indicates that there have been different proper places for a deposition in different eras, something which is not only related to building technology.

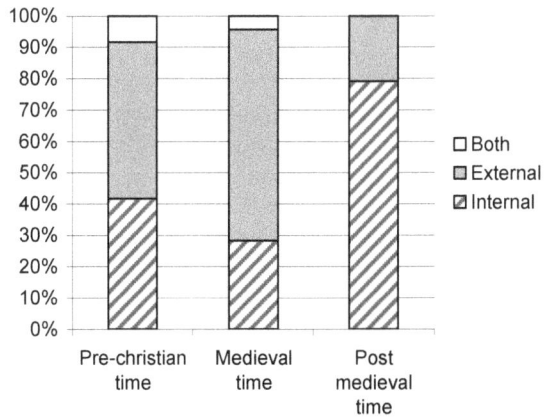

Figure 2. Depositional pattern over time. The table is based on the catalogued material presented in Falk 2007.

Changes and continuity

The studied ritual is an activity performed in a small closed group, probably a household. Each participant might have taken part in such a ritual a few times in a lifetime. The material is stretching over almost 1500 years, and the depositions are going through changes in depositional patterns and in chosen object.

To understand this ritual in the Middle Ages we will have to begin a little bit further back and study the reference material from Iron Age. I believe that changes and continuity both are important, but it might be easier to break through at a point of changes; I see changes in a ritual activity as a re-negotiation, derived from changes in social order. I will demonstrate two different kinds of changes, one episodic, and one slowly developing alteration. These changes are visible in the pattern of the material residues, and as I have argued above, the material residues should be viewed both as facilitating for and constraining of human behaviour.

Ritualization as means of a strategy

The first visible alteration in this activity occurs in the late Iron Age. After the year 500, the number of chosen artefacts starts to increase. This coincides with the first remarkable findings from great hall buildings. This is also the time when the first hall building appears in Scandinavia. At this time there were changes in the social order and on the social arena. Due to alterations in daily life and the organisation of political power the ritual activity is negotiated and the ritual depositions found in the archaeological record are also altered.

But how did ritualization empower and who got empowered? To answer that question we have to know who the controller of the rite was. The controller was most probably the initiator to the building project, the head of the family, both in small scale and in bigger scale. The ritualization empowered the head of the family, through the fact that he or she took the responsibility of ensuring the house and the family of good fortune. The responsibility also gave him/her the right to judge over the family. The activity was a legitimating of power, and the ritualization was a way of using the power of tradition to ensure power. The remarkable depots that we have found in the hall-buildings are probably an expression of political disturbances. The leaders have used an "old" tradition to legitimate and appropriate power, in a way which was well known and understandable for everybody. At this point "the ritual" was already a significant action, practiced and known to the people, a way to settle the relations concerning the household. When consolidating the new political rearrangements there was perhaps a need for doing this in a manner that confirmed the rightfulness of the new order. When building the new extraordinary hall-buildings it was a way of manifesting the new household, new responsibilities and privileges. By using an already existing ritual with strong traditional values invigorating it with new wealth, they could settle the new power-relations in consent. In this case it is not only the ritualization that is the means of strategy. I also interpret the reuse of an existing ritual, the tradition, in it self a means of strategy.

Building offerings as means of evil aversion

At the beginning of the Middle Ages the numbers and types of chosen artefacts are generally the same as before, if something the variation gets even bigger. It even seems like the new religion contributed to the vividness of the tradition. New patterns of symbolic associations were added to the common culture and created new possibilities. The Christianization in Scandinavia was no drastic revolution at heart. A new liturgy and set of rituals were adapted but nobody knows what people really believed in. The conformity of the ritual during and after the "Christianisation" is most remarkable. Does this imply that there were no Christianisation at heart, or that this ritual has very little to do with religion? As mentioned before there is one visible modification in the material pattern, the variation gets even greater. I interpret this as if the possible artefacts for deposition have increased due to the new religious influences, an assimilation of new elements. I understand this such as there were no drastically changes in the social arena. At least there were no considerably modifications concerning the relations that were created and regulated by the ritual. According to my previous interpretation social life in the household wasn't affected that much by Christianisation.

During the Middle Ages there is a gradual alteration of the spatial depositional pattern. In pre-Christian times the quote of "internal" and "external" depositions is almost one to one. During the Middel Ages almost 80% of the offering gifts are placed in an external position. This might be seen as an accentuation of a pattern, which I interpret as a gradual negotiation of a ritual activity dependent of changes on the social arena. Perhaps this was due to the fact that Christianity gradually permeated the medieval society. Each individual's action gets more and more important for his destiny and his time in the afterlife. With this new condition the threat from the outside takes material form and becomes a reality. During this era the "devil him self" becomes a personality, and hell and purgatory are created (Oestigaard 2003).

Another more practical change in society by this time is the development of building techniques. The technique of building one-aisled buildings instead of three-aisled buildings caused internal rearrangements as for the place of the fireplace, where you slept and how you moved inside. The houses shell became in a sense thinner, it was more important to mark the boarder-lines of the house, and these lines where marked already by the foundation. In this era there is an alteration of the cosmology, which influences human behaviour and interaction. At the same time there are visible alterations in the materiality mediating the conditions of living. The new one-aisled buildings changed the prerequisites on the social arena. Accompanied by the ontological movements the deposition was relocated to the boarder-lines of the house.

Conclusion

In this article I have discussed building offerings in terms of ritualization. Ritualization is not only empowering those in control of the rite, the participation is also negotiated. Change is about negotiation and creative actors. In my examples I have tried to epitomize ritualization and tradition as means of strategy as well as negotiation and consent. The power of tradition is immense and it can be manipulated as a strategy.

I have tried to show that ritual practices not always directly reflect religion or belief, but are also dependent of social activity, politics and economics. Obviously, alterations in social order have an effect on social activity and ritual practice.

In the beginning of this article I wrote about the tension field between written sources and archaeological records. In this instance it is the lack of written sources that create the tensions. How come that a ritual practised repeatedly like building offerings did not deserve a single note in the medieval written sources?

The fact that Christianity didn't have that impact on the ritual is both surprising and expected. It indicates that it is a profound ritual, the ritual it self, or the fact that it is a superior activity constructing superior relations, is important enough to continue practise the ritual, irrespective of public religion. Building offerings is a ritual built on, and controlling social relations. The content of the ritual has probably followed hand in hand with cosmology. The important thing in performing the ritual was not to confirm cosmology but to create and confirm social relations. In a patriarchal medieval Christian society, this ritual has coexisted with Christianity. A ritual burdened with tradition, orchestrating responsibilities and obligations. A ritual like this is no threat to the Christian church; it might not even have been viewed as religious.

References

Andersson, G. 1999. Varför sko med runda stenar? Om en reproduktionsritual i Arlandastad. Andersson, K., Lagerlöf, A. & Åkerlund, A. (eds.) *Forskaren i fält – en vänbok till Kristina Lamm.* Riksantikvarieämbetet. Avdelningen för arkeologiska undersökningar. Skrifter nr 27. Stockholm. 91-98.

Barrett, J.C. 2001. Agency, the duality of structure and the problems of the archaeological records. Hodder, I (ed.) *Archaeological Theory Today.* Cambridge. 141-164.

Bell, C. 1992. *Ritual Theory, Ritual Practice.* Oxford University Press. Oxford, New York.

Bourdieu, P. 1977. *Outline of a Theory of Practice.* Cambridge University Press, Cambridge.

Bourdieu, P 1999. *Praktiskt förnuft: bidrag till en handlingsteori.* Göteborg.

Carlie, A. 2004. *Forntida byggnadskult. Tradition och regionalitet i södra Skandinavien.* Riksantikvarieämbetet. Arkeologiska undersökningar Skrifter no 57. Malmö.

Clunies Ross, M. 1998. *Hedniska Ekon. Myt och samhälle i fornnordisk litteratur.* Uddevalla

Clunies Ross, M. 2002. Närvaro och frånvaro av ritual i norröna medeltida texter. Jennbert, K., Andrén, A. & Raudvere, C. (eds.) *Plats och Praxis. Studier av nordisk förkristen ritual.* Vägar till Midgård 2. Lund. 13-30.

Egardt, B. 1950. Problem kring hesteskallar. *Rig* 1950. 149-159.

Falk, A-B. 2005. Building offerings – the remains of a ritual. *Lund Archaeological Review 2002-2003, vol8-9.* Lund. 63-76.

Falk, A-B. 2006. My home is my castle. Andrén, A., Jennbert, K. & Raudvere, C. (eds.) *Old Norse religion in long-term perspectives. Origins, changes and interactions.* Vägar till Midgård 8. Nordic Academic Press. Lund.

Falk, A-B. 2007. En grundläggande handling – byggnadsoffer och dagligt liv i medeltid. Unpublished licentiate thesis. University of Lund, Institution of Archaeology and Ancient history. 2007.

Giddens, A. 1984. *The constitution of society: outline of the theory of structuration.* Berkeley.

Habbe, P. 2005. *Att se och tänka med ritual: kontrakterande ritualer i de isländska släktsagorna.* Vägar till Midgård, 7. Nordic Academic Press. Lund.

Hauge, H-E. 1965. *Levande begravd eller bränd i nordisk folkmedicin.* Stockholm.

Henninger, J. 1987. Sacrifice. Eliade, M. (ed.) *The Encyklopedia of Religion, vol 12.* New York.

Karsten, P. 1994. *Att kasta yxan i sjön - en studie över rituell tradition och förändring utifrån skånska neolitiska offerfynd.* Acta Archaeologica Lundensia series in 8, no. 23. Lund.

Kitzler, L. 2000. Odensymbolik i Birkas Garnison. *Fornvännen* 2000/1, Stockholm. 13-21.

Nordström, K. 1997. Problems and Ideas concerning Ideology in the Construction of "Religion and Ritual" as Analytical Concepts. Normalized categories in archaeology and other disciplines. *Lund Archaeological Review, 1997, vol 3.* Lund. 49-57.

Oestigaard, T. 2003. *An Archaeology of Hell. Fire, Water and Sin in Christianity.* Bricoleur Press. Göteborg.

Paulsson, T. 1993. *Huset och lyckan: en studie i byggnadsoffer från nordisk järnålder och medeltid.* C-uppsats, University of Lund, Institution of Archaeology and Ancient history. 1993.

Paulsson-Holmberg, T. 1997. Iron Age building offerings. A contribution to the analysis of a die-hard phenomenon in Swedish preindustrial agrarian society. *Fornvännen 92, 1997/3-4.* Stockholm. X-x.

Renck, A.-M. 2000. Den helgade marken – ritualen som dokument. Ersgård, L. (ed.) *Människors platser – tretton arkeologiska studier från UV.* Riksantikvarieämbetet arkeologiska undersökningar, Skrifter No 13. Stockholm. 209-227.

Siech, S. & Berggren, Å. 2002. *Rapport över arkeologisk slutundersökning Öresundsförbindelsen. Petersborg 6.* Malmö Kulturmiljö. Malmö. 134-140.

Offering practices at two holy stones in Setomaa, south-east Estonia

Heiki Valk

Introduction

In prehistoric societies, ritual activities most often were related to holy natural places. Sanctuaries of pre-Christian origin may have been involved in popular ritual practices even in the Middle Ages, especially at the time of transition to Christianity. Considering this, the topic of holy natural places should not be neglected also in medieval archaeology, or, more precisely, in the archaeology of medieval religiosity and popular forms of Christianity.

Due to long-lasting Christian practices, the holy natural places have totally disappeared from oral tradition in most parts of Europe and are sometimes reflected in landscape or written records merely as toponyms. In such a general context, the question of natural sanctuaries has greatly been disregarded in European archaeology, except for natural bodies of water – sites which have attracted the attention of archaeologists due to the Germanic and Scandinavian weapon offerings (e.g. Bradley 1990). Although the topic of holy natural places has been raised also on a broader scale (Bradley 2000), the scantiness of tangible archaeological material, as well as the lack of research tradition have still kept it in a most marginal position.

Because of an early and profound Christianisation and due to the fact that only a very limited part of the former complexity of rites and rituals can be observed in the archaeological record, the chances on unearthing the former meaning of holy natural places are most limited in the core areas of Europe. They are somewhat bigger in its peripheries where cultural processes had a slower course, where old traditions did survive much longer and where comparative data can be obtained from the written sources, folkloric and ethnographic data. The Eastern Baltic Area does belong to such a peripheral region: in Lithuania (Vaitkevičius 2004), Latvia and Estonia holy natural places were in use up to the 19th century and locally even in the 20th century.

The research area and the context

Although from a western European viewpoint Estonia is commonly seen as a peripheral part of Europe, located on the border of the West and the East, somewhere on the fringe of Western civilization, from a closer perspective there are peripheries also within peripheries. The research area of this article –Setomaa (Setumaa) County a frontier district of south-eastern Estonia directly at the Russian border – can be regarded just as such territory (figure 1).

The Setos, a Finnic ethnic group speaking a southern Estonian dialect, presently ca. 5 000 people in their native area, have until 1920 never been involved in the sphere of the Western culture. The whole ethnic Seto territory (ca 500 km^2) since Christianisation belonged to the realm of Orthodox Christianity and was politically subordinated to Russian supremacy. The Seto community, presently split by the state border between Estonia and Russia, has lived in isolation since medieval times. From the Russians the Seto were separated by language and cultural and identity – from the Estonians by a religious and political border. Due to these historical reasons, we can speak of a most conservative society, which mentally still lived in the Middle Ages until 1920 when Setomaa became part of the new-born state of Estonia. The peripheral situation and isolation from the neighbours have contributed to the long continuity of several ancient traditions. The homemade national costume was worn in everyday life until World War II and the last bearers of this tradition died only in the early 1990s. Ritual communication with the ancestors in form of meals on the graves (Valk 2006) and the archaic *runo*-song (*regilaul*) tradition have existed, on the basis of continuity, until now. As a whole, the traditional popular religiosity of the Setos can be characterised as a religious syncretism, of which some features have survived among the older generation up to the present time (Valk, Västrik 1996).

The monuments

This article offers an insight into the complexity of rites, rituals and beliefs related to two holy offering stones in Setomaa where the tradition of gift-giving existed up to the 20th century and has not ended even nowadays. The two stones under discussion – *Jaanikivi*, i.e. St. John's stone in Miikse (Meeksi) and *Annekivi*, i.e. St. Anne's stone in Pelsi, both small villages, – are located within the Estonian territory, close to the border of medieval Livonia and Russia, 3 km to the south-east and 4 km to the east-south-east of the ruins of medieval Vastseliina (Neuhausen) Castle.

Jaanikivi is situated on the historical border, on the Livonian side of Miikse stream, flowing at its foot. The Miikse village itself belonged, as all Setomaa, to Russia up to 1920. According to popular concepts, the stone has got its name from *Pühä Jaan*, i.e. St. John (John the Baptist) who was believed to have once rested on it. The low flat stone is overgrown with turf and its exact measures are unknown. Presently, only its highest top and vertical side facing the stream can be observed. In the 1930s, however, when the stone still was in active use and having an Orthodox chapel on its top, it seemed higher (figure 2).

In fact, the stone has originally been bigger. According to the oral tradition, it was exploded, to get building

Figure 1. Location of Setomaa.

material for a cow house of the adjacent Miikse manor. As a punishment for the sacrilege, the cattle started dying. The disaster stopped only when the pieces of the stone were broken out of the wall and returned to their original place. This legend, which is recorded in the Estonian folklore archives in numerous versions, is remembered among the native population also nowadays, as an evidence of the miraculous power of the stone. The ruins of the cow house from the first half of the 19th century are still standing in a distance of ca. 500 m from the stone.

Of big importance is also the stream at the foot of *Jaanikivi* (figure 3). Fragments of the exploded stone in its water confirm also nowadays the above-mentioned legend of breaking the stone The water of the stream is believed to have healing qualities. The archaeological complex also includes a medieval village cemetery, located on a hill called *Jaanimägi* (St John's Hill) or *Pühäkivi mägi* (the Hill of the Holy Stone), which begins immediately beside the stone. A legend tells us that once upon a time there ran a holy spring out of the hill and that it disappeared as a result of sacrilege – washing dirty clothes there.[1]

Before World War II three orthodox chapels belonged to the sanctuary – one stood on the stone, and the others in the vicinity. In 1952 the local people built a new church of John the Baptist in a distance of ca 100 m from the holy stone and after that the old chapels were deserted and demolished. The cultural layers of the medieval settlement begin ca. 150 m from the stone. The village of Miikse is first mentioned in the written sources in 1342, when a big battle between Russian and Livonian troops took place on its fields.

The other stone, *Annekivi* in Pelsi village, is a rather small, thin and flat granite slab (figure 4). On the stone there was a wooden chapel which was replaced by a new one of stone nearby in 1896. According to the legend, St.

---

[1] ERA II 267, 576/578 (14). Setumaa, Meremäe v., Vinski k., Tammiste t. – Stepan Lendla < ema Marie Lendla, 55. 1940.

Figure 2. Chapel on Jaanikivi (St John's stone) in Miikse. Photo: Villem Kirss 1939. ERA 1073

Anne, the protector saint of sheep, rested on the stone and had mutton there for lunch. The legend also tells that the stone was under an old tree and that the saint has given sheep to the people, taking them from its hollow (Loorits 1951, 340). Thanks to popular beliefs related to St. Anne, sheep play a special role in the rites related to her stone.

An old folklore note also says that the present-day *Annekivi* is not the original stone and that rites have been transferred to it only later. The small slab, "Anne's gift-stone" is stated to have overtaken the name of the original stone.[2]

In the Estonian Folklore Archives there are several notes – the oldest from the second half of the 19th century – about the popular meetings which occurred at the two holy stones. Some of these texts that are presented below enable us to re-construct a picture of the events on holidays related to the name saints of the stones – on St. John's day (July 7th) in Miikse and at St. Anne's Day (August 7th) in Pelsi. Both holidays are celebrated in the local Orthodox tradition still after the old, i.e. Julian calendar.

The events at Miikse – the former situation at St. John's stone

The earliest of the notes about the activities at *Jaanikivi* goes back to the third quarter of the 19th century. According to the eyes of a witness, the events were as follows:

Figure 3. St. John's stone and the stream at its foot in Miikse. Author's photo, 2003.

---

[2] H II 69, 817/822 (5). Seto, Vilo v., Alaotsa k. – Jaan Sandra. 1903.

Figure 4. St Anne's stone in Pelsi. Author's photo, 1994.

/---/ Bei meiner Ankunft fand ich schon eine recht zahlreiche Versamlung von Bettlern welche sich alle um den Stein gelagert hatten, mit entblössten Häuptern, und leise wie in heiliger Scheu, mit einander flüsternd vor. Nach einigen gestellten Fragen erfuhr ich das alles nur den Aufgang der Sonne erwarte, um die Feierlichkeiten zu beginnen.

Nun so war es, den auch mit dem Aufgang der Sonne strömten die Settu, aus dem gegenüber gelegenen Dorfe Meeks zahlreich zusamen. Es waren sogar Leute aus der Ostrowschen und Pleskauschen Gegend hingekomen. Alsbald erschien ein alter Steltzfuss, der aus dem heute geöffneten Bethause Wachskertzen mitbrachte, und dieselben zahlreich auf dem heiligen Steine verkaufte. Die Bettler begannen alte nie gehörte Lieder anzustimen, welche zwar einen christlichen Anstrich hatten, aber dennoch nicht rein christlich waren. Das Volk, festlich geschmückt, wogte nun zum Stein, Kesemilch und Butter als Opfergabe hintragend. Diese Gaben hatten aber zuvor in dem gegenüberligenden Bethause von einem daselbst befindlichen Priester eine Weihe erhalten, bei welcher Gelegenheit dem Priester ein Theil der Gaben zufiel. Die beim Stein befindlichen stellten nun die Butter und Kesemilchgeschirre auf denselben, umstellten die Geschirre mit neun brennenden Kertzen, und verneigten sich kreutzigend und kniend vor dem Stein, indem sie manches vor sich hinflüsterten. Alsdann wurden die Lichter verlöscht, die Geschirre in die Hand genomen und mit denselben dreimal der Stein umkreist, nachdem auch dieses geschähen, vortheilten sie den Inhalt der Gefässe unter den Bettelnden, welche von allen Seiten ihre Geschirre (lännik) entgegen streckten. Ein jeder von ihnen erhielt nun drei Löffel foll, und gab sich damit sehr zufriede. /---/

Jetzt kehrte ich wiederum zum Steine zurück, und sah abermals das vorher gesagte. Aber auch wie die kleineren Bruchstücke des Steines verwerthet wurden. Einige trugen dieselben auf der Schulter, Andere auf dem Rücken, wieder Andere dieselben auf dem Magen haltend drei Mal um den Hauptstein. Ein jeder trug den Stein an der Stelle die ihm krank oder schmertzhaft war, in der festen Überzeugung dadurch zu genesen.

Nach 12 Uhr Mittag zog sich der ganze Volkshaufe zum Kruge hin, woselbst die verschiedensten Tänze aufgeführt wurden (vor dem Kruge auf einem freien Platz). Werend des Tanzes werden die alten Volkslieder von den Weibern und Mädchen abgesungen, die in einem Kreise eine festen Krantz bilden. Hinter ihnen stehn in geschlossnen Gruppen ihre Männer oder Freier. /---/

Um nicht zu weit von der Heiligkeit des Steines abzuschweifen, komme ich wieder auf denselben zurück. Die Butter und Kesemilch welches zu demselben getragen wird, erhält schon vor seiner Bereitung eine Art Weihe; indem man die Milch welche zu diesem Zwecke gemälkt wird, an vier Donnerstagen mälkt. Dieses geschieht dann imer kniend und dabei werden die Worte gesprochen:

Dear Holy John,
keep the animals of my cattle,
when coming home
and when going out of home,
behind the bush
eating green grass.
Keep from damages of the forest,
from wild beast!
Dear Holy John,
Give milk to my cows![3]

Thus, we get evidence of crowds gathering at the stone on Midsummer Eve, people coming even from big distances. In a note from 1928, the number of participants is estimated around a thousand people, about one hundred of them being beggars.[4] In addition to the Government of Pskov, the old records mention participants even from Vitebsk (in Byelorussia) and Kiev in the Ukraine. In one case a Seto narrator tells how he guided a pilgrim to the holy stone: the man had come by foot for some 500 km

---

[3] *ELM: H, Wiedemann 1, 45/5. All presentations of folklore texts in English are author's translations.*
[4] *H, Jõgever 2, 175/181. – Jakob Orav, 1928. Since the text tells about visitors from Russia, the numbers reflect, probably, the situation before 1920.*

Figure 5. The beggars at the stone. Photo: Villem Kirss 1939. ERA 1072.

from the surroundings of Moscow.[5] The event attracted beggars both from the Pskovian Land, especially those related to the Pechory (Petseri)[6] monastery, as well as from Lutheran Livonia. The poor gathered at the holy stone already on the fortnight of the event, in hope to get the gifts which were brought there (figure 5).

But there were so many beggars in Meeksi around this Jaanikivi that there was no place for them at the same time. Then some were sitting there for half a night and the others were waiting there before the morning. If someone laid anything on the stone, you had to have very quick hands to get the gift. Who had quicker hands, got more of that stuff, but there were infinite and huge amounts of butter and curds.[7]

The old records give evidence of a noisy atmosphere. In addition to the songs of the beggars whose *lamentation makes listeners frighten*,[8] we can imagine their screams when quarrelling for the gifts: *A hag put a scroll of cloth upon the stone that was attacked by the stronger beggars who were fisting until the senior from Miikse village was called who chased away the quarrellers.*[9] We also can hear the voices of Seto women shouting at the priest: *Everyone can hear there how the Seto women, loudly curse and scold the priest at the village chapel, because of small gifts of the poor: "Dear poor, this gift (either butter, curds, handful of wool, edge of a cloth or something else) really remained so few and small – but what to do, if the priest, the evil one, took so much for himself. He, unfilled blackguard, does not notice at all that the poor do not get anything of it!"*[10]

An extra contribution to the atmosphere was added by the nearby dancing party of the local youth: *The youth who had gone there and who did not do anything, who gave no gifts or nothing, those danced there for the whole night. The whole night there was a big party. But early in the morning the sermon began again at 8. Such was the Jaanikivi in Miikse.*[11]

In the Seto tradition, *Jaanikivi* was a most multi-functional source of help, both in case of human and animal diseases, as well as in questions of general luck and misfortune. Although the main communal offering practices occurred at Midsummer, the stone was visited individually in case of need also in other cases and some piece of money, a little milk, a wisp of wool or something else could be found there.[12]

Since St. John is the protector of cattle in popular Orthodox Christianity, many of the gifts brought to the stone were dairy products – milk, butter, home-made cheese and curds. People greased the stone with butter and cheese all around, asking for much milk and good luck for the cattle.[13] Old descriptions mention among the gifts also eggs, grain and meat, as well as money, cloth and clothing items. The latter, e.g. mittens, towels and

---

[5] ELM: H II 70, 557/561 (12). Setu, Vilo v., Radaja k. – Jaan Sandra < Radaja Timmo. 1904.
[6] The monastery of Pechory, founded in 1473 in the settlement area of the Seto population, is one of the most famous Orthodox monasteries of Russia.
[7] ELM: RKM II 290, 365/370 (13) Setu, Meremäe v., Korski k. – Lilia Briedis < Hilda Kadakas. Vastseliina khk. 1972.
[8] ELM: H, Jõgever 2, 175/181 – J. Orav. 1928.
[9] ELM: H, Jõgever 2, 175/181. – J. Orav. 1928.
[10] ELM: H II 61, 661–663. – J. Sandra. 1898.
[11] ELM: RKM II 14, 298 (11). – Liis Pedajas < Pelagei Sõrm, 85. 1946.
[12] ELM: H II 60, 769/71 (1). – J. Sandra. 1897.
[13] ELM: H II 60, 769/71 (1) – J. Sandra. 1897.

head-dresses were brought to the stone for healing purposes and represented the diseased parts of the body.

In Miikse manor, behind Vastseliina manor there is a big stone in the stream. Every Midsummer Eve many Russians and Setos began to gather there. They came there only if some part of the body was ill: if there were scabs, if the neck, feet and hands were aching. They cast all their old clothes to the stone from where they were removed by the beggars.[14]

According to their disease, then they lay there upon the stone: who the shirt, who socks, who the head-dress[15]*.*

I also brought for children. Put their small shirts upon Jaanikivi because of children. Their health was poor, now they are better. That was last year.[16]

I brought socks. My feet, the bones of my feet started to cramp, then I brought the socks. There I took off my shoes on the shore, put on others [socks], laid the socks on the stone, took them away from the stone again and then gave to the poor. You say so: "Dear Holy John, give me health!" [---]. It is laid on the stone, since it is John's stone; John was sitting there. The clothes or socks are put upon the stone because of illness.[17]

And also I have. My foot was also very bad once. And it was before, in the time of Estonian rule.[18] *Yes, and then my mother-in-law said that "Oh, there is nothing to do. Let us go to Jaanimägi." And then the soft healless leather shoes were worn. Well, and I cut one rag for the foot and took it along from home and went there. But there were such poor people. Widowers and boys and such troubled people and... I put it first upon Jaanikivi and then gave it to someone: "Pray for me as well – I have a bad foot!" And since that time my foot became better, became well. And also now people keep the custom. I have not been there for 3 years now. We also visited Jaanimägi.*[19]

A most common way of healing was direct contact with the holy stone: pressing the aching part of the body against it (figure 6).

Well, then very many people went there, likewise to heal, people did it. It was a very big help if you pressed against that stone and washed in the stream. Then people became well. In olden times there were no hospitals... then people

*Figure 6. A Seto woman healing her head.
Photo: L. F. Zurov 1938. ERA 1185.*

could not allow healing for big money. Then people got health there.[20]

One of them has become the candle-seller from whom everyone who celebrates the "holy stone" buys a candle ant puts it upon the stone where "Holy John" himself is said to have sat. And everybody can even see some men and women coming to the holy stone in a shameless way, revealing the lower part of the body and pressing their lumbers and other parts against the holy stone there.[21]

For healing also pieces of the stone were used:

A newly-married Seto woman who was the first, put her 5-stoup bowl, its lower part filled with curds and the upper part with butter, upon the stone, pressed a lighted candle burning on the stone, took from among the pieces of the stone one of about 5 pounds, and pressed with it the aching parts of her body, as breast, back and head (those with bad teeth must gnaw the stone). Then she laid the stone down again and put three spoonfuls from there upon the [big] stone. That was taken by the stronger beggars, after the right of the fist, and they put butter and curds in their vessels. Then the newly-wed Seto woman went with her bowl to the chapel of Miikse village where the priest from Taelova Church had come to pray

---

[14] *ELM: ERA II 247, 160 (3). 1939*
[15] *ELM: RKM II 14, 127/128 (27). 1944*
[16] *ELM: RKM II 22, 207 (1). Petseri. – Liis Pedajas < Irina Targa. 1949.*
[17] *ELM: RKM II 14, 294/295 (7). – Liis Pedajas < Pelagei Sõrm, 85. 1946.*
[18] Between 1920 and 1940.
[19] *ELM: FAM 302 (35) Petseri raj., Ungavitsa küla. – Heiki Valk < Tatjo Õuna, 80. 1996.*

[20] *ELM: EKRK I 74, 221/222 (11) Setumaa, Võru raj., Meremäe k/n, Palo k. < Poksa k. – Paul Hagu < Stepanida Vahvik, 80. 1973.*
[21] *ELM: H II 61, 661–663. – J. Sandra. 1898.*

(because at that day the priest takes from the people of that area the tithe of milk). With the rests of the milk which remained after blessing she came back to the stone and distributed her gift by spoonfuls among the beggars.[22]

Most often the stone was visited also if there were problems with cattle:

And now all go to Miikse to the stone at Midsummer night. Who feels to have misfortune with cattle or if there is no luck with life, the animals die or if there is a bad disease, illness of back or headache, or if one feels especially bad, with bad feet, then he goes there, takes new shoes to Miikse, puts them upon Jaanikivi stone. And then the Seto had linen scarves on their head or headscarves. Then they took either a new linen scarf or headscarf on Jaanikivi. And for cattle people took curds, butter there – in most large amounts – with full bowls – and the more there was, the more proud it was. Then God had to help and the stone had to bless all the diseases that were there.

Because of the horses no prayer is prayed. People did not go [to Jaanikivi] because of hen. Because of sheep they took wool, because of cattle – milk and butter – so that God should protect the animals and have all well.[23]

But their misfortune with cattle was overcome, indeed. They wasted a big vessel of curds, another vessel of butter, but there was help also. What else than the praying God by the poor or the water poured over the holy stone could help this much. Otherwise, they could have not a single cow to bear a calf in a normal way, as other people's cows do. Who kicked the calf, which had the calf cross, who had the calf born with big trouble and both died together. But now they had got all the four cows to bear at night. /---/ In the morning when going to see the cattle they found a calf dancing in the cow house.[24]

Supernatural help in case of trouble might be gained also after promises to visit the stone:

In the old time, if there were many worries or troubles, then the old people promised. Who had some diseased animal of something wrong in the family, then promised to go to Jaanimägi if it would get well. Well, people went because of that promise on Jaanimägi and there was help also.[25]

Also here Ohkrim from our village has promised again to be in Miikse every Midsummer. He had three years ago also big misfortune with cattle and then it was taught: you promise to start visiting Jaanikivi. He did so as well. Since that time he has no bigger problems with cattle, animal disease. There is sometimes something unimportant – a calf of piglet gone wrong – but that is nothing. Earlier – a year – a cow, a year – a cow. It became terrible even to look upon it from aside, but what to bear it?[26]

If you have promised, then you take, put a rouble or what you have. I had a wound on my leg – if it gets healed by St. John's day, I would go to Jaanikivi. In my heart I promised – God, make it well![27]

Promises have even been regarded as a general explanation for visiting the stone: *The servants of John's stone or holy offering stone have all surely promised to be there every year and bring their promised gifts there.*[28]

All is laid there as promised gifts, what is surely promised at the time of and due to misfortune and from what help is gained already in case of promising. But the misfortune is said really to return, if you cheat the holy stone and do not take the promised things there.[29]

The former situation at Jaanioja – the stream of St. John

Healing was also practiced at the stream whereby its water was believed to have miraculous qualities only in sacred time, i.e. on St. John's Day (or old Midsummer). The water was considered to have healing powers also in other places of the stream downwards of Miikse, until its flowing into the Piusa River about 4 km further down.[30] Betterment took place as a result of washing whereby naked bathing in the stream was practiced in the past. The earliest description of Midsummer events at *Jaanikivi* depicts it as follows:

Darauf entkleideten sich Männer, Weiber, Mädchen, Jungen auch Kinder und gingen in den Fluss, in welchem sie dreimal tauchten. Von gegenseitiger Scham war keine Rede. Der Fluss wird an der Stelle "pühhä lette" [holy spring] genannt. Dieses heilige Wasser soll vor Krankheiten schützen, und gegen Krankheiten vorbeugen. Nachdem nun ein solches Bad genomen war, wurden die aus dem Wasser steigenden von Bettlern beglückwünscht, und von denselben ersucht ihnen auch etwas zukomen zu lassen, – wogegen sie versprachen auch für das Wohl der Gabenspendenden zu beten. Dieses geschah denn auch imer, und gewöhnlich bestand die Gabe in einem Hemde welches die vom Bade erquickte Person angehabt hatte.

---

[22] ELM: H, Jõgever 2, 175/181. – J. Orav. 1928.
[23] ELM: RKM II 14, 298 (11). Setu, Meremäe v., Obinitsa k. – Liis Pedajas < Pelagei Sõrm, 85. 1946.
[24] ELM: H II, 70, 557/561 (12) Setu, Vilo v., Radaja k. – Jaan Sandra < Radaja Timmo. 1904.
[25] ELM: FAM 309 (28) Petseri raj., Setu, Petseri v., Truba k. – Tea Vassiljeva, Aimar Ventsel < Ilvese Olga, 75. 1996.
[26] ELM: H II, 70, 557/561 (12) Setu, Vilo v., Radaja k. – Jaan Sandra < Radaja Timmo. 1902.
[27] ELM: RKM II 14, 291/294 (6). Setu, Meremäe v., Meeksi k. – Liis Pedajas. 1946.
[28] ELM: H II 60, 769/71 (1). – J. Sandra. 1897.
[29] ELM: H II 60, 769/71 (1). – J Sandra. 1897.
[30] Personal comment by Eevi Kambrimäe, Miikse village, 2005.

Dieselbe hatte sich imer mit einem zweiten Hemde vom Hause versorgt, welches sie alsdann anzog.[31]

Into that stream go bathing all the seekers for health who feel something wrong. Let him be a man or a woman, a boy or a maiden. But everyone tries to wash himself at the place of the stone. When bathing, there is no difference between men and women. After bathing some give all their old clothes away, hoping to get rid of their troubles together with those, and put on new clothes which they have brought along. Some give some of their clothes, some give money, but no one leaves without assisting help.[32]

Some washed themselves in the stream – feet and faces. A young woman brought a child, washed him in the stream and put sitting on a stone for a while.[33]

And there the small stream or river was flowing. Who were crippled or ill, they washed themselves. And there really was help! One child – she was not from this village, she was from Sokolova, where I lived – the small girl did not see. She had eyes but they were not good eyes. And then Mother carried her there in her arms and carried her back as well. And when she came back from Jaanimägi, she washed her eyes in the water.[34] And how far it was – two-three kilometres, Mother wanted to rest as well – the child was in her arms. And she put her there on the grass – at Midsummer there are flowers – and the child went, saying "Mother! Look, which flowers! I go and pick the flowers!" As Mother said, how many times she bowed then deeply backwards for [St.] John – she was so happy that the child began to see! So it was![35]

In a record from 1946 the combination of the healing qualities of the stone and the water is stressed:

In a small chapel on the shore of the stream there was a barrel of water, a low cask where water was brought from the spring. That was done by the church assistant who stood there with candles and offertory box. There were loose pieces of stone, of fist size, in the chapel. People came there in succession. Water was taken with a piggin, it was poured over the stone and people washed themselves – hands, feet, face. Some seekers for help did it themselves. The person who poured water over the stone was one of the beggars who, when pouring water for the people over the stone on their hands and into the bottles, said: "Holy Jaanikivi, make clean, make clean, make their lives clean!" Some let the beggar press them with the stone, with a piece of the stone which was made wet – one the breast, the other – the back, the third – the hand. Some pressed themselves their diseased places with a piece of stone, a young woman – her stomach. Coins were cast into the cask. Someone doubted, said that he does not know what to do – to throw money into the water or put it into the offertory box. Some who take the water and use the stone light a candle in front of an icon.[36]

For persons who could not participate in the event, miraculous healing was believed to arrive also after dousing their clothes into the water of Jaanioja: *People go there on St. John's Day [=Midsummer] to have a sermon and look for help against the diseases. If somebody is ill [at home], then some clothing item, likewise a shirt, is taken from him. In the river it is dipped into the water, saying: "Dear Holy John, heal him!" Then it is given to the poor who have gathered there. Many people go there to look for help. Some have become cleansed as well.*[37]

In addition to health, bathing in the stream was expected to give good luck for getting married for maidens: *The Seto girls bathe there in the stream, after blessing, and give all their clothes worn before to the beggars who have gathered there in a big crowd that night. Thus they hope to get, for the coming year, good luck for getting married.*[38] Also water which was taken along from the stream in vessels or bottles was believed to have miraculous qualities – both for cattle and people.[39]

The present situation

The popular meetings and healing practices at St. John's stone continue also nowadays (Valk 1999). The number of participants of the event – sermon, healing practices and following commemoration of the dead by meals on the graves – varies between ca 400–500 up to 700–800 persons, depending on occasional factors, but mainly on the weekday and the weather.

Visiting the stone begins at 9–10 in the morning; at the time of the sermon in the church most of the time the stone is occupied by one or two persons. Since access to the stone is hindered by the stream and the bushes there is seldom more than two people involved in the healing.. Throughout the sermon, unless the Orthodox crosses' procession has not come out of the church, the stone is attended by people, either healing or queuing for it. As in former times, people press their heads, hands, backs or feet against the stone, in order to get help and release. This process lasts for some minutes and then a gift is laid on the stone (figures 7, 8). Food gifts have disappeared and also clothing items (socks, handkerchief, headscarf, a candle) occur only rarely. Simultaneously people go to the stream, washing their faces or legs; some take water

---

[31] *ELM: H, Wiedemann 1, 45/5.*
[32] *ELM: H, Jõgever 2, 175/181. – J. Orav. 1928.*
[33] *ELM: RKM II 14, 291/294 (4). Setu, Meremäe v., Meeksi k. – Liis Pedajas. 1946.*
[34] The popular nomination of the water taken from the stream *jaanivesi* has a double meaning: it reflects relations both to Midsummer and St. John.
[35] *ELM: FAM 309 (28) Petseri district, Setu, Petseri community, Truba village. – Tea Vassiljeva, Aimar Ventsel < Olga Ilves, 75. 1996.*
[36] *ELM: RKM II 14, 291/294 (3). – Liis Pedajas. 1946.*
[37] *ELM: ERA II 248, 675 (6) Setumaa, Petseri v., Mosküla, Sillaotsa t. – Aleksandra Lepisto < Daria Lepisto, 46. 1939.*
[38] *Mss 74.*
[39] *ELM: FAM 129 (5) Setu, Meremäe v., Palande k. Ergo Västrik & Veinika Raabe < Kõlli Nasta, 82. 1994.*

Figure 7. Laying gifts on St. John's stone. Author's photo, 2001.

Figure 8. Gifts on St. John's stone. Author's photo, 1997.

home in bottles. After taking water, a coin is thrown in the stream (figures 3, 9). While the stone is visited mainly by elderly people, casting coins and taking water is performed by most different age groups.

A big difference to the situation as described in the old sources is the absence of beggars nowadays: they are said to have disappeared in the Soviet time, due to stately pensions for the retired. The atmosphere and space have changed also, since the chapels have been replaced by a church. Thus, a distance of ca. 100 m between the ecclesiastical and non-ecclesiastical side of the rites has been created and the priest is not participating in the activities related to the stone any more. The attitude of the Church towards activities at the stone is neutral – neither supporting nor hindering.

Healing at the stone and the stream ends mainly with the crosses' procession coming out of the church. During the final stage of the sermon the stone is visited only rarely.. The end of the sermon means also the end of activities at the stone. Now people gather on the graves to commemorate the relatives with foods and drinks (see Valk 2006). The money brought to the stone is taken into the church when the sermon and gift-giving has ended.

Rites at St. Anne's stone

Data about *Annekivi* are limited in the records from the folklore collections. In contrast to the site of *Jaanikivi* the tradition at St. Anne´s stone ended during the Soviet period, and only a modest revival (sermon at the local village chapel) has taken place during the last years. As in Miikse, the gifts, especially wool, feet and heads of ram, were blessed by the priest in the village chapel before bringing upon the stone (Wiedemann 1876, 411/12, 416). Also here the event was attended by crowds of beggars who received the gifts after they had touched the holy stone.

A long folklore text from 1902 describes the events as follows:

Last year (1902) I went on St. Anne's Day to Pelsi, to see with my own eye how gifts and offerings are brought to St. Anne's stone. A big crowd of people, mostly women, stood clustered around the stone where all of them laid head and feet of sheep which they had brought with them. On the next moment after laying the gifts were quickly seized by the stretched hands of the beggars and were put into their bags. There I heard several maidens pleading:

Figure 9. Offered coins in the St. John's stream. Author's photo, 2001.

"Oh you, worldly! Let those ram feet lay at least for one moment on the holy stone!" In such a tone and way several "generous givers" were moaning under the quickness of the beggars who tried to grasp the ram heads and feet laid upon the stone, as well as wisps of wool, from each other.

It was both sad and funny to see the trouble a Seto guy of about 15–16, who, when distributing wool at the stone, was pulled and dragged about with his wool by the crowd of beggars. The boy was, because of trouble and shame, red in face as a boiled crayfish, but he still was grabbed and torn from one and the other side, so that his clothes crackled, by the hands and claws of the beggars, who were permanently rebuking: "Give me! Give me! Me!" The beggars seemed to have the victory. The boy retreated with big trouble from among the beggars and the people, so that his head was wet and he left – or, more correctly, had to leave – his half-new red cotton shirt to be tattered and quarrelled among the beggars, in order to escape with unharmed flesh and bones.

I saw also a pair of men, carrying ram heads in their hands, approaching the holy stone, knocking both with the ram head against the stone and going onwards with all towards the chapel. One of them seemed to have even a bloody ram head. The crowd of beggars gazed at both men with a half-bitter gaze, since they had to be deprived of the valuable spoils. In the mind and heart of every giver of gifts and offerer there was luck with sheep – how to keep or gain it. Only rarely some religious Seto men remembered with their gifts also St. Anne who had had lunch there. /---/

Such are the stories and faith of the Seto concerning St. Anne's stone. That Holy Anne, when going to Petseri, had lunch there, is for them as sure truth, as that two by two is four, although at that time when St. Anne lived and walked, even the name of Petseri did not exist in he world. It is strange that they can be so childlike and truly believe in fairytales as real events. A dual thinking seems to have, in questions of faith, no place among them.[40]

In one text, telling about former times, also slaughtering a ram at the holy stone is mentioned: *Earlier also living animals – living sheep and ram were brought here. Who brought, that slaughtered. The ram was ever blessed.*[41] Animal sacrifices which are never mentioned in the case of *Jaanikivi* give evidence of the deep temporal stretch of rites related to St. Anne's stone.

Character of the rites

The folklore notes and descriptions of the rites performed at the holy sites give evidence of a mixture of different traditions. Since St. John's Day has the meaning of Midsummer, several beliefs, rites and rituals at *Jaanikivi* evidently originate from pre-Christian Midsummer

---

[40] ELM: H II 69, 817/822 (5) Setu, Vilo v., Alaotsa k. – Jaan Sandra. 1903
[41] ELM: RKM II 14, 159/160 (60) Setu, Meremäe v., Pelsi k. – Liis Pedajas < Aleksei Annemäe, 62. 1944.

festivities. Considering this even the ritual of bathing to get good luck for marriage might have its origin in ancient fertility rites. Of most ancient origin is the treatment of the stone as the healer, as well as the principle of reciprocity, clearly expressed in gift-giving rituals. Christianity has furnished the pre-Christian sacral complex with the chapels, with the participation of the priest in the holidays, and with legends about the saints and trust in their aid.

Also part of medieval Christian traditions is the gift-giving to beggars and the poor, as well as the knowledge about their thanksgiving and prayers as a source of bliss. A similar role is performed by the poor in Orthodox Karelia (Stark 2002). The origins of promises to visit the stones in case of help remain unknown. They may belong both to the context of popular Orthodox Christianity as well as to the pre-Christian religion. It is also impossible to say whether the rites related to pre-Christian calendar festivities were originally related to the cult of some pre-Christian deity or merely with the sacredness of the area and the stones as sacred and living natural objects. The approach to the stones, expressed in several texts, enables to suggest the latter version.

It seems likely, that compared to pre-Christian times knowledge of the sacredness of the stones has spread out to cover a wider area during the Christian period.. It may have spread in course of long-distance collective pilgrimages, participated by large numbers of people – events deeply rooted in the Orthodox traditions. It was probably in this course the fame of Jaanikivi has stretched deep into Russia, Byelorussia and the Ukraine.

The descriptions of rites express not only the special meaning of sacred time and sacred space (Eliade 1961) but also of their intersection: just this makes a quality, most different from ordinary life situations. In case of both stones the activities are concentrated in a limited span of sacred time, expressed simultaneously both in the pre-Christian and Christian context. The special situation also causes the lack of the shame of being naked at the presence of the other gender.

The reasons of attending the festivities and gift-giving – getting good luck to the cattle, to the sheep or gaining health – express, however, not this much religious but practical backgrounds. The folkloric data enable to suggest that when giving gifts, people often do not think about the origin and sources of help: most important is to follow the rites and rituals. The latter, as well as attitudes and behaviour are of practical character and free of religious pietism. Even attitude towards the priest might be quite irrespective in the past – the scolded clergyman was not regarded as a person of a high social status but just as an ritual actor who furnished the gifts by blessing with special qualities, contributing, thus, to communication with the supernatural.

When regarding the events from an archaeological perspective as related to certain singular objects, we should also not forget their meaning in a broader context. Religious syncretism with offering to holy stones, springs and stone crosses, related to animatistic approaches is a common feature for popular Orthodox Christianity (Panchenko 1998). Thus, the rites related to *Jaanikivi* and *Annekivi* are not exceptional single cases somewhere in the periphery but an expression of the tolerance of the Orthodox Church to popular rites of pre-Christian origin, embedded in the Christian context.

Conclusions

Since peripheral areas offer a chance to meet phenomena, forgotten long ago in and near the centres, *periphery* and *isolation* are keywords of special meaning for the study of history of religion, especially when combining archaeology with folkloric and ethnological data and written sources. The situation which has persisted in the peripheries, in exceptional historical conditions enables the researcher to meet the complexity of such rites and rituals which are forgotten long ago in the central areas, offering also an insight into the mental background of ritual practices.

The folkloric and ethnological data give evidence of the practical character and pragmatic purposes of the rites and rituals performed at Setomaa. Since several practises represent phenomena, occurring trans-culturally in different areas, times and contexts, the examples presented above have also a wider meaning. Data from Setomaa allow us to sketch a broader picture about the popular religiosity at the transition from pre-Christian times to Christianity, enabling us to get in touch with the mentality and atmosphere, related to popular offering practices at holy natural places, and revealing the nature of religious syncretism – a phenomenon so characteristic for medieval rural mentality. Religious syncretism appears in space, time and rites. In space it is expressed in the co-existence of pre-Christian and Christian sanctuaries, in time – in the transformation of ancient holidays into Christian ones, and in rites – in the survival or pre-Christian practices, principles, attitudes and mentality in a Christian context.

Data related to two sacred stones from Setomaa show that the whole atmosphere of popular offering rites, as well as related mentality, can never be reconstructed by means of archaeology only. For interpreting the natural sanctuaries, as well as for re-constructing the mentality of the Medieval period, the value of written, ethnographic and folkloric sources, especially from the peripheries, can/should in no way be underestimated.

Unpublished sources

ELM – Estonian Literary Museum, Estonian Folklore Archives (Tartu).
Mss – Collection of letters sent to amateur archaeologist Jaan Jung (1835–1900) and Estonian Literary Society in the archives of the Institute of History (Tallinn).

References

Bradley, R. 1990. *The passage of arms: an archaeological analysis of prehistoric hoards and votive deposits*. Cambridge.

Bradley, R. 2000. *An archaeology of natural places*. London – New York.

Eliade, M. 1961. *The Sacred and the Profane. The nature of Religion*. New York.

Loorits, O. 1951. *Grundzüge des estnischen Volksglaubens*. Skrifter utgivna av kungl. Gustav Adolfs Akademien för folklivsforskning 18: II. Uppsala – Köpenhamn.

Панченко А.А. 1998. *Исследования в области народного православия. Деревенские святыни Северо-Запада России*. С.-Петербург.

Stark, L. 2002. *Peasants, Pilgrims, and Sacred Promises. Ritual and Supernatural in Orthodox Karelian Folk Religion*. Finnish Literature Society. Helsinki.

Vaitkevičius, V. 2004. *Studies into the Balts' Sacred Places*. BAR International Series 1228. Oxford.

Valk, H. 1999. Mälestusi Meeksi Jaanipäevast. Mäetagused, 9. Tartu, 146–174.

Valk, H. 2006. Cemeteries and Ritual Meals: Rites and their Meaning in the traditional Seto World-view. – Old Norse Religion in long-term perspectives. Origins, Changes and Interactions. Ed. A. Andrén, K. Jennbert, C. Raudvere. Vägar till Midgård, 8. Lund, 141–146. Nordic Academic Press.

Valk, H. and Västrik, E. (Eds.) 1996. *Palve, vanapatt ja pihlakas*. Vanavaravedaja, 4. Tartu.

Wiedemann, F, J. 1876. *Aus dem inneren und äusseren Leben der Ehsten*. St. Petersburg.

The Medieval Udmurt Sacred Sites: An alternative interpretation

Alexei Korobeinikov

Introduction

The archeological site known as the Kuzebaevo settlement is located in South of the Udmurt Republic (Russian Federation). The site is characterised by bank and dikes, judging by their archeological traces these facilities could not have served as a forceful obstacle.

Considering this I pose the question: "Could pagan ceremonies leave any traces to be subsequently registered by means of archeology?" It is well-known that many rites of Udmurt people are related with animal sacrifices. This fact is proven by ethnographic sources. In many occasions blood and parts of bodies (primarily bones) of the sacrificed animals may turn to out be found in a pit adjoining to the fire-place and sacrificing post.

All the aforesaid allows to assume that archeological finds around the Kuzebaevo village can be identified as remnants of pagan altars. Regular distribution of altars (a straight line with equal intervals between fire-places) reveals that we deal with an attempt to use the available space in the most efficient way, so dozens of bread and meat offerings could be cooked at the same time.

Thus the applied ethnographic data combined with modeling of supposed archeological traces of sacrificing facility allows us to interpret it as a shrine. I hope, that the proposed method of comparative analysis of ethnographic/archeological data may re-determine the purpose of other known archeological objects.

Initial archaeological data

The archeological site known in literature as the Kuzebaevo settlement is located in the South of the Udmurt Republic (Russian Federation) in approximate coordinates 56°5´N. and 52°45´E. Half of a square of this promontory site is investigated by means of excavations. Results of these activities as well as inventory of finds are released in publications. Director of excavations Professor Taisia Ostanina comes to the following conclusion: "For the first time this settlement was inhabited by Finnish-Ugric people of Mazuninskaya culture at 4th-5th centuries A.D. By 7th century A.D. the settlement becomes the most North-Eastern fortified hillfort attributed to the Imenkovskaya culture (inhabited by Slavonic or Baltic people?) (Ostanina 2002:5) According to her opinion "Judging by available archeological traces and findings, the purpose of the Kuzebaevo settlement was a multi-functional one. It was dwelling area… Probably it also carried ritual functions. The main purpose of the discussed settlement was defense and protection of residents and their property. To achieve this goal the Kuzebaevo settlement had a series of substantial earthworks" (Ostanina 2002:16).Prof. Ostanina also notes: "Population of the modern Kuzebaevo settlement calls this promontory as "Lud-gurez" (translated from Udmurt language it means "Sacred hill"). For several centuries until now the residents of the Kuzebaevo village have been praying here for pagan gods" (Ostanina 2002:109). In spite of the protective characteristics of bank and dike, their archeological traces (the average of their levels in ancient time equals to 1 meter) ensures us that these facilities could not have served as a forceful obstacle. Based upon the above-said, the function of the discussed site is likely to be interpreted as a shrine.

Ethnological analogies

Examination of the cited hypothesis requires an analysis of the excavation scheme (Ostanina 2002:figure 26) – which coincides with figure 6 of the present work. When ordering the groups of post holes interlinked with straight lines it is obvious that most of them are distributed as a straight chain. Besides that, many of the holes are accompanied with scorches of soil. This peculiarity allows to make two admissions: a) distribution of the holes is subordinate to some regularity and b) each post being accompanied with a hole may be identified as a pagan altar. To verify or falsify such assumption we should address to ethnographic sources.

Ethnographer Gregory Vereshagin who witnessed pagan prayers among the Udmurt people in late 19th century narrates: "At sacrifice ceremony for each (sacrificed) animal an individual fire-place is build – they look as a straight chain oriented in the Eastern direction. All fire-places are separated from each other with the same interval which equals to 7 feet. Each sacrificed animal is put into a the firer-places make a group of 7 - which corresponds with the sacral number of (sacrificed) animals – i.e. seven (Vereschagin 1996:95-96).

Ethnographer Pavel Luppov in his book published in 1927 reveals schemes of sacrificing sites from the South of Udmurtia (Luppov 1927). I sugest that these schemes should be compared to the supposed archeological traces of such activities (see figures 1, 2 and 3).

Field data acquired by ethnographers at present time in the South of Udmurtia reveal the following:

A scheme of excavations (see figure 6) contains all kinds of objects being found by ethnographers at praying sites

FOLK BELIEFS AND PRACTICE IN MEDIEVAL LIVES

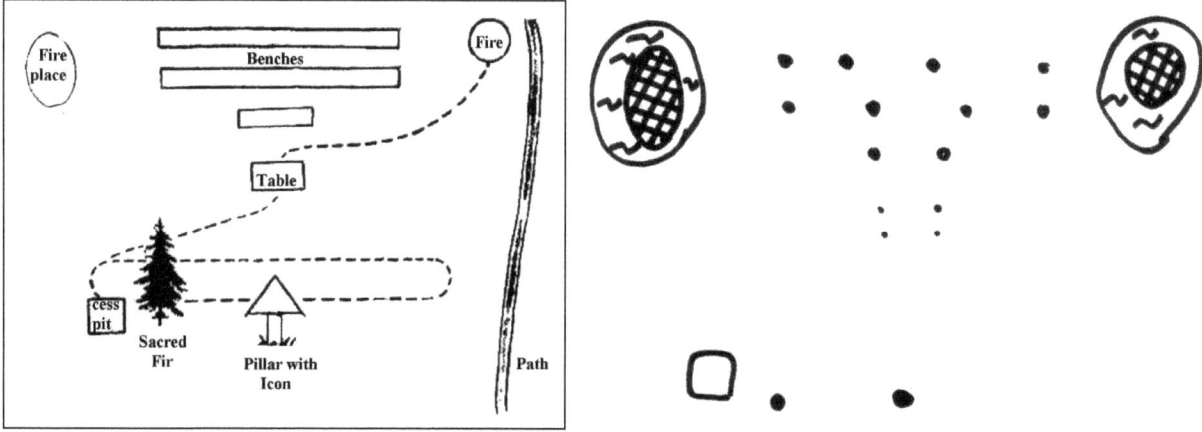

Figure 1. Left: Scheme of pagan ritual meeting place in the neighborhood of the Varzi-Yatchi village by Pavel Luppov. I have re-oriented the scheme northwise and translated original notes into English. Right: The supposed archeological traces of the same object: Cesspit, possible bread table, post holes (hole of the sacrificing stake (post?) is marked with a bold point), scorches of soil. © Copyright 2005, Alexei Korobeinikov.

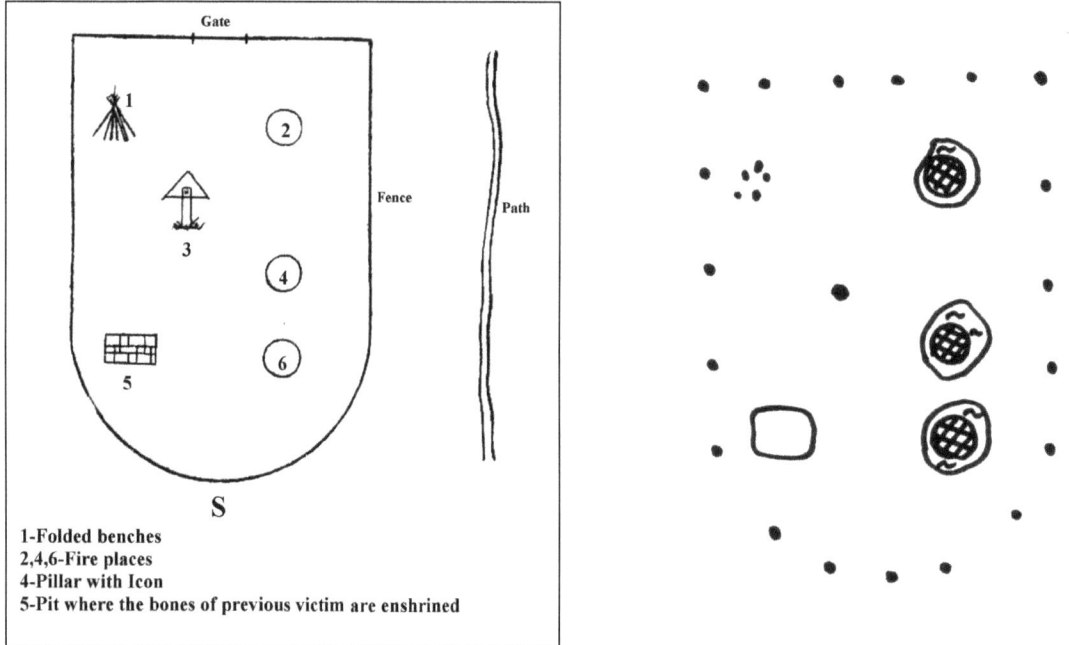

Figure 2. Left: Scheme of pagan ritual meeting place "Bulda" in the area of the Varzi-Yatchi village by Pavel Luppov. I have translated original notes into English. Right: The supposed archeological traces of the same object: Cesspit, Idols corches of soil corresponding to the chain of fire-places. © Copyright 2005, Alexei Korobeinikov.

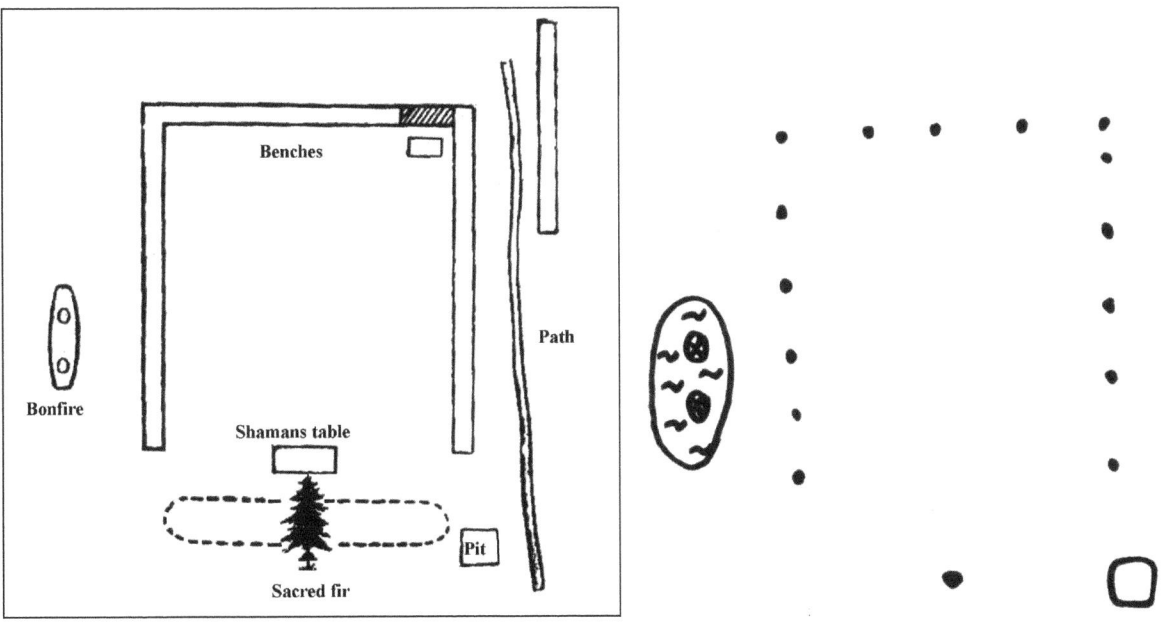

Figure 3. Left: Scheme of woodcraft pagan convent near Kibya and Bodya villages by Pavel Luppov. I have re-oriented the scheme North wise enlarged original notes and translated into English. Right: The supposed archeological traces of the same object: Cesspit, Idols, Table for Consecrated bread. © Copyright 2005, Alexei Korobeinikov

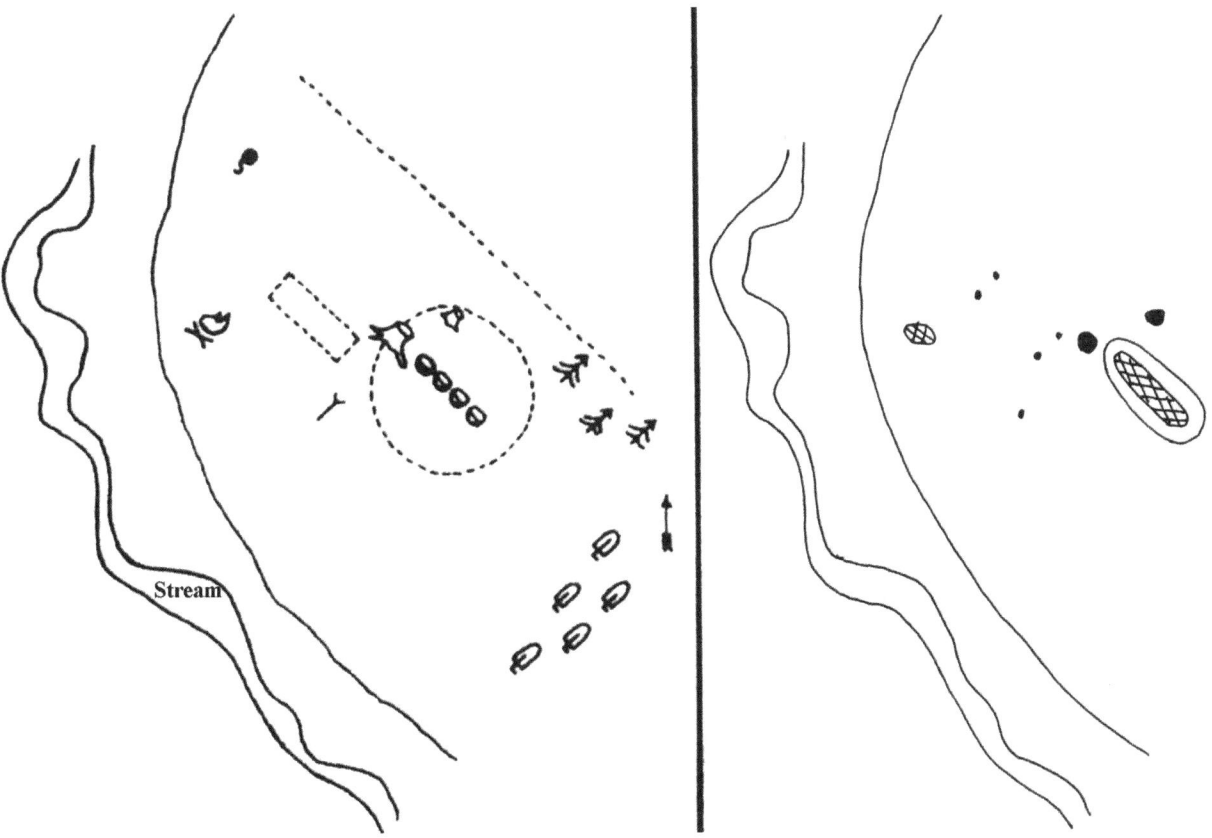

Figure 4. Left: Scheme of pagan shrine "Lud" in the Kuzebaevo village by Vladimir Vladykin (SHUTOVA 2001:50). I have re-oriented the scheme North wise according to the author's polar point. Chain of fire-places possesses azimuth about 130° which is close to azimuth of sunrise at winter solstice. Right: The supposed archeological traces of the same object: Post holes, scorches of soil (traces from a chain of fire-places each purposed for cooking ritual repast). © Copyright 2005, Alexei Korobeinikov

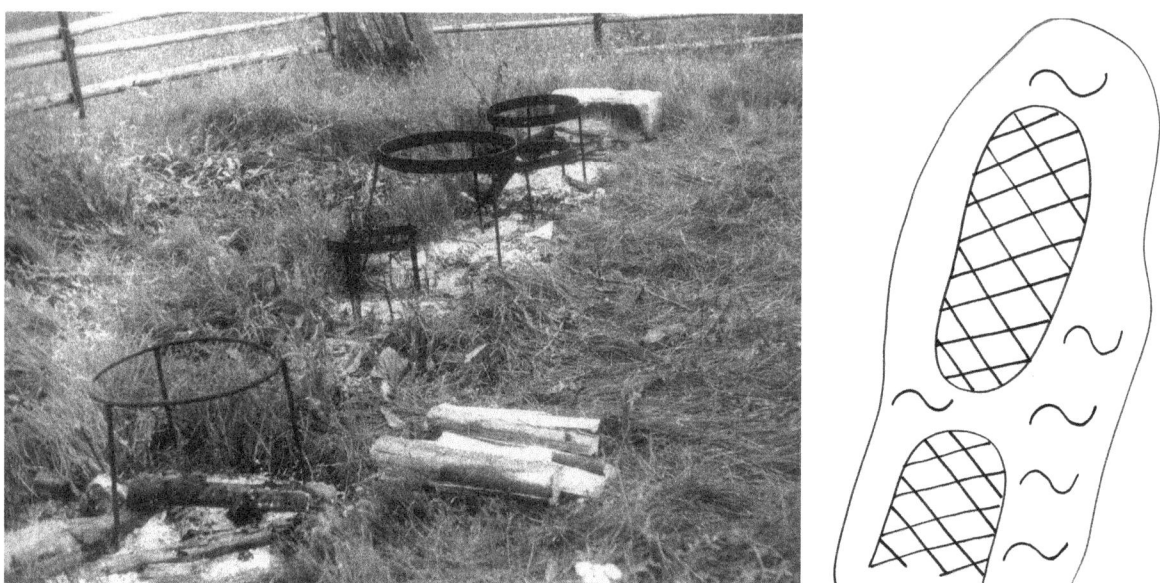

Figure 5. Left: Image of pagan shrine "Lud" in the Kuzebaevo village photographed by Taisia Ostanina in 1988 (SHUTOVA 2001:PHOTO 9) Group of fire-places purposed for ritual repast evidently looks as a straight line which makes a contracted scorched soil. © Copyright 1988, Prof. T. Ostanina Right: the supposed archeological traces of such fire-place: Several closely built individual fires may produce an elongated large scorch of soil being surrounded with ash deposits. © Copyright 2005, Alexei Korobeinikov

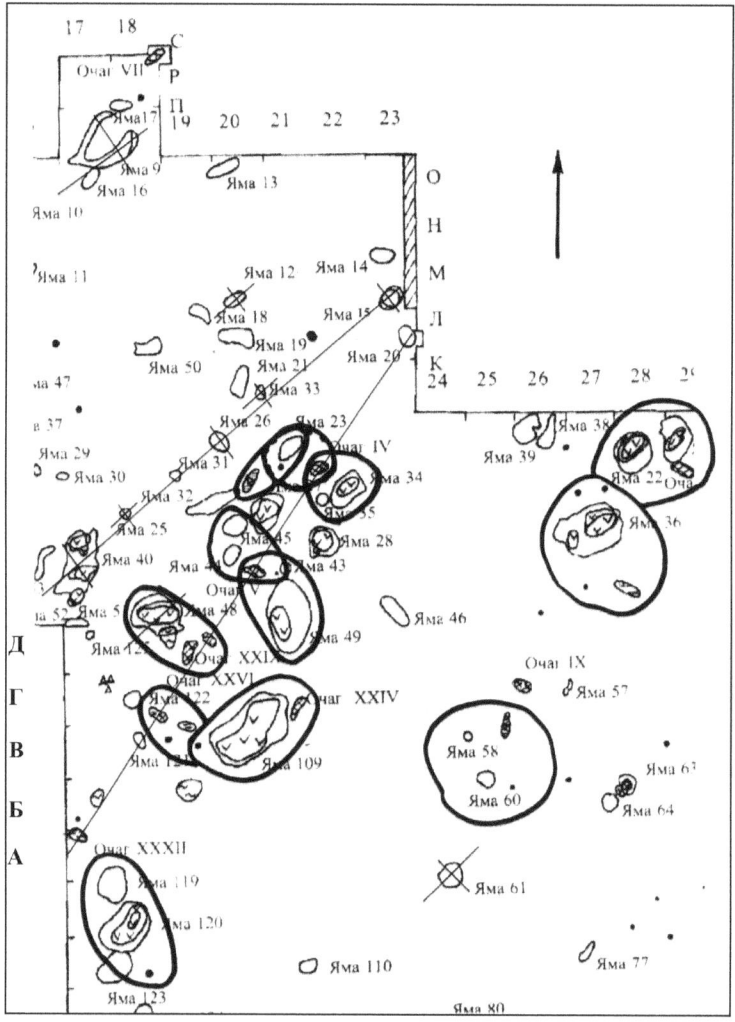

Figure 6. Excavation scheme. © Copyright 1988, Prof. T.Ostanina; 2005, Alexei Korobeinikov

e.g. combination of post holes, pits and fire-places.

An alternative interpretation

All the aforesaid allows to assume that archeological finds around the Kuzebaevo village can be identified as remnants of pagan altars. Regular distribution of altars (straight chain with equal intervals between fire-places) reveals that we deal with an attempt to use the available space in the most efficient way, so dozens of bread and meat offerings could be cooked at the same time. When describing sacrifices in the South of Udmurtia in late 19th – early 20th century the ethnographers note: "Hereabouts the Nirya village (Mamadysh county of Kazan gubernia) the number of sacrificed animals reaches 80 cattle, the same number of horses and just the same number of flocks and herds" (Vasiljev 1906:21). The quantity of oblational buildt fires coincides with the number of families in particular settlement (Pervukhin 1988:97-98). This evidence proves an assumption that the distribution of individual altars through the shrine area reveals peculiarities in ancestral structure of people who used this shrine.

Considering the above mentioned I pose the question: "Could pagan ceremonies leave any traces to be subsequently registered by means of archeology?" It is well-known that many rites of Udmurt people are related with animal sacrifices. This fact is proven by ethnographic sources (Vasiljev 1906, Pervukhin 1988, Luppov 1927, etc.) In many occasions blood and parts of bodies (primarily bones) of the sacrificed animals may turn out to be found in a cave adjoining to the fire-place and sacrificing pole (see figure 1, 2, 3). The discussed schemes of excavations near the Kuzebaevo village shows caves whose purpose was interpreted by the director of excavations as "household facility aimed at camouflaging a secret storage of corn, meat and milk products" "At excavations of the pits a lot of ceramic fragments, bones and other things were encountered" (Ostanina 2002:7-10). I selected only those holes where bones had been found. Then I pointed these holes with a colored marker. When doing that I attributed each marked hole with its nearest scorch of soil and post. In occasions where an evident straight chain of holes is accompanied with the lack of scorches (chain of holes: 15, 33, 26, 25, 40) I allocated them to an intersection of the chain's trend and perpendiculars to it (see figure 6).

I assume that the selected complexes (each consisting of hole with bone remnants, fire-place and posts) or just only holes may have served as pagan altars. Figure 6 clearly shows that such altars present several straight chains whose axis is close to the azimuth of sunset at winter solstice in this particular region (considering magnetic declination it is about 210-220°). The observed chains of altars are separated from each other with a trend of regularly distributed scorches (quadrate: А17-Л23) which possesses azimuth about 215° too. Each fire-place of the mentioned group of altars may have been used in combination with a specific pit (located on one of its sides) or with both pits at the same time (see aforementioned evidence of Grigory Vereshagin about 7 feet intervals between fire-places). Obviously, at medieval times (i.e. before converting groups of population of local folks to Christianity) each post within the sacrificing complex was surely purposed for idols, not for Orthodox icons.

Some of the selected complexes "post-cave-fire-place" may occasionally coincide with each other. It implies multiple use of the area for the needs of sacrificing. Once traces of altars throughout the surface got faded a new group of such facilities might be built. But since the orientation of altar chains remained invariable, it means that participants of ceremonies were able to maintain it (to find it again and again) by applying to such fixed reference points like, for instance, celestial objects.

Conclusion

Available ethnographic data of the present time let us to make the following conclusions:

1. All of the above discussed altars purposed for pagan ceremonies of Udmurtian people consist of post,, cave, and fire-place (or several fire-places). These shrines must have left archeological traces (e.g. bones and scorches) which were incorrectly identified [2] as "pits of household purpose".
2. An elongated scorch of soil is the sequence of either multiple building of fires or simultaneous building of several fires.
3. Those shrine sites, whose orientation is measured by means of instruments, are evidently oriented at cardinal points of solar path through celestial sphere.

Thus the applied ethnographic data combined with modeling of supposed archeological traces of sacrificing facility disapproves purpose of so-called "Kuzebaevo settlement" as a fortified hill fort and allows interpreting it as a shrine. The discussed facility was used by ancestors of Finn-Hungarian folks for the needs of sacral ceremonies. I hope that proposed method of comparative analysis of ethnographic/archeological data may re-determine the purpose of other known archeological objects.

References

Luppov P.N. 1927. *Iz nabludenij nad bytom udmurtov Varzi-Yatchinskogo kraya Votskoi Avtonomnoi oblasti»*, Trudy Noivk, Izhevsk.

Ostanina T.I. 2002. *Kuzebaevskoe gorodische IV-V, VII B.C.*, Izhevsk.

Pervukhin N.G. 1998. *Eskizy predanij i byta inorodcev Glazovskogo uezda: Eskiz II: Idolozhertvennyj ritual drevnikh votyakov*, Vyatka.

Shutova N.I. 2001. *Dokhristianskije kultovye pamyatniki*

v udmurtskoi religioznoi tradicii, Izhevsk.
Vasiljev I. 1906. *Obozrenie yazycheskikh obryadov, sueverij i verovanij votyakov Kazanskoi i Vyatskoi gubernii*, Kazan.
Vereschagin G.E. 1996. *Votjaki Sarapulskogo uezda Vjatskoi gubernii*, Izhevsk.

Symbolic meanings of the slip decoration on medieval and post-medieval redware

Marianna Niukkanen

Redware vessels for all

Redware vessels glazed on the inside were probably in use in almost every kitchen in the Baltic region from the late Middle Ages right up to the beginning of the 20th century. Apart from a few luxury articles, redware was primarily designed and made for everyday use, and it can be categorised according to its intended use, as being for cooking, storage or for serving food. This intended use is reflected in the shape of the vessel, the size, decoration and marks of use. Vessels intended for preparing and preserving food were generally simple in shape and decoration, while serving dishes were more ornamental (Elfwendahl 1999:60-64, 110-117; Niukkanen 2000: 73,76.). A particular shape of vessel or decoration could also be traditionally associated with a specific festive occasion, such as a wedding or the birth of a child.

Archaeological finds indicate that, at the end of the 15th century, the amount of redware grew greatly, especially in towns. Vessels were more abundantly glazed, and the glaze was of better quality than before, with painted slip decoration becoming common (Bartels 1999:119; Carlsson & Rosén 2002:94). During the 16th century, more attention was paid to the showiness of the vessels: glossy surfaces, decorative shapes, and copious, multi-coloured painted decorations were pleasing to the eye of the Renaissance diner. The middle classes gradually adopted the manners of the aristocracy, which they imitated using cheaper materials. The various ceramic vessels were used as a mark of social status and fashion-consciousness. In comparison with vessels made out of other materials, cheap redware with painted decorations gradually became the vessels particularly of poor townsfolk and peasants (Bartels 1999:417-418; Elfwendahl 1999:40-41; Rosén 2004:106-109).

Painted decorations were executed particularly on the inner surfaces of dishes and bowls, and to some extent on the outer surfaces of jugs and cooking pots, generally on their upper parts. The decoration was done using various slip techniques. 'Bolus' decoration was done by thinning white pipe-clay with water to make a somewhat runny slip. This was, for instance, used in a cowhorn instrument to paint patterns on the still-wet surface of a vessel before the bisque firing. Pigment was not generally added to the slip, but in the finished vessel the white decoration took on the colour of the lead glazing on top of it. In addition, green copper oxide powder could be sprinkled onto the vessel's surface as a highlighting pigment. In 'engobe' decoration the whole vessel is dipped in white clay slip. This technique was, for instance, used to try to imitate white earthenware and faience. 'Sgraffito', meanwhile, is a technique in which patterns were scratched into the vessel's white-slipped surface using a burin, so that the dark tone of the red clay showed through from beneath the slip (Augustsson 1985:92; Pihlman 1989:90; Niukkanen 2000:76).

The painted patterns and pictorial motifs that appear on redware vessels have not generally been analysed in any great detail in research on ceramics. Decorations are usually dealt with in a brief mention indicating the type of pictorial motif, such as "geometrical patterns", "decoration with plant motifs", "animal motif", "bird" and so on. In reality the pictorial motifs were significant to the people of the day, and identifying and investigating them tells us a lot about people's, especially the women's, worldview, beliefs and ways of managing reality. The purpose of this article is not to give precise answers to the question of what the various pictures painted on vessels mean or symbolise, but to air some ideas about the colourful world of beliefs that may lie hidden behind these apparently simple patterns.

Witchcraft in everyday tasks

People who lived in the Middle Ages thought very differently from the way we do. This included a strong Catholic religiosity, mingled with ancient pagan superstitions, with their spirit powers, omens, charms and curses. Existence was seen as being a continual dualistic battle between good and evil, a battle that was also portrayed in art either concretely or cloaked in the language of symbols (Stigell 1974:75; Garthoff-Zwaan 1988:37). No material or immaterial thing was necessarily solely what people were capable of perceiving with their senses, but could also have a magical dimension. An object could thus be used to establish contact between the sensible and insensible worlds. Consequently, everything that could be perceived had both a functional and a symbolic significance. Also, the imagery linked with an object was an attempt to control good and evil: life and death, health and sickness, success and ill fortune (Garthoff-Zwaan 1988:25-27).

Information about the everyday folk magic practised in Finland and Sweden comes, for instance, from cases recorded in the 17th century court 'judgement books'. In them we find charms, descriptions of various rites, and accounts of witches' sabbaths on the mythical Blåkulla hill. On the other hand, we can say that the Karelian epic poems, e.g. *The Kalevala*, recorded in the 19th century, and the mental world embodied in the set of spells known in Finland, which lived on in a secret tradition, reflect a substantially older era, the Middle Ages or even the late Iron Age. People attributed meanings to their actions and were constantly reshaping and interpreting reality in an effort to understand and control it. The means they used, which included witchcraft and magic, were common knowledge, as were the related symbols, and people were generally able to read the alternative meanings associated with them (Eilola 2004:138-139).

One of the main dividing lines drawn in cases of witchcraft was between the inside and the outside of the household. Jobs within the household, such as cooking, milking and churning, were primarily the responsibility of the mistress of the house and the other womenfolk. With her work, a woman created order within the home, and failure in this work signified a loss of control and an upsurge of ill-omened chaos. The smooth running of household tasks was ensured with the aid of magic. The same means could also be used to disrupt the actions of others, as can be read in the accusations of witchcraft in the judgement books. Suspicions of witchcraft in a household were instigated and spread specifically through the mediation of women – when someone had overstepped her own bounds and specifically entered the domain of other women. Even though this intrusion into the system by an outsider might have lasted only a short time, it could be used to explain subsequent misfortunes (Eilola 2004:155-159; see also Nenonen 1992).

Evil could enter the inner circle of the household from outside through the agency either of a person with evil intentions or of a bewitched object. Once the evil had entered, things began to go wrong, for example, baking, brewing or distilling. Fire and borrowed tools were prime instruments of this kind of witchcraft. The treacherous object might be hard to recognise, because it could be very innocent-looking – for example, a cabbage leaf that someone had dropped in a farmyard and which had begun to have an adverse effect on the specific entirety around it. The function of the object could not be known for certain, since any object at all could be given a magic significance, which was not outwardly visible. The use of objects in a way that diverged from their original purpose was a central element in witchcraft and magic (Eilola 2004:156-158).

By using magic means it was possible to manipulate boundaries, for example, that between the inside of the household and the threatening outside world. Magic made what was inside more solid, more ordered and more resistant to external chaos. On a mythical level this was about a threat to the human world, i.e. to Christendom, from the Beyond. On the social level the threat mainly focused on the household, on the functions carried out within its precincts, and on the people who lived there and their health (Eilola 2004:166-167). Seen against this background it is possible that the ordinary objects used in household work, such as vessels, and the pictures on them, were associated with magical meanings, which were used, for instance, to ensure there was enough food, that it was safe to eat, and to guarantee the success of food preparation.

Christian and magical significance

The seemingly simple decoration on the redware vessels tells us a great deal about the experiential and mental world of people of former times. Pictorial expression was probably of great importance to the people of the beginning of the Middle Ages and the post-medieval period, most of whom were illiterate. An ordinary member of the common people only saw art proper in church, but the everyday visual environment was richer than we might now be able to imagine. Only chance examples of the wide variety and colourfulness of the designs and decorations of carved-wood furniture and utensils, parts of buildings, textiles and leather items – all demonstrations of the craftsman's skills – have survived to the present day.

A large part of the pictorial emblems used in the Middle Ages are ancient, chronologically and geographically widely distributed, and appear in numerous variants. The same symbol could have different meanings, depending on the time, the place and the context, and it is not now possible to decipher all these meanings. Several symbols have both a Christian and a magical, as well as a positive and a negative, meaning, and we cannot always know which interpretation to choose. A confusion of meanings occurs, for example, when Christian content is attributed to an emblem for some pagan power (Stigell 1974:45,66; Garthoff-Zwaan 1988:43). The meaning of some symbols was diluted with use, and they turned into common decorative motifs with no particular meaning content. People of that time could, nevertheless, presumably tell the difference between sacred and profane images (Stigell 1974:45,65). Distinguishing between orthodox religion and magic had no relevance for Christians of the Middle Ages, since the two were not seen as being opposites or as unconnected categories. People, nevertheless, did make a distinction between asking God for help, resorting to demonic magic, and making use of the occult powers of nature (Katajala-Peltomaa 2004:103-104).

Abstract pictorial symbols in medieval ceramics

The pictorial world of the painted decorations on medieval redware is abstract and geometric. The patterns are visually dominant, but simple and frequently painted with only a few strokes inside the bottom of a bowl or on the side of a jug or cooking pot. We must assume that the simpler the mode of presentation, the more potent its symbolic import was at the time (Garthoff-Zwaan 1988:43).

According to the Dutch researcher Maria Garthoff-Zwaan, in the painted decorations on Dutch redware three main meanings for symbol can be distinguished: fertility, regeneration, and defence against evil (Garthoff-Zwaan 1988:10). Symbols representing fertility are among the most common in vessels. A typical sign is formed out of two semicircles on top of each other, side by side or facing in opposite directions, and usually intersecting, this sign possibly being repeated several times on the surface of the vessel to form an ornamental pattern. The origins of the sign may lie in the *ing*-rune in ancient Germanic futhark runic alphabet, which signifies marriage, offspring and fertility, while also being a symbol of heaven and earth, sun and moon, and maleness and femaleness (Garthoff-Zwaan 1988:29). (figure 1)

Figure 1. In medieval vessels fertility may possibly have been symbolised by this commonly occurring arc pattern. Drawing M. Niukkanen.

In the symbology of rebirth and resurrection, a common pattern is the three-leaved "sprouting plant", many of which could be combined into a single image, for example, into a picture the shape of a Greek cross. One variant on this triple-leaf design is a pattern made of three circles. Triple patterns may also refer to the Holy Trinity. Rebirth is also depicted by the Tree of Life, which can conversely be seen as a symbol of fertility and of sin and grace. The revolving wheel is an ancient sign, also familiar from oriental religions, which is an emblem of the sun, motion and the passage of time. Regeneration may also possibly be referred to by the s-patterns repeated one after another in the surface of the vessel, the origin of this possibly being the ancient Germanic *odal* rune (Stigell 1974:48,59-61; Garthoff-Zwaan 1988:33). (figure 2)

Warding off evil (demons) was extremely important for people of the Middle Ages. At times of peril, they prayed to the saints, but these efforts were also reinforced by means of witchcraft. People protected themselves from evil by casting counterspells, by manipulating sensorily perceptible manifestations of the Devil. Magic signs for warding off evil are known, for instance, from a Dutch

Figure 2. The sprouting-plant-like patterns on the sides of medieval tripod pipkins refer to the symbolism of rebirth. Concentric circles may represent the sun or the universe. Drawing M. Niukkanen.

vernacular manuscript from the 15th century, and they are closely linked to medieval astrology. Astronomical phenomena were observed closely so as to measure time and so as to forecast, not just the weather, but also the future, since what happens in Heaven, would also happen on Earth. The sun is symbolised, apart from by a revolving wheel, by a six-pointed star pattern, i.e. a hexagram, and a circle divided into six segments, which is also the Monogram of Christ. Circles within circles symbolise the sun, too, and possibly also the universe. Ancient emblems of the moon are the crescent and the circle divided into four segments, which can also of course be understood as being a cross (Stigell 1974:47,50-52,61; Garthoff-Zwaan 1988:37-39). The Sign of the Cross was used to drive away demonic apparitions, and the Greek cross was the calendar symbol for religious holidays (Stigell 1974:113). The five-pointed star, i.e. the pentagram, was very commonly used, and over a very long period, as a protective emblem. Another pictorial element that warded off evil was the lattice, made up of horizontal and vertical lines (Garthoff-Zwaan 1988:37). (figure 3)

Animal motifs

Extremely popular in the High Middle Ages were the 'bestiaries', the illuminated "animal encyclopaedias". These gave accounts of all the real and imagined animals in creation, and of their physical features, character and behaviour. The works were a mixture of fact and fiction. The roots of the animal tales lay in Antiquity, but the church began to use this animal imagery for its own pedagogical purposes. There was a belief that God had given animals certain characteristics in order, via them, to teach people Biblical values. The animal tales in fact always contained a moral, metaphorical lesson. Pictures

Figure 3. Magical patterns that ward off evil include the Greek cross in several variants and the lattice. Drawing M. Niukkanen.

of animals were used abundantly in different contexts to symbolise Christ, the Devil and various Christian virtues and vices, according to the nature of each particular animal. Thus, an important lesson could be transmitted to the illiterate population, too (e.g. Voisenet 1994 & Bianciotto (ed.) 1980).

Redware was also painted with stylised animal pictures. Bird motifs were quite common on bowls. The pictures are allusive to the extent that it is not possible to identify with certainty each individual bird species depicted. Nevertheless, they are not usually small birds; in many cases the bird looks like it might be a cockerel, which is a recognised symbol of Christian vigilance and spiritual observance. The cockerel was also a protection against fires (Biedermann 1989:175-177). In some cases the bird probably represents a dove, an emblem of the Holy Spirit and bringer of the good news of Christianity. Conversely, in many bowls the bird is disconcertingly reminiscent of a parrot. And yet, this in itself apparently outlandish idea is not necessarily purely a matter of chance, since from the 15th to 17th centuries, in the cities of the Baltic region, and presumably including Finland, highly popular parrot-shooting competitions were held. These were sharp-shooting competitions, in which people tried to shoot a dummy parrot down from the end of a spear with a musket or crossbow. This originally southern French tradition is best known from the Nordic countries, where it arrived via the Hansa cities, possibly as early as the 14th century (Lamberg 1998:13-16). (figure 4)

Another very common pictorial motif is the stag or hart. In Christian iconography interpretations were based on Psalms 42:1, which says: "Man thirsts for God like a hart in its thirst seeks the water of a brook." This animal symbolised the battle against evil, since it is the enemy of the serpent, i.e. the Devil, and is able to purge itself of its venom by drinking water from a spring. Deer horns can be seen as the tree of life or as purifying, as running water, and were considered a powerful remedy. The deer is also an emblem of regeneration, since each year it grows new antlers to replace the ones that it has shed (Biedermann 1989:194-197). (figure 5)

Figure 4. Bird patterns often appear to portray a cockerel. Drawing M. Niukkanen.

Figure 5. Red-deer stag, the enemy of the snake, i.e. the Devil, was a common pictorial motif especially in the 16th and 17th centuries. Drawing M. Niukkanen.

The third animal motif common in painted decorations is the fish, which is one of the oldest symbols for Christ. Fish were associated with many Bible tales. The apostles were fishers of men, and fish appeared along with bread as allegorical raw material for a divine meal, while also being a symbol of the Eucharist. Fish also survived the Flood, just as the baptised are saved from God's punishment (Biedermann 1989:142-145).

Images on vessels in the 16th and 17th centuries

In the countryside old magic ornamentation continued in use for a long time, but in the urban environment the significance of motifs rooted in nature, cosmology and folk beliefs dwindled during the 16th century, with new figurative motifs beginning to take their place. The common Christian pictorial symbols and Biblical allegories, and others based on classical mythology, spread widely via printed pictures. At the same time, the magical occult meanings of the pictures faded (Garthoff-Zwaan 1988:43-45).

Tulips could represent the resurrection; frequently, many tulips form a pattern reminiscent of the tree of life on the surface of a bowl. Fertility and sensuality were symbolised by fruit, especially seed-packed pomegranates and grapes, which conversely also suggested marital fidelity, virginity and moral striving for virtue and for the bountiful blessings of God (Garthoff-Zwaan 1988:44-45; Biedermann 1989:169-170). Fertility symbolism can be seen both in decorative motifs, and in the shapes of some vessels, such as in money boxes and drinking flasks shaped like women's breasts. The designs of the tubular handles on tripod pipkins could also possibly have phallic connotations. In fact, it is very possible that a connection was seen between the preparation of food and fertility – with the cooking pot as the womb, the creator of the sustenance that sustains life, and the male organ as its protector – or then this may just be folk humour (Bergold, Bäck et al. 2004:20-22). Another interesting feature is that in the visual art of the 16th and 17th centuries redware itself often appears as an emblem of fertility and eroticism (Garthoff-Zwaan 1988:57). (figure 6)

At the beginning of the 17th century, coats of arms, years and initials appeared in decorations. Especially in redware dishes and fire covers given as wedding presents, combinations of several motifs can be seen: man and woman (Adam and Eve), between them the tree of life and around them pomegranates, birds and so on (Garthoff-Zwaan 1988:45). Corresponding themes appear, for instance, in the relief panels on stoneware jugs. We might even speak of a common European Renaissance iconography, which spread to bourgeois homes via practical items and utensils.

Living and changing meanings

A lot of redware vessels were brought from Holland and Northern Germany to Scandinavia, at least until the second half of the 16th century, and the same pictorial motifs spread as far as Sweden and Finland. They were also incorporated into the decorations on locally made ceramics. The decoration is generally surprisingly similar, regardless of where in the Baltic region the vessel has been made. But, of course, it is often difficult to trace where a vessel was made.

Figure 6. A seed-filled pomegranate was a symbol of fertility and marriage as early as Antiquity. Drawing M. Niukkanen.

Nor, of course, can we know with any certainty to what extent the emblematic world of vessel decoration was understandable, for example, to small traders in Finnish towns, or what meanings people of the time actually attributed to the vessels and pictures. Were they explicitly aware of the symbol language, or is the decoration to be seen chiefly as the common pictorial language of the age, whose original, possibly symbolic, meaning had become obscured over time? Especially after the mid-16th century, simple, repeated ornamental decorative motifs, such as concentric circles, wavy lines and spiral patterns in which it is hard to see any symbolic content became common on vessels. The Reformation may have contributed to this development – perhaps there was a desire to remove from the visual environment all reminders of the previous, proscribed ritual practice of religion.

In Finland, too, the significance of runes and simple symbolic meanings was presumably fairly well known among the common people of the Middle Ages, for instance, through owner's marks, calendar pictures painted on church walls and calendars drawn on wood, including on runesticks (Stigell 1974:15-20,45). Rune writing was used in the Nordic countries alongside the Latin alphabet in some contexts well into historical time, at least up to the 18th century. Research has traditionally associated futhark rune writing with magic elements. More recent research views rune magic as in part being an exaggerated overinterpretation, but it, nevertheless, appears indisputable that at least some runes were associated with magical meanings in certain contexts (See e.g. Oldenstedt 1992; Fjellhammer Sein 1994).

We should remember that the decorative motifs described here did not appear solely on vessels, but were also common in textiles, utensils, furniture, details of buildings and so on. The new pictorial motifs adopted by urban society in the Middle Ages and at the beginning of the post-medieval period gradually found their way into the rural environment. As the context changed, the significance of the pictures may have changed, too. Identical pictorial motifs were still appearing, for instance, in Finnish peasant rya rugs, in wooden utensils and in painted decorations on furniture in the 19th century (See Sirelius 1924). The ancient tradition of charms and magic is also known to have lived on among the people well into that same century (Talve 1990:264-267).

Translation: Mike Garner

Bibliography

Augustsson, J-E. 1985. *Keramik i Halmstad ca. 1322-1619. Produktion – distribution – funktion.* Hallands länsmuseer skriftserie no. 2. Lund.

Bartels, M. 1999. *Steden in Scherven – Cities in Sherds 1-2. Vondsten uit beerputten in Deventer, Dordrecht, Nijmegen and Tiel (1250-1900).* Amersfoort.

Bergold, H., Bäck, M. et al. 2004. Redware tubular tripod pipkin handles. *Muinaistutkija* 2/2004. Helsinki. 2-25.

Bianciotto, G. (ed.) 1980. *Bestiaires du Moyen Age.* Paris.

Biedermann, H. 1989. *Knaurs Lexikon der Symbole.* München.

Carlsson, K. and Rosén, C. 2002. *Stadsbornas kärl – keramik I västsvenska städer från 1400-tal till 1700-tal.* Urbaniseringsprocesser i Västsverige. GOTARC Serie C, Arkeologiska Skrifter No. 44. Göteborgs Universitet. Arkeologiska institutionen.

Eilola, J. 2004. Rajojen noituus ja taikuus. Katajala-Peltomaa, S. & Toivo, R.M. (eds.) *Paholainen, noituus ja magia – kristinuskon kääntöpuoli. Pahuuden kuvasto vanhassa maailmassa.* Tietolipas 203. Suomalaisen Kirjallisuuden Seura. Helsinki. 136-186

Elfwendahl, M. 1999. *Från skärva till kärl. Ett bidrag till vardagslivets historia i Uppsala.* Lund Studies in Medieval Archaeology 22. Lund.

Fjellhammer Sein, K. 1994. Var futharken en magisk formel i middelalderen? Testing av en hypotese mot inskrifter fra Bryggen i Bergen. Knirk, J.E. (ed.) *Proceedings of the third international symposium on runes and runic inscriptions.* Runrön 9. Institutionen för nordiska språk. Uppsala universitet. Uppsala. 278-300.

Garthoff-Zwaan, M. 1988. *Communicerende vaten. Beeldtaal van slibversiering op laat-middeleeuws aardewerk in de Nederlanden.* Museum Boymans-van Beuningen. Rotterdam.

Katajala-Peltomaa, S. 2004. Paholainen, demonit ja riivatut raukat – keskiaikaisia käsityksiä sielunvihollisesta. Katajala-Peltomaa, S. & Toivo, R.M. (eds.) *Paholainen, noituus ja magia – kristinuskon kääntöpuoli. Pahuuden kuvasto vanhassa maailmassa.* Tietolipas 203. Suomalaisen Kirjallisuuden Seura. Helsinki. 78-115.

Lamberg, M. 1998. Kun tärkeintä ei ollut voitto, vaan voitosta kertominen – keskiajan tarkkuusammuntakilpailut sosiaalisen viestinnän kanavina. Halmesvirta, A & H. Roiko-Jokela, H. (eds.) *Urheilu, historia ja julkisuus.* Suomen urheiluhistoriallisen seuran vuosikirja 1998. Helsinki. 11-23.

Nenonen, M. 1992. *Noituus, taikuus ja noitavainot Ala-Satakunnan, Pohjois-Pohjanmaan ja Viipurin Karjalan maaseudulla 1620-1700.* Historiallisia tutkimuksia 165. Suomen historiallinen seura. Helsinki.

Niukkanen, M. 2000. Jacoba-kannusta ja jyllantilaispadasta seltteripulloon – historiallisen ajan keramiikkaa Laukon kartanosta. Uotila, K. (ed.) *Vesilahden Laukko – linna, kartano, koti.* Archaeologica Medii Aevi Finlandiae IV. Turku. 73-84.

Oldenstedt, B.1992. Om uppkomsten av den yngre futharken. En diskussion av några huvudteorier.

Blandade runstudier 1. Runrön 6. Institutionen för nordiska språk. Uppsala universitet. Uppsala. 67-80.

Pihlman, A. 1989. Saviastiat. Kostet, J. & Pihlman, A. (eds.) *Turun Mätäjärvi – Mätäjärvi i Åbo.* Turun maakuntamuseon raportteja 10. Turku. 83-104.

Rosén, C. 2004. *Stadsbor och bönder. Materiell kultur och social satus i Halland från medeltid till 1700-tal.* Riksantikvarieämbetet Arkeologiska Undersökningar Skrifter 53, Lund Studies in Medieval Archaeology 35. Lund.

Sirelius, U. T. 1924. *Suomen ryijyt: tekstiilihistoriallinen tutkimus.* Helsinki.

Stigell, A-L. 1974. *Kyrkans tecken och årets gång. Tideräkningen och Finlands primitiva medeltidsmålningar.* Finska fornminnesföreningens tidskrift 77. Helsingfors.

Talve, I. 1990. *Suomen kansankulttuuri.* Suomalaisen Kirjallisuuden Seuran toimituksia 514. Helsinki.

Voisenet, J. 1994. *Bestiaire chrétien: l'imagerie animale des auteurs du Haut Moyen Âge (Ve–XIe s.).* Toulouse.

www.ingramcontent.com/pod-product-compliance
Lightning Source LLC
Chambersburg PA
CBHW061545010526
44113CB00023B/2808